During the twentieth century the number of people who

speak English as a first or second language has increased dramatically. The covers of

the Voyages series reflect the fact that English is the most widely read language in the world.

This year our Voyages in English book takes us to Asia.

VOYAGES in English

Revised Edition

Carolyn Marie Dimick

General Editor

Marie T. McVey

Revision Editor

Loyola University Press · Chicago

Contributors	Carolyn Marie Dimick
	Susan Mary Platt
	Joan I. Rychalsky
	Margaret O'Toole
	Marie T. McVey
Managing Editor	Juanita Raman (revision)
Production / Design Manager	Carol Tornatore
	Frederick Falkenberg (revision)
Designer	William A. Seabright

ISBN 0-8294-0764-2

Preface

In every grade, language development challenges teachers and students to explore their world through the spoken and written word. Language in all its aspects is essential to the development of the individual on both personal and social levels. We use language as a vehicle for expressing wonder and delight, a tool for exchanging ideas, a medium for transmitting information, and a resource for bridging the differences among peoples. These are the ultimate goals of language and the underlying philosophy of *Voyages in English*.

Integration of the language arts

The revised *Voyages in English* series is designed to include the major areas of the language arts curriculum: writing, grammar, correct usage, mechanics, dictionary and library skills, speaking and listening skills, and literature. These areas should not be considered separate and distinct from one another even though, for purposes of instruction, the skills may be taught in isolation.

The challenge of the teacher is to present the areas as integrated so that the students can perceive the seemingly discrete parts of the curriculum as an interrelated whole. Ultimately, students should view the entire program as essential to building competency and success in other curricular areas.

Parts I and II. Before teaching the material in *Voyages in English*, the teacher should become acquainted with the format of the textbook. There are two distinct sections: writing and grammar. (Literary selections are incorporated into each chapter of the grammar section.) Neither section is meant to be taught in continuity without reference to the other. Familiarity with the chapters in both areas will enable the teacher to move with ease between the two sections.

For example, when working with the students in the proofreading stage of the writing process, the teacher will discover areas of weakness in correct usage and mechanics. At this point it is recommended that the teacher turn to the lesson in the grammar section that corresponds to the particular problem area and teach the concept in the context of the writing activity.

While teaching an area of grammar such as adjectives, teachers might refer to the lessons on word substitution, sentence expansion, or descriptive writing in order to integrate grammar and writing effectively. The correlations are many, and at all times the instructional goal should be integration, not isolation.

Illustrations. The full-page illustration that opens each chapter relates directly or indirectly to the chapter that follows, but it may often be as appropriately used with other subject matter.

In the writing section of the book, the captions are "lead" questions designed to serve as a springboard for class discussion. The ideas explored through the illustrations can often inspire a composition. Teachers having an overview of the illustrations in the book can refer to a specific one to prompt a writing activity.

In the grammar section a credit line identifies photographs and fine art. Illustrations may inspire a poem, a theme, or different kinds of sentences (declarative, interrogative, exclamatory, imperative). A simple sentence about the picture might be expanded with words, phrases, or clauses—all of which might include various types of figurative language or the use of verbals. The regionalist (especially American) and other art from different periods provides opportunities for cross-curricular links.

Sharpening Your Skills. This feature provides a skill-extension or a writing activity following each grammar lesson. Sometimes it is simply writing sentences or completing a review exercise; at other times it is writing a brief paragraph or poem. With teacher assistance, the students should come to realize the importance of integrating correct grammar, usage, and mechanics with writing skills.

You Are the Author. This feature extends the integration of the language arts, replacing the final Sharpening Your Skills activity in each chapter with an assignment related in some way to the literary opener. The students learn to apply the grammatical concept taught in the chapter to writing that draws on the genre, subject, or content of the literature. In addition, students engage in cooperative learning, which teaches them to take pride in sharing both their individual skills and the rewards of group achievement.

The writing process

Exploring and discovering meaning through written language should be part of every child's educational experience. Schools that make the development of writing skills a high priority foster the writing process within the curriculum.

Developing good writing skills is essential at every grade level. The teacher should become familiar with the elements of the writing process. The goal is for writing to be a natural, enjoyable means of expression in which the students engage frequently.

When the writing process is begun in the early school years, children have no fear or anxiety about writing. Instead, building on their ability to communicate through speech, they find writing an exhilarating and happy experience. There is a sense of satisfaction in knowing a piece is well written and has expressed exactly what the writer intended to say. Although research on the composing, or writing, process is ongoing, most authorities agree that the process has four stages: prewriting, writing or drafting, revision, and editing. These are not mutually exclusive, however, so should not be taught in isolation. Writing is a cyclic process; thus its components overlap, allowing the writer to wander in and out of all stages at will.

Prewriting. Observing, discussing, reading, journal writing, note-taking, interviewing, brainstorming, imagining, and remembering are some activities that take place before the writer begins an actual draft. In this stage the writer hones in on a subject, narrows it, and makes decisions about the purpose and audience of the piece. Why is it being written? For whom? (The teacher, parents, principals, other students, and the community are all appropriate audiences.) What form should the writing take? In this stage enthusiasm is generated. Interaction between student and teacher helps attest to the value of the project. Teachers should encourage students to share their ideas so as to "hear" their own ideas and others', ultimately helping them to evaluate their material, to be selective about it, and to make associations.

Writing. During the creation of the first draft, the student puts the information on paper. At this stage the writer should be encouraged to keep the ideas flowing without worrying about sentence structure or correct usage. Maintaining momentum is important, so completing this process at one sitting is the ideal. The first draft is the visible form of what took place in the pre-writing stage. It allows the student to see a dim shape of what the material is to become. Teachers should encourage students to write without making corrections—on alternate lines so as to provide room for revision.

Revision. This can be the most difficult stage of writing yet the most vital to its success. Here students look over the work again and again. First drafts are rarely well organized or cohesive. Ideas need clarification, sentences need variety, and vocabulary needs development. Such refining takes more than one revision. Teachers should encourage students to write as many drafts as necessary.

Editing and proofreading. In the final stage before "publication," the students must look to the correctness of the piece. Correct punctuation, spelling, capitalization, and usage are important if the work is to be convincing. The students should be taught to review their own work but not to get caught up in refining content—which is not the domain of proofreading—rather than proofreading and attending to mechanical details. The teacher can help control the proofreading process by suggesting four or five areas to check so that all the students proofread for at least those specific prime areas of concern.

Having another student proofread the work is another way to help avoid major revisions at the proofreading stage. To increase objectivity and foster cooperative learning, students should be encouraged to do what real publishers do: select "a second pair of eyes." Teachers may wish to assign a team of students who are good in proofreading to serve as a class resource in this area.

Remember that writers wander in and out of the writing stages. One may begin to revise while writing a first draft. Another may return to prewriting so as to gather more information or rethink an idea. Proofreading can be done while revising. No student should be locked into writing stage by stage, although it is often productive to restrict the critical faculty during a creative time.

Finally, students are ready to publish their work—as close to perfection as possible. The audience has the right to require that finished writing be comprehensible and stylistically consistent. The students can learn a great deal from total involvement in the process of writing. If the audience receives the work well, the students learn to take pride in achievement.

More to Explore. This extension of the activities in each writing lesson may or may not be completed by students, depending on their ability to manage the assignment. Some will respond to the challenge. Others may perform better on a version modified to address individual interests, learning styles, or needs.

Grammar, usage, and mechanics

Part II of the *Voyages in English* program offers the students a traditional approach to grammar in a handbook-reference format. Lessons include definitions, explanations, and then exercises that allow for abundant practice in each concept. The activities and recurring features build on learning by providing opportunities for practical application and language-arts integration.

Recalling What You Know. A few review questions in the first lesson of each grammar chapter set the stage for learning and relate loosely to a literary selection in the chapter. The questions are intended not to test students' previous learning but to remind them of what they already know, to show them that they can do the exercises that follow, and so to instill self-confidence.

Chapter Challenge. At the end of each grammar chapter is a paragraph that incorporates all the grammar skills the students have learned in the chapter. Identifying various grammatical structures is more difficult in paragraphs than in isolated sentences. In most cases, therefore, this feature should be teacher directed rather than used as a testing tool.

Literature

New to the *Voyages in English* program is literature-based traditional grammar. The series' ample poetry component has now been expanded to include other literary genres drawn from a broad range of ethnic backgrounds, social contexts, and historical periods. Not only is the literature integrated into the other language arts; it suggests many cross-curricular applications as well.

Literary opener. The literature that opens each chapter in the grammar section of the book includes fiction, drama, history, fables, folktales, fantasy, and biography. Topics often relate to other academic subjects. Exciting, thought-provoking subject matter stimulates discussion of current issues, introduces students to new cultural perspectives, and has personal relevance.

The Writer's Craft. This feature relates the literary selection the students have just read to their experience. Open-ended questions stimulate discussion and encourage interpretation, teaching students to think and developing an appreciation for writing style. By eliciting the students' feelings, opinions, and judgments, the reader-response questions create interest and reinforce the literary intent. Subsequent questions highlight the author's application of the grammatical concept being taught in the chapter.

The Teacher's Edition

The teacher's text sets the objectives and presents directives for the lessons. Some lessons may require two or three days of instruction. The pacing depends on class as well as individual needs.

Enrichment. This section in Part I, to be used at the discretion of the teacher, provides a challenge for more-advanced students. Many exercises in Part II also contain an extended application.

Voyages in English 8 will provide students with a thorough knowledge of English and will lead them to appreciate language as a gift. The textbook, together with a teacher's own love of language and attentiveness to its many nuances, can be a vehicle for growth and development in all areas of the curriculum.

Teacher-student interaction is vital in the writing process. When trust is built up, students readily share their work. The teacher can guide by asking questions: What are you writing about? Should you say more about your subject? Have you expressed what you have written in the best way you can? What part do you like best? least? Deleting, adding, and rearranging ideas are essential to the revision process.

Students should be taught to look for specific things as they examine their own work: Is the opening sentence effective? Is there one topic sentence? enough sentence variety? strong action verbs? Does the ending sentence draw the whole to a close?
Peer response is important, so students should ask these questions when critiquing one another's work too. The more response from others, the better the revision will be. Language at this point is exciting and challenging. Trying to select just the right word in the right place is the challenge of revision.

Likewise, teachers creating original pieces of writing *along with* the students reinforce the feeling that the challenge and effort involved in the writing process are worthwhile.

The satisfaction that comes from creating a good piece of writing is immeasurable. The hard work is well worth the effort.

Contents

Part II   Grammar, Correct Usage, Mechanics

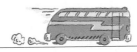

Exploring Our Language

Part I

Chapter 1

Building the Paragraph

Lesson 1 Selecting a Topic

A topic is the idea about which a composition is written.

Did you ever wonder where authors get their ideas? They get them from the same place you will get your ideas for writing: the experiences of life. Every person's life is filled with joyful, sorrowful, and many ordinary events. These events provide subject matter that can be developed in writing class.

Activity A

Let's begin by exploring some life experiences.

Was there ever a time when you were lost? Try to remember all the details, and especially how you felt.

Did you do something during vacation that was exciting, frightening, or funny?

Were you ever in a hospital? Were you a patient or a visitor? How did you feel?

Did you ever see a blazing sunset, a tree covered with snow, a butterfly landing on a flower? Try to remember exactly how it looked and describe it.

Did you ever try to convince your parents or teacher to let you do something or go somewhere? What arguments did you use? Did you win or lose?

What kind of books do you like to read? Why do you enjoy them?

Did you ever travel in a plane? How did you feel the first time? Why did you feel this way?

What approach to life and to writing is suggested by
this photograph of white water rafters?

1

Do you have a secret fear? Are you afraid of the dark, of heights, or of failing in school? What events in your life may have caused these fears?

What kinds of things make you angry? Did you ever want to tell your side of the story?

What kind of music do you like? To what kind of music do you listen when you are in a bad mood? A good mood? Why?

How do you feel when you wake up on Saturday morning and it is raining outside? What do you do all day?

What sports or games do you know a great deal about or play well?

Did you ever have one of "those days" when everything went wrong?

Think back to the last time school was canceled because of bad weather. How did you feel when you heard the news? What did you do all day?

The answer to one of these questions could very well be a good topic for you to develop and write about. Remember, authors write from their own experiences of people, places, things, and events. These experiences can either be firsthand or through reading. So look to your *own* interests and events in life to supply you with your ideas.

Activity B

Now, let's explore some interests you may have. Below is a list of topics. On a separate sheet of paper, copy each topic. If you have firsthand experience of the topic, write *experience* next to it. If the topic is something about which you have read, put the word *read* next to it. If you know nothing about the topic, write *nothing* next to it.

1. A snowball fight
2. A personal computer
3. The death of a pet
4. Playing on a team
5. Photography
6. Working parents
7. Tennis
8. Vampire bats
9. Niagara Falls
10. Making a cake

Sometimes in school, topics will be assigned to you, or you may be given several topics from which to choose. Before you choose a topic, ask yourself these questions:

1. Do I know something about this topic from experience or reading?
2. Does this topic interest me enough to find out something about it?

If the answer to either of these questions is yes, then you will probably enjoy the writing experience and produce a better composition.

More to Explore

Listed in pairs are some topics that could be assigned in social studies, science, or math class. If you had to choose *one* from each pair, which would you choose and why? Write your answers on a sheet of paper.

1. The Great Depression *or* The New Deal
2. Earthquakes *or* Volcanoes
3. World War I *or* World War II
4. The Emancipation Proclamation *or* Woman suffrage
5. How a computer works *or* How to write a computer program
6. Nuclear power plants *or* Solar energy
7. Job programs for youth *or* Job programs for the handicapped
8. Poverty in our cities *or* Crime in our cities
9. Environmental protection *or* Urban development
10. United Nations *or* The League of Nations

Lesson 2 Narrowing the Topic

A topic must be narrowed to a specific idea.

Once you have found a topic that interests you and with which you feel comfortable, the next step is to limit your topic to a specific idea. How do you begin to narrow down your topic? Suppose you chose the subject "food." Innumerable things could be written about food, so you must first *brainstorm for ideas related to the topic.* Your scrap paper might look something like this:

CHICKEN STORES JUNK FOOD
DELI FOOD HAMBURGERS
POPCORN PIZZA
DESSERTS RESTAURANT SNACKS

Read over the ideas you have written down and decide which appeals to you the most. Suppose you choose "desserts." Since this is still a large topic, you might ask yourself, what kind of desserts? You find yourself thinking of ice cream cones, sundaes, and chocolate-covered ice cream on a stick, so your answer is "ice cream desserts." That's still too much to write about in a short space, so you ask yourself, What kind of ice cream desserts? You decide sundaes are your favorite ice cream desserts.

Now you have to ask yourself one last question: What can I say about sundaes? Well, you know you don't like just *any* sundae; for you, there is a perfect *kind* of sundae. Therefore, you might decide to write about "what makes the perfect sundae." You have put the topic "food" through a strainer and come up with one specific idea about which to write. In chart form, your thinking process would look like this:

Food
Desserts
Ice cream desserts
Sundaes
What makes the perfect sundae

4

Activity A

On a separate sheet of paper, draw two charts like the one in the example. Narrow down the categories in 1 and then do the same for 2. The broadest topic should be on the first line, and the narrowest on the last line.

1. Books

A. Library books
B. *The Pigman*
C. Fiction
D. How John and Lorraine take advantage of Mr. Pignati

2. Trees

A. Deciduous trees
B. Blights that affect maple trees
C. Maple trees
D. Trees in the United States

Activity B

The broadest and narrowest topics are given on the charts. On a separate sheet of paper, complete each chart by putting in three more items that show the "sifting" process.

1

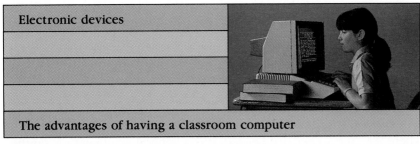

Electronic devices
The advantages of having a classroom computer

2

Famous people
Washington's military strategy at Valley Forge

More to Explore

Because limiting the topic to a specific idea will help you to write a better paragraph, it is important to practice this technique. To improve your skills, draw four more charts on a sheet of paper. Choose any four of the six topics listed below, brainstorm for ideas, and then reduce them in four or five steps to one narrow idea. Share your results with the class.

Sports   Animals
Dancing   Cars
Money   Clothes

Lesson 3 Writing Topic and Beginning Sentences

Topic Sentences

A topic sentence states the main idea of a paragraph.

Why is a topic sentence important? A topic sentence tells the reader where you, the writer, are headed. It is a general statement giving the reader an overview of the paragraph. If you were asked to summarize a paragraph or tell its main idea in one sentence, it would be your *topic sentence*.

Activity A

A *topic sentence* should include the *topic* as well as the *narrowed topic*. Read each of the following sentences and write the topic and narrowed topic on a separate sheet of paper. The first one is done for you.

Down into the cool depths of tropical waters go dauntless swimmers whose dangerous occupation is pearl diving.

What is the topic? Pearl diving

What is the narrowed topic? Pearl diving is a dangerous occupation.

Family members filter in from all parts of the country, each contributing some delicious surprise to the Thanksgiving dinner.

What is the topic?

What is the narrowed topic?

I slowly began to unravel the hidden workings of my home computer.

What is the topic?

What is the narrowed topic?

Activity B

Here is some practice in writing original topic sentences. The topic and narrowed topic are provided. On a sheet of paper, write a topic sentence for each example that expresses both ideas. The first one is done for you.

Topic: A deserted mansion
Narrowed topic: The mystery surrounding the deserted mansion
Topic Sentence: The deserted mansion with its banging shutters and broken windows was shrouded in mystery.

Topic: Climate
Narrowed topic: How climate affects people's lives
Topic sentence:

Topic: Stringed musical instruments
Narrowed topic: The harp is the oldest of the stringed instruments.
Topic sentence:

Musicians, detail from
an ancient Greek vase

7

Activity C

A topic sentence may come at the *beginning* of a paragraph, *stating the main idea*, or it may come at the end of the paragraph, *summarizing the ideas*. In the paragraphs below, the topic sentences have been omitted. On a separate sheet of paper, write an original topic sentence for each.

_____

_____. After he overthrew his father, Jupiter divided the world between his brothers, Pluto and Neptune. Pluto dominated the underworld, and Neptune, the seas. For himself, Jupiter kept the heavens and controlled the actions of both gods and men.

Decide: What is the topic?
      Narrowed topic?

    Gingerly I walked out to the end of the diving board. The instructor carefully stepped behind me and gently bent my body at the waist, encouraging me to almost touch my toes with my fingertips. With a light nudge he pushed me over, and miraculously I landed head first in the water. _____

_____

Decide: What is the topic?
      Narrowed topic?

Beginning Sentences

A beginning sentence may be, but is not always, a topic sentence.

Sometimes the beginning and topic sentences are one and the same, and sometimes they are two separate sentences. A good beginning sentence will have the following qualities:

    Attract the reader's attention
    Arouse his or her curiosity
    Encourage him or her to read on

In order to incorporate these qualities into your beginning sentence, there are several possible ways of writing one. It can be:

A *descriptive sentence:*

The engine sputtered and spat a few empty syllables, dying a slow death.

An interrogative sentence:

Does the abominable snowman really exist?

A *direct quote:*

"Are you *sure* there's a social studies test today?" inquired the pale-looking student.

Activity A

Listed below are topics and narrowed topics. On a separate sheet of paper, write three different beginning sentences for each one, modeling them on the three kinds of sentences given in the example. REMEMBER: the beginning sentence does not have to be the topic sentence.

Topic: Rock stars
Narrowed topic: Why _____ is the most popular rock star today
Beginning sentences:

    Descriptive: _____
    Interrogative: _____
    Direct quote: _____

Topic: School
Narrowed topic: Some of my best moments in school
Beginning sentences:

    Descriptive: _____
    Interrogative: _____
    Direct quote: _____

Topic: Computers
Narrowed topic: How computers work
Beginning sentences:

    Descriptive: _____
    Interrogative: _____
    Direct quote: _____

Activity B

Below are five topic sentences. Write a more interesting beginning sentence for each one. Use one of the three different ways you have been taught.

1. The desert can be a very dangerous place.
2. Every year a new fad comes into existence.
3. The pioneers faced many difficulties as they traveled west.
4. _____ is one of the best books I've ever read.
5. The principal sent for me at 9:00 A.M.

More to Explore

Below are three topic sentences. Write one beginning sentence for each. Next are three beginning sentences. Write one topic sentence for each.

Topic Sentences

1. I found out that wearing the proper shoes can make all the difference in the world.
2. Riding on the back of an elephant is truly a unique experience.
3. When I saw the envelope marked "Winner's Award," I could not contain my excitement.

Beginning Sentences

1. Our new family member caused us a few surprises.
2. Have you ever gone around in circles?
3. "Only thirty seconds left!" shouted Kim.

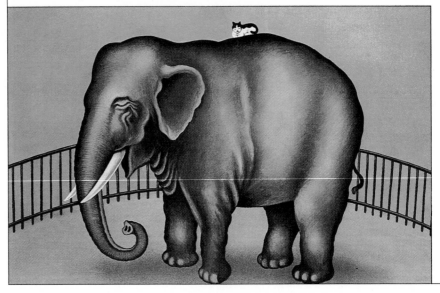

Lesson 4 Collecting Supporting Details for Middle Sentences

The details of a composition are those ideas that support the topic.

Once you have narrowed your topic to one idea, you are ready to continue with the next step in writing: gathering the details that support your topic. Let's presume you chose the topic "computers" and narrowed the topic to "how computers work." You are now ready to list the things that are related to your narrowed topic. There are several ways to do this. The example below uses a method called "word mapping."

1. Write your narrowed topic and draw a ring around it.

2. Around the ring, name ideas that are related to your narrowed topic. These ideas are called *subtopics*. Draw lines connecting each subtopic to the topic in the center.

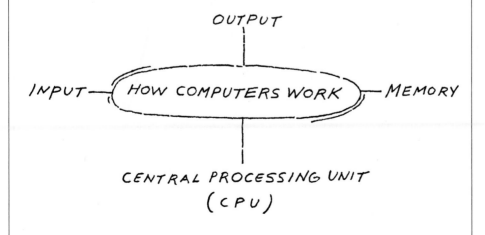

3. Around each subtopic, write any details relating to that particular subtopic. These details may be things you already know, or you may need to discover them through research.

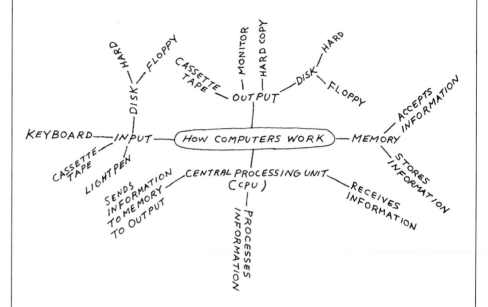

4. Examine your word map and decide if you have too much information for one paragraph. If so, eliminate some of the least important details about your subtopics.

Before you begin writing your paragraph, examine the relationship between your subtopics and your topic. Is there any particular order or arrangement that the subtopics should have? For our topic "how computers work," there is a definite process involved: the input comes first, the memory and CPU interact next, and the output comes last. *It is important to write about the subtopics in the same order in which they naturally occur.*

In the preceding lesson, you learned how to develop a good topic/beginning sentence. Now you will write sentences about your subtopics. These will be your *middle sentences.*

How computers work	→	The working of a modern computer appears to be simple, but is actually a complex operation.
Input	→	Material enters the computer by means of a keyboard, light pen, diskette, or cassette, and is referred to as the input.
Memory	→	The information enters the memory, where it is either stored or transmitted to the Central Processing Unit to be processed.
CPU	→	The CPU performs the required function and returns the information to the memory for storage or for retrieval by the operator.
Output	→	The processed information can be saved as hard copy (printout) or stored on a diskette or cassette.

The sentences you have written will not automatically form a good paragraph. Some words will have to be changed and others added in order for the sentences to flow smoothly from one to another. Watch particularly for words that are repeated, and use synonyms to replace them. After several revisions and peer/teacher consultation, your paragraph might resemble this one:

Title

topic sentence The working of a modern computer appears to be simple yet is actually a complex operation. [Material is entered into the computer by a trained operator using a device such as a keyboard, light pen, cassette tape, or floppy or hard disk. This is referred to as the *input*. Once it is entered, the information passes to the *memory* function of the computer, where it is either temporarily stored or transmitted to the CPU to be processed. The *Central Processing Unit* performs the required function and returns the processed information to the memory for temporary storage, or directly to the operator for immediate retrieval. This finished copy, or *output*, may appear in several ways: on a monitor, as hard copy (using a printer), or on a diskette or cassette tape.]

middle sentences containing supporting details

ending sentence

Activity

Below are some topics. Use a textbook or encyclopedia and make a *word map* for each.

1. Wind instruments in the orchestra
2. The parts of a flower
3. The branches of the federal government
4. Types of clouds
5. Olympic Games
6. Number systems (e.g., whole, rational, irrational, integers etc.)

More to Explore

Select any *one* of the topics above and compose a paragraph using the details in your word map.

Lesson 5 Writing the Ending Sentence

The ending sentence draws the paragraph to a close.

After the topic, beginning, and middle sentences have been completed, it is necessary to draw all that you've written to a close. Your reader must feel satisfied and know that you have finished what you started out to do. This is called the ending sentence. There are different ways of writing an ending sentence. It can express an *emotion* or *feeling* about what you have written:

Next time I'll think twice before examining a beehive.

When the class bell rang, Cathy uttered a sigh of relief, knowing she was safe for another day.

It can also *summarize* what you have written and restate in other words what the topic sentence has already expressed:

It is no wonder that Edgar Allan Poe's short stories have become a favorite of teenagers everywhere.

The entire process takes less than a second, but involves the complicated interaction of highly sophisticated electronic equipment.

Activity A

Choose the ending sentence that would best complete the ideas expressed. Discuss your answer in class.

Martina had always feared traveling by plane. After her first flight, she wrote a paragraph telling how she lost her fear of flying. Select the best ending sentence.

1. Now I am anticipating my next opportunity to see Wichita from the air.
2. I was terrified as the attendant said, "Fasten your seat belts; we're about to take off."
3. Wichita looked like a toy village from the air.

Ben is writing about why he likes football. Which ending sentence do you prefer for Ben's topic?

1. Football is a very invigorating sport.
2. Is it any wonder, then, that every autumn finds me practicing football, my favorite sport?
3. Everyone likes the color, the fast-moving action, and the exhilaration of a Saturday afternoon football game, and I am no exception.

Activity B

On a separate sheet of paper, create original endings for the following paragraphs. For one paragraph, try to express an emotion; for the other, restate the topic.

A Jack of All Trades

Our school janitor, Claus Jansen, is a very special person. Because he takes pride in his work, our walks are always cleanly shoveled and our corridors shine. He unjams stubborn locker doors and repairs broken desks with skill and good humor. As if these qualities weren't enough, Claus also shows an uncommon creativity. He designed and built a fascinating wooden playground structure for the younger children, and has guided the construction of wonderfully imaginative sets for our school plays. He is willing to share his talents and workshop space any time we need help, whether it be with a complicated science project or with something as minor (but embarrassing) as the day the heel came off my shoe. _____

_____

The Mighty Peanut

Most persons have probably enjoyed eating the crisp, brown delight known as a peanut. It is doubtful, however, if they are familiar with the variety of other uses for this delicious tidbit. Though chiefly a food substance, peanuts also are used in manufacturing processes. Cosmetics, soaps, explosives, and plastics are but a few of the commercial products derived from the peanut. In fact, several hundred uses have been documented for this versatile seed. _____

_____

Activity C

Below are four narrowed topics for possible paragraphs. On a separate sheet of paper, write an ending sentence for each and tell whether you have expressed an emotion or feeling, or restated the topic.

Narrowed topic: Why reading books is a worthwhile pastime
Ending sentence: _____

Narrowed topic: Humorous antics of my pet
Ending sentence: _____

Narrowed topic: Why students need a longer lunch hour
Ending sentence: _____

Narrowed topic: Why driving is important to a sixteen year old
Ending sentence: _____

More to Explore

Write an ending sentence that would express each one of the following emotions: anger, fear, joy, surprise, confusion.

Lesson 6 Creating a Title

The title is the name of a written work.

The title of any work is usually a short, creative expression of the composition's main idea. A title that is cleverly worded will catch a potential reader's eye and draw him or her into the work. Sometimes clever titles come to an author's mind as a flash of creative insight. At other times, titles must be written, revised, and refined until the author is satisfied.

Some professional writers employ figures of speech in creating their titles: *Alliteration* is used by Edgar Allan Poe in his title "The Tell-Tale Heart"; Lenore Kendel uses a *play on words* in her poem "Wonder Wander"; *allusion* to a child's story is apparent in A.A. Milne's "The Ugly Duckling," a play about a princess; "The Crystal Moment" by Robert Tristram Coffin introduces the *metaphor* that is implied in his poem; and Vachel Lindsay uses *personification* in the poem title "The Potatoes' Dance."

Besides being short and creative, the title should reflect the main idea of the work. It can do this in two ways:

1. The title can name the person, place, thing, or event around which the main idea takes place.
2. The title can indicate the theme or underlying message of a work.

"The Kitten," by Richard Wright, is an excerpt from the author's autobiography, *Black Boy*. In this story, the main idea centers around the killing of a kitten and the effect this had on the author when he was young. *The title directly names the kitten—the animal around which the main idea takes place.*

"Top Man," by James Ramsey Ullman, is a story that revolves around a mountain climbing expedition. Two men stand out in the story; one is young and ambitious, the other, older and more cautious. The younger man, Osborn, foolishly attempts to reach the top of the mountain despite the warnings of Nace, the older and wiser man. Although in the end Osborn does reach the top, he is only able to do so because Nace loses his life saving him from a life-threatening fall. *The underlying message is suggested by the title: who IS the "Top Man"?*

Begin creating your titles by brainstorming all the ways you can use different figures of speech or clever words to state your main idea. Remember to follow these guidelines:

1. Keep your title short.
2. Be creative.
3. Focus on the main idea.

Activity A

Below are some titles that could be used for paragraphs. Read the topic given and choose the title you think would be best. Tell why.

1. A composition about being lost in a cave
   a. Trapped Inside the Earth   b. The Lost Boy
2. A short story about a large raccoon raiding a campsite at night
   a. Raccoon Raider   b. A Beastly Fright in the Night
3. A personal experience story about a girl's first attempt at skiing
   a. Downhill Daredevil   b. Gliding Down the Slopes
4. A composition about catching a home run ball
   a. Prize Possession   b. The Best Baseball Game Ever

5. A narrative composition about a serious bike accident
   a. The Day I Got Hit by a Car   b. Almost Fatal!
6. A descriptive composition about a subway ride
   a. Speeding through the Dark   b. Traveling Underground

Activity B

Below are several paragraphs that need titles. Read each and create a title that would arouse a reader's interest.

_____

Writing can be a very tiring experience. Sometimes when I sit down to write, I can't think of anything to say. When that happens, I have several options. I can stay in my chair, twiddle my pen, and look out the window. I might pick up a book and read for a while to stimulate my thinking. The best thing for me to do, however, is put on my shorts, t-shirt, and running shoes, and head out the door. Once I am outside, I relax. I think better. Still, I often have to run many miles before I can go back to my desk and put those thoughts on paper.

_____

The first morning of my summer vacation found me speeding to a frightening seaside adventure. After a short run down the beach, I felt the cool water cover my ankles and the misty spray of foam fan my face. With the sun bright above, I was totally delighting in my first swim of the season. My enjoyment soon faded, however, when I spied a shark dangerously near. Land seemed miles away. Suddenly a giant wave thrust me to the bottom, and I came up gurgling and choking. Gripped by fear, I struck out for the shore. Surely, I thought, the shark must be near enough to capture me with its sharp teeth. Just then another wave engulfed me. When my blurred vision cleared, I found myself on the beach with my pursuer lying close beside me. To my surprise and relief, I discovered it was nothing more than an inflated rubber shark.

As I reached the high rocky shelf, I paused and turned for a better view of the beautiful valley through which I had come. Far below, a little creek pushed insistently past its banks. Wild ducks moved swiftly through the clear water, their blue-green plumage gleaming with an almost metallic brightness. Warm sunlight shining through the trees cast lacy patterns of light and shadow on the ground. The trees themselves stood proud and tall, conscious of their riotous coloring, and paid to every passing breeze a gracious tribute of drifting leaves. As I gazed down upon this lovely valley, I was filled with a deep sense of gratitude for this beautiful country of ours.

What is personality? It is certainly something that everyone has. In fact, personality is what distinguishes one person from another. It is a combination of social, physical, intellectual, and emotional characteristics. Personality shows itself by the way people interact with others and the way they face certain situations. Although personalities are not fixed, but grow and develop, experts seem to agree that people are born with certain traits. This can be seen most clearly in a set of twins, who grow up in exactly the same environment. It can even be seen in animals, who also have personalities, though to a lesser degree. Anyone who has watched a litter of kittens develop, for instance, will have noticed how one kitten might be aggressive and daring, another timid, and yet another very affectionate. Of course, the most interesting thing of all about personality is that every one is unique. No two people have exactly the same combination and degree of personality characteristics.

More to Explore

Create a title for a paragraph on each of the following topics:
1. The day the smoke alarm went off
2. The year your team won the championship
3. Being chased by a huge dog
4. The time your friends gave you a surprise party
5. Catching a prize-winning fish

Word Study 1

Prefixes

A prefix is a syllable or syllables added to the beginning of a word that changes the meaning of the word.

Many of our prefixes come from other languages, such as Latin and Greek. This symbol [<], meaning "taken from," is found at the beginning or end of the dictionary entry.

Activity A

Listed below are six prefixes. Using your dictionary, discover whether the prefixes are derived from the Latin or Greek language. Write your answers on a sheet of paper.

1. pan–   all   <
2. semi–   half   <
3. mono–   one   <
4. intro, intra–   inside of   <
5. multi–   many   <
6. poly–   many   <

Detail from an ancient
Greek vase

Activity B

Copy the chart below. Using your dictionary, give three new words for each prefix listed in Activity A and write the meaning next to each new word. Make certain that the meaning uses the definition of the prefix. The first one is done for you.

Prefix	New Words	Meanings
pan	panacea	cure for all difficulties
	_____	_____
	_____	_____
semi	_____	_____
	_____	_____
	_____	_____

(Continue in same manner with remaining prefixes.)

Activity C

Think of a word that would best complete each of the sentences that follow. The prefix of the word is given for you. Some sentences will be easy to complete, while others may require looking through the dictionary for appropriate words beginning with the prefix shown.

1. My birthday gift was a mono_____ sweater.
2. In the play, the main character read a mono_____ .
3. I would like you to intro_____ me to that girl with the red hair.
4. Intra_____ sports are popular at our school.
5. Everyone said that John was an intro_____ because he was so shy.
6. The multi_____ banner attracted our attention.
7. A multi_____ of people gathered outside the theater.
8. Sometimes a semi_____ is used to divide a compound sentence.
9. The basketball team made it to the semi_____ .
10. His pants were made of poly_____ and cotton.
11. A poly_____ is commonly called a "lie detector."
12. On weekends, we always have eggs and pan_____ for breakfast.
13. Pan_____ broke out when the lead singer threw his hat into the crowd.

Chapter 2

Developing Your Writing Skills

Lesson 1 Unity

A paragraph has unity when all sentences relate to the topic or main idea.

When you read the paragraph below, look for the topic sentence, the related middle sentences, and the misfit sentence.

Among the world's greatest treasures are exquisite diamonds owned by governments, royalty, and museums. The United States proudly displays the Hope diamond in the Smithsonian Institution. In the Louvre Museum in France is the beautiful Regent diamond, while the Koh-i-noor remains secure in the possession of Great Britain. Some diamonds can even be produced by artificial means under the right conditions. Russia's prize, the Orloff diamond, was supposedly stolen from the eye of a Hindu idol. Such rare gems are surely the earth's gift to humankind.

1. Which is the topic sentence?
2. What is the general topic?
3. What is the narrowed topic?
4. Is the topic sentence the beginning sentence?
5. Which are the supporting middle sentences?
6. Which sentence is not related to the topic?
7. Why doesn't this sentence relate to the topic?
8. Which is the ending sentence?
9. Does the ending sentence express a feeling or restate the topic?

Now read the same paragraph, omitting the misfit or unrelated sentence. When all middle sentences relate to the topic, this is called *unity*. Since all the sentences in the paragraph now tell about the great diamonds of the world, the paragraph has the quality of unity.

Do you think this photograph of a butterfly wing suggests the value of looking closely at everyday wonders? In what ways?

25

Activity A

Read the following paragraph. Look for the topic sentence, the related middle sentences, and the misfit or unrelated sentence.

   The students' voices soar as they try to squeeze in a quick word with their friends. One girl's voice rises above the others as she reminds participants about the bicycle ride to support the zoo, and two boys can be heard desperately trying to discover who made this year's football squad. Teachers, chatting loudly, race to the faculty room to rescue forgotten test papers or grab a quick sip of coffee. The coffee was brewed early in the day. Needless to say, at the change of class the noise level is at a feverish pitch.

On a sheet of paper,
   1. write the topic sentence.
   2. give the general topic.
   3. give the narrowed topic.
   4. write the sentence that is not related to the topic.
   5. compose a sentence that would relate to the other middle sentences and take the place of the misfit sentence.

Activity B

Read the following two paragraphs and discuss the qualities that give them unity.

Rocking Chair Saga

   Household furnishings often occupy a prominent place in the memories of an individual. Many of the recollections of my early years are built around a comfortable wooden rocking chair that stood in the corner of our big kitchen. What opportunities it offered for three imaginative children! Disguised by a blanket and turned on end, it became a smugglers' cave inhabited by buccaneers who were a constant menace to the pantry shelf. Without the covering, a patient steed groaned under the weight of three sturdy riders. If other pieces of furniture could be pressed into service, the rocker was transformed into a locomotive hauling a train of startling appearance. The chair in its natural position, however, holds the dearest memories of all. Then it became the place where mother soothed her tired children and rocked away the cares of a weary day. Pirates' cave to haven of comfort and love—could anything but a sturdy pine rocker have stood the strain?

White Magic

In spite of keen competition from a variety of newly invented materials, cotton continues to hold its own as a most versatile product. Many who appreciate the usefulness of ordinary cotton cloth are unaware of a lengthy list of other uses, ranging from explosives to mayonnaise. Yes, it is true; the oil from the cotton seed is employed in the making of salad dressing, and the cotton linters become the powerful guncotton so necessary in quarrying and in mining. A strong cloth called canvas is woven from cotton and used for such purposes as bookbinding and the manufacture of heavy duty items like awnings and mailbags. If cotton canvas is waterproofed with tar, paint, or other materials, it becomes tarpaulin and is used to protect boats, machinery, and the like. Raw cotton has a large percentage of cellulose, which is used to make paper, glue, paint, and various plastics. For many years cotton was the leading fiber, and today it still continues to play an important role in our everyday lives.

More to Explore

Choose one narrowed topic from the list below. Write four or five supporting details, including one misfit sentence. Then write a topic sentence and an effective ending sentence.

1. The first time I tried to ski (skate, waterski, windsurf, etc.)
2. How my sister (brother) and I managed to ruin dinner
3. Music that makes me want to dance
4. Why _____ makes me laugh (supply own idea)
5. Where I go when I need to think things over

Lesson 2 Coherence

A paragraph has coherence when it is in logical and natural order.
Coherence means "sticking together."

A paragraph will have coherence if it flows naturally from one idea to the next. In other words, there must be a sense of order in the paragraph. Order can be *sequential* (time, order of importance, directions) or *spatial* (space).

Sequential Order

When a paragraph is written in *sequential* order, the sentences follow a logical pattern. Most often the pattern is according to time (chronological order) or order of importance. Many "how to" compositions (how to plan a trip, how to use a VCR, etc.) are written according to sequential order. Read the following paragraph and note the words that signal sequence.

> Almost all things in nature can be recycled. The leaf is a perfect example of nature's recycling process. First, the leaf must fall to the ground to allow the autumn rains to soften it. Next, bacteria breaks down the materials that make up the leaf. Then rain water dissolves the matter and slowly washes it back into the earth. All this decayed substance provides food for the soil and, finally, leaves the ground fertile for the new plants that will grow there. Recycling is just one of nature's many phenomena.

1. Name all the words that indicate a sequential order.
2. Read the paragraph again, reversing sentences three and four. What happens to the coherence in the paragraph?
3. What transition word signals the conclusion of the process?

Activity B

Even when ideas are put in spatial order, they will not automatically form a well-worded paragraph. You may find some short, choppy sentences, just as you did with sequential order. Certain transition words can tie these sentences together and give a clearer sense of the order of ideas. Listed below are some of the most commonly used transition, or signal, words for spatial order.

above	farther	to the left
across	here	to the right
before	in front of	under
behind	next to	underneath
below	opposite to	

After studying these transition words, use them to connect the ideas in Activity A. Write a topic sentence, put the middle sentences in spatial order, and then write a concluding thought. Use extra words and ideas to make the paragraph more interesting.

Activity C

Below are twelve topics for paragraphs. Decide if the ideas for each should be organized by sequential or spatial order. Indicate your choices on a separate sheet of paper by writing the number of each topic and the word *sequential* or *spatial.*

1. To explain how to get to your home from school
2. To explain the arrangement of the furniture in your bedroom
3. To describe the design of a flag
4. To trace the history of the automobile
5. To explain how to make a banana split
6. To outline the steps in the writing process
7. To explain what makes a volcano erupt
8. To describe the clothes on a model
9. To explain how a computer works
10. To explain how to set a table
11. To trace your roots back to your great grandparents
12. To show how you have matured from first to eighth grade

More to Explore

To reinforce your skills in writing coherently, choose one of the topics in Activity C, or make up one of your own, and write a brief paragraph about it.

Lesson 3 Comparison

Many of your high school writing assignments will involve comparing and contrasting. You might be asked to compare and contrast such things as poems, historical periods, or the results of experiments. To help get you started in writing of this kind, let us first look at what we mean by *comparison*.

Comparison is a method of writing that shows the similarities among persons, places, or things.

In order to organize your thoughts and ideas, it is wise to map out on a piece of paper the similarities among the objects being compared. Here is an example. In the circle are two objects being compared: a small truck and a station wagon. The lines coming from the circle show the many ways in which the two are similar.

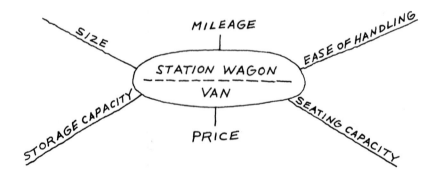

Once you have your ideas mapped out, you can put them into paragraph form.

Activity A

Here is a paragraph someone wrote about the similarities between a van and a station wagon. As you read the paragraph, look for the things mentioned in points 1–4 on the next page.

Decisions! Decisions!

Like many adventurous Americans, the Wilders decided to try camping for recreation. Knowing that a new form of transportation would be required, the family faced a dilemma: should it be a van or a station wagon? They compared the two vehicles. The van was roomier than their present car, but compact and easy to handle on the highway. So was the station wagon. The station wagon had the capacity to transport all the family members and their camping gear, just as the van did. In the same way, the highway mileage of both vehicles was comparable. Furthermore, the van and the wagon had almost identical sticker prices. The family realized they were going to have to find more factors on which to base their decision.

On a sheet of paper,
1. write the first three words of the topic sentence.
2. write the first three words of the beginning sentence.
3. list the transition words that signal points of comparison.
4. tell how many points of comparison were made.

Here is a list of possible transition words for comparison writing.

also	like	similarly
furthermore	likewise	so
just as	in the same way	resembles

Activity B

Ready for mapping are four sets of topics for comparison. On your sheet of paper, draw the circle, write in the topics to be compared, and then on lines coming from the circle, write in all the similarities you can think of.

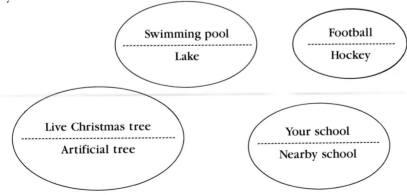

Swimming pool

Lake

Football

Hockey

Live Christmas tree

Artificial tree

Your school

Nearby school

More to Explore

Choose one of the topics from Activity B, or create an original set, and write a short paragraph showing *comparison*. Use transition words to keep the paragraph unified and coherent.

Lesson 4 Contrast

Contrast is a method of writing that shows the differences among persons, places, or things.

Showing the differences among topics is a more difficult task than showing the similarities, but it can be a very rewarding way of writing. In order to point out differences, the subjects must be alike. This sounds like a contradiction, but it is really a very logical statement. Things cannot be compared unless they have similar natures. You can contrast a daffodil with a tulip, but you can't logically contrast a daffodil with a butterfly. You can contrast a lobster with a crab because they are both shellfish, but a lobster and a cat have no mutual points on which they can be compared.

Activity A

Copy the following ten topics onto a sheet of paper. Next to each topic, write the name of something that can be sensibly contrasted with it.

1. piano
2. lizard
3. collie
4. word processor
5. candle
6. dictionary
7. pencil
8. toothbrush
9. cheddar
10. ballet

Activity B

As you read the following paragraph, look for the things mentioned in numbers 1-5 below.

All the Better to See You With

Without a doubt, contact lenses are a vast improvement over glasses. Lenses can correct every visual defect that glasses can and, because lenses are worn directly on the eye, can correct some defects that glasses cannot. Lenses move with the eye, so they give better peripheral (side) vision. They never slide down one's nose or make a mark on it. Neither do they fog over in cold or damp weather. Where sports are concerned, contact lenses definitely show their superiority. They can be worn with almost no fear of breakage. Glasses, on the other hand, cannot solve as many visual problems. Because their position is fixed, they also give poorer peripheral vision. More often than not, they are at the end of one's nose, leaving a little red mark at the top. In cold or damp weather, the lenses on glasses quickly steam up, impairing vision. Furthermore, glasses are very easily broken during active play. It's no wonder contact lenses have become so popular.

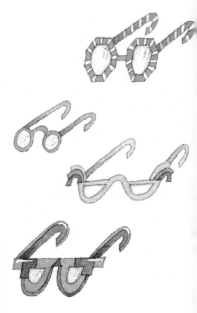

On a sheet of paper,
1. write the topic sentence.
2. name the two topics being compared.
3. list the points of differences discussed.
4. name the transition phrase used to show contrast.
5. choose the outline that best fits the paragraph you just read. Select Plan A or B and tell why you made the choice.

PLAN A
1. **Contact Lenses**
   —ability to correct visual defects
   —peripheral vision with
   —comfort of
   —effect of weather on
   —breakage of

2. **Eyeglasses**
   —ability to correct visual defects
   —peripheral vision with
   —comfort of
   —effect of weather on
   —breakage of

PLAN B

1. **Contact Lenses**—ability to correct visual defects
2. **Eyeglasses**—ability to correct visual defects
1. **Contact Lenses**—peripheral vision with
2. **Eyeglasses**—peripheral vision with
1. **Contact Lenses**—comfort of
2. **Eyeglasses**—comfort of
1. **Contact Lenses**—breakage of
2. **Eyeglasses**—breakage of

Activity C

As you read the following paragraph, look for the things mentioned in numbers 1-6 below.

Different Where It Counts

Although the Thoroughbred and the Clydesdale are about the same height, there are striking differences between these two breeds of horses. The Thoroughbred is lighter with longer legs, enabling it to be one of the swiftest creatures in existence. The Clydesdale, on the other hand, is a heavier and stronger animal, able to pull hefty loads. While the Thoroughbred is considered to have a nervous temperament, the Clydesdale, in contrast, is known for its good disposition. The unique features of these two horses have been bred into them over the years so that they could serve humankind in different ways. The Thoroughbred developed from the Arabian horse and has always been a saddle animal, whereas the Clydesdale is a descendant of the early draft, or workhorses of central Europe. These handsome creatures are just two of the many interesting breeds of horses found all over the world.

On a sheet of paper,
1. write the topic sentence.
2. name the word in the topic sentence that signals a contrast.
3. name the two topics being contrasted.
4. name the points of differences discussed.
5. name the transition words used to show contrast.
6. choose the outline that best fits the paragraph you just read. Choose Plan A or B and tell why you made the choice.

PLAN A

1. **Thoroughbred**
   —body build
   —temperament
   —origins
2. **Clydesdale**
   —body build
   —temperament
   —origins

PLAN B

1. **Thoroughbred**—body build
2. **Clydesdale**—body build
1. **Thoroughbred**—temperament
2. **Clydesdale**—temperament
1. **Thoroughbred**—origins
2. **Clydesdale**—origins

Thoroughbred

You can see that either plan is effective and both can be formed into well organized paragraphs. Both plans utilize transition words, but one plan uses more than the other. Which one is that?

Here are some transition or signal words you can use in contrast writing.

but	on the other hand	whereas
however	unlike	in contrast

Clydesdales

Activity D

Listed below are some possible topics for contrast. First see what they have in common, and then determine the differences. On a piece of paper, write one point of comparison and three points of contrast for each set of topics.

1. Movies at the theater
   Movies on a VCR

2. Motorcycle
   Automobile

3. Cello
   Violin

4. Table
   Desk

5. Elevator
   Escalator

6. Digital watch
   Traditional watch

More to Explore

1. Choose a set of topics from Activity D, or create an original set, and compose a short paragraph stressing *contrast*. Use transition words to keep the paragraph unified and coherent. Make sure you choose the plan that works best for you.

2. Redo the paragraph "All the Better to See You With" according to Plan B, and then do "Different Where It Counts" according to Plan A.

Lesson 5 Revision

Revision means "the act of seeing again." To revise a piece of writing means to take a second look at it and decide whether you should *Change* sentences around, *Add* or *Remove* words, or *Substitute* new ones (CARS).

All writers revise their work. When they first put their ideas down on paper, they end up with what is called a *first draft*. They then read over the first draft and see how they can improve it. There will sometimes be several drafts before the final version.

As a writer, your goal is to create paragraphs that will express your ideas in a clear and interesting fashion. It is important to revise your writing until it reads exactly the way you want it to. When you read over your first draft, you should check for unity, coherence, appropriate word choices, and effective transitions. It is also helpful to ask yourself the following questions:

To *whom* am I writing?
—myself
—my teacher
—other students
—the local community

What is the subject of my writing?

Why am I writing?
—to describe
—to inform
—to tell a story
—to persuade

The following paragraph needs to be revised. Read it over and decide what changes you would make. Discuss these ideas with your teacher or with other students. Use the Checkpoints for Revision at the end of the paragraph to help you focus in on your revision.

First Draft Paragraph

My cat, whose name is Ariel, misses me when I am not at home. When I go to school, she tries to follow me. If she gets out the door, I have to get her back in the house. Then she sleeps in the sun and looks out the window and plays with her toys. I have some friends who let their cats follow them to school. Ariel gets particularly upset when I go away for a weekend, even though I leave her food and water. She likes my company. I know how she feels. I get lonely when I'm by myself too much, too.

Checkpoints for Revision
—Is there a topic sentence that clearly states the main idea of the paragraph?
—Are there enough supporting details?
—Do all of the details fit the topic?
—Are the details in the correct order?
—Are effective transitions used?
—Are there different kinds of sentences?
—Are the words precise and accurate?
—Is there a strong ending sentence?

Now read a revised version of the paragraph about the cat. What did the writer do to improve the paragraph? What is changed around, added, or removed?

Revised Paragraph

My cat, Ariel, misses me when I am not at home. As I leave for school in the morning, she tries to follow me. Sometimes she squeezes out the door, and I have to chase her back in the house. She is particularly upset if I go away for a whole weekend, even though I make sure she has plenty of dry food and water. When I am gone, Ariel passes the time by sleeping in the sun, looking out the window, or playing with her toys. She likes all those things, but seems to enjoy my company most of all. I know how she feels, because I also get lonely when I'm by myself too much.

Activity A

Combine the following sentences to create a paragraph. Then revise and rewrite the paragraph by adding or deleting words, moving sentences around, or substituting new words. Use the Checkpoints for Revision to help you discover where improvements are needed.

Topic Sentence	People have different approaches to doing homework, some more effective than others.
Supporting Details	1. Andrew refuses ever to do homework. 2. Cynthia does everything that is assigned, as soon as it is assigned. 3. Jon reads the beginning and the end of every assigned reading, and glances at the middle. 4. Nicole takes good notes in class and studies those for tests, but never reads anything else. 5. Tod tries to decide what is most important and does that.
Ending Sentence	Tod and Cynthia get the best grades. Do you think their grades are related to how they study?

Activity B

Consider how the following paragraph might be revised, and then rewrite it on a separate sheet of paper.

Building a house requires many different kinds of workers. An architect creates a plan for the house. Cement workers pour the foundation. Roofers climb around on the nearly completed outer structure to put on shingles. Carpenters put up studs and beams to compose the frame. A contractor hires workers of many kinds. An electrician puts in the wiring. Painters are needed for both the inside and the outside of many houses. Other times a stone mason or bricklayer puts finishing touches on the outside.

More to Explore

Look over the paragraphs you have written in past lessons and choose one that you feel could be improved. Exchange paragraphs with another student and practice the revision process on each other's work. Afterwards, discuss why you made the changes you did.

Lesson 6 Proofreading

Proofreading is the last step in the writing process. It is at this point that you make a final check for:

Punctuation: periods, commas, colons, semi-colons, apostrophes, hyphens, question marks, exclamation points

Capitalization: first word of each sentence, proper nouns, proper adjectives

Spelling: start at the last word and work backwards; consult dictionary for problem words

Correct usage: subject-verb agreement, consistent verb tenses

Smoothness: copy all words correctly from last revision; read composition aloud, give work to another person to read

Appearance: handwriting neat and legible, appropriate margins on paper, name at the end of your work

Here are some symbols that a proofreader uses when going over a paper for the last time:

Symbol	Meaning	Example
¶	begin a new paragraph	over. ¶Begin a new
◡	close up space	close u p space
∧	insert	students ∧think _should_
℘	delete, omit	that the the book
/	lower case letter	Mathematics
∽	letters are reversed	letters are reversed
≡	capital letter	washington

Activity A

There is one error in each of the sentences below. Copy the sentences onto a sheet of paper and use appropriate proofreaders' symbols to indicate the corrections that need to be made.

1. We always have a family cookout on the fourth of July.
2. Mt. St. Helens is an active Volcano.
3. Beach combers are on the sand early in the morning.
4. The actor who played the theif was superb.
5. The flag will be raised each morning 8:30 A.M.
6. The King Tut exhibit wass quite fascinating.

Activity B

Proofread the following paragraph. On a separate sheet of paper, note each error by writing down the two words preceding it and the two words following it. With a different color pen, mark in proofreaders' symbols to indicate the corrections needed. There are fifteen errors in the paragraph.

Nowadays I sail every chance I can get, but I didn't always feel that way abut the sprot. My first sailing lesson did not go well from the very beginning. After my Instructor, Mike, introduced himself, he told me to toss my canvas bag into the dinghy. I tossed a little too enthusiastically, and mike had to row out to save my bag from certain death by drowning Things didn't improve wh en we finally got out to the sailboat. I caught my pantleg on a on a hook and literally fell into the boat. After Mike carefully showed me how to put the small sail on correctly, I puttt it on upside down. I also managed to dip hafl the mainsail in the water, bang my shin on the anchor, and flip an ore over the side (they float!). I began to regard the Boat as an enemy, and was sure it felt the same way about me. Mike managed to get us ready sail despite me but I felt no real pleasure as we moved away from our mooring. Instead I looked mournfully back at familiar landmarks I was sure i would never sea again.

Because there are so many errors in this paragraph, it should be rewritten once more. If there were only one or two errors, they could be corrected by erasing and using the same color ink.

More to Explore

Take a paragraph you have written that is in final form and rewrite it, inserting seven errors. They should be the kind of mistakes that can be corrected by the proofreaders' symbols you have just learned. Trade paragraphs with another student and see if you can find each other's deliberate errors. Use the proofreaders' symbols to indicate corrections that need to be made. Return paragraphs and check that all errors were found and that you both used the symbols correctly.

Word Study 2

Root Words

A root word is a base word from which other words are built.

Root words have their own meanings. Some can stand alone as words; others need to be added to a prefix or suffix in order to form a word.

Activity A

Listed below are five root words. Using your dictionary, discover whether they are derived from [<] the Latin or Greek language. Write your answers on a sheet of paper.

ped–	foot	<
meter–	measure	<
chrono–	time	<
duct–	lead	<
scribe–	write	<

Activity B

Copy the chart below. Using your dictionary, create three new words from each root word listed in Activity A, and then write the meanings of the new words.

Root	New Words	Meanings
ped	_____	_____
	_____	_____
	_____	_____
meter	_____	_____
	_____	_____
	_____	_____

(Continue in same manner with remaining roots.)

Activity C

Complete each of the following sentences by using a word based on the root shown in parentheses.

1. The little boy (scribe) all over the painted wall.
2. The secretary (scribe) the letter perfectly.
3. Please arrange everything in (chrono) order.
4. When your feet hurt, see a (ped).
5. All (ped) are to cross the street at the corner.
6. If you wish to know what the temperature is, check a (meter).
7. A (meter) is one tenth of a meter.
8. Water is an excellent (duct) of electricity.
9. The (duct) in Rome carried water throughout the city.

Chapter 3

Refining Your Writing Skills

Lesson 1 Combining Independent Clauses

Combining independent clauses varies sentence length and makes paragraphs more interesting.

If a paragraph contains too many short sentences, it will not read smoothly. When two short sentences are closely related in thought, they can be combined to form one longer sentence. The longer sentence is called a *compound sentence* because it contains two simple sentences, or *independent clauses*, properly connected. Most independent clauses are connected by *coordinate conjunctions*, each of which varies slightly in meaning and changes the thought of the sentence.

Coordinator	Function	Example
and	suggests ideas that are of equal importance	The safe was open, and the money was gone.
but/yet	suggests opposite or contrasting ideas	Dan often travels by plane, yet he is afraid of flying.
or	suggests options or alternatives	I could paint the walls, or I could put up wallpaper.
nor	suggests no possible option or alternative	My sunglasses weren't in the house, nor were they in the car.

There is a surprise in the hatbox in this painting. Tell about a surprise you have had that has made life more interesting.

Activity A

On a sheet of paper, combine the following simple sentences by inserting an appropriate conjunction. Tell the function of the coordinator.

1. Jeanne could take a course in early American history. She could take a course in modern poetry.
2. The mechanic used all his skills. Nothing corrected the engine problem.
3. Suddenly the wind started blowing strongly. It began to rain.
4. Jack does not walk to school. He does not ride a bus.
5. The tomato is treated like a vegetable. It is really a fruit.
6. Peter could pitch in tomorrow's game. He could pitch next Saturday instead.

Activity B

Write five original sentences showing the proper use of *and, but, yet, or,* and *nor.* Try to draw on information from your science, math, or social studies classes. Be able to identify the function of each coordinator.

More to Explore

Write a short paragraph about an incident that happened at school or at home. Include at least three compound sentences using different coordinators.

Lesson 2 Sentence Combining with Adjectival Clauses

In a complex sentence, the principal clause is the more important idea expressed. The dependent clause is the less important idea. An adjectival clause is a dependent clause.

You have learned that you can use a coordinate conjunction to form two simple sentences into one compound sentence. When this is done, each sentence remains an independent clause. Another way of combining sentences is to make one of the sentences an *independent clause* and the other sentence a *dependent clause*. When you combine an independent clause and a dependent clause, you create a *complex sentence*.

An *adjectival clause* is one kind of dependent clause. It can be added to a principal clause by means of a relative pronoun. The principal clause, or *independent clause*, always contains the *main idea*. The adjectival clause, or *dependent clause*, expresses the *idea of lesser importance*. Look at the following sample sentence:

> Florida, which is one of the leading tourist states, is located in the southeastern part of the United States.

The writer wishes to stress the location of Florida. The main idea of the sentence is: *Florida is located in the southeastern part of the United States*. The adjectival clause, beginning with the relative pronoun *which*, states an idea of lesser importance: *Florida is one of the leading tourist states*.

Suppose the writer wished to stress the fact that Florida is a leading tourist state. In that case, the writer would subordinate the idea that Florida is located in the southeastern part of the United States. An appropriate relative pronoun would introduce this statement. The complex sentence would now look like this:

> Florida, which is located in the southeastern part of the United States, is one of the leading tourist states.

Now compare the two sentences.

Activity A

Following are some complex sentences. Each contains an independent and a dependent clause. Read each sentence and then write its main idea on a sheet of paper.

1. The Parthenon, which stands on the Acropolis, overlooks the city of Athens.
2. The earliest type of armor, which was made of animal skins, protected the body from clubs and axes.
3. Ferdinand Foch, who was a French military leader, was one of the greatest Allied generals of World War I.
4. The flounder has a flat body that blends in with its surroundings.
5. Castles, which are fortified dwellings, played a prominent role in the life of the Middle Ages.

Activity B

For each sentence, locate the clause containing the less important idea and copy it onto a sheet of paper.

1. The Sears Tower, which is located in Chicago, is 110 stories high.
2. The name *Florida*, which in Spanish means "full of flowers," was given by Ponce de Leon.
3. Fog is a low cloud that rests near the ground or a body of water.
4. Animals that live in the polar regions are usually hairy with thick hides.
5. The centaur was a mythological creature that was half man and half horse.

Activity C

On a sheet of paper, rewrite the sentences in Activities A and B so that the clauses are reversed. This means that the importance of the ideas will also be reversed. What was formerly the main idea will become the less important idea, what was less important will become the main idea. The first sentence is done as an example.

adjectival clause

The Parthenon, [which overlooks the city of Athens,] stands on the Acropolis. ──▶ main idea

Activity D

Combine each pair of sentences, making the sentence in italics the principal clause. Connect the dependent clause to the principal clause with an appropriate relative pronoun: *who, whom, which, what, that.* Some words will be omitted when the sentences are combined.

1. *Atlantis was a mythical island in the Atlantic Ocean.*
   Atlantis was destroyed by earthquakes and floods.
2. John Adams was the second president of the United States.
   John Adams was the first president to live in the White House.
3. *Students should know about the encyclopedia.*
   The encyclopedia contains many interesting facts.
4. Babe Didrikson was a great athlete.
   Babe Didrikson set world records in the 1932 Olympic Games.
5. A dingo is a wild dog of Australia.
   The dingo may have been brought to Australia by prehistoric settlers.

Babe Didrikson *(Right)*

More to Explore

Write five original complex sentences. The principal and the dependent clauses should be joined by a relative pronoun. Use information from your other subject areas.

Lesson 3 Sentence Combining with Adverbial Clauses

In a complex sentence, the principal clause is the more important idea expressed. The dependent clause is the less important idea. An adverbial clause is a dependent clause.

An adverbial clause is a type of dependent clause. It can be added to a principal clause by means of a subordinate conjunction. The subordinate conjunction establishes the relationship between the two clauses. Look at the sentences below and note the different types of relationships. The adverbial clauses are italicized.

Carlos has an extensive vocabulary *because he is an avid reader.* (cause and effect relationship)

As soon as I pack my suitcase, I'll be ready. (time relationship)

An Olympic athlete performs better *than an amateur college athlete does.* (comparison relationship)

Sandra works *as though there will be no tomorrow.* (relationship of manner)

Although Monica wanted to be a great gymnast, she was unwilling to practice every day. (conditional relationship)

Changing the subordinator can change the meaning of a sentence. Read the sentence below, using a different subordinator each time. Discuss the shades of meaning.

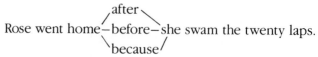

The entire subordinate clause, which includes the subordinate conjunction, may be placed before or after the principal clause. This provides sentence variety. Look at the example below.

The old, weathered prospector built a fire [because the temperature dropped to 30°.]

[Because the temperature dropped to 30°,] the old, weathered prospector built a fire.

Activity A

The relationship between the sentences in each set is given in parentheses. Show this relationship by using the proper subordinate conjunction to combine the two sentences.

1. Paper was scarce and expensive in the Middle Ages. It had to be used sparingly. (cause and effect)
2. Little children went to school. The children were given a hornbook. (time)
3. The hornbook was a flat board with a hole in its handle. The hornbook could be worn around the neck. (cause and effect)
4. The hornbook was used in England and America. Printed books became cheaper. (time)
5. Some hornbooks were made of gingerbread. Children could eat the letter of the alphabet they had mastered. (cause and effect)

Activity B

Combine each of the following sentences by making the italicized words into an adverbial clause. Introduce the clause with an appropriate subordinator from the list below and tell what relationship is established.

although	for	since	then
after	if	so	unless
because	provided	than	when
before			

1. Chess is a difficult game to learn. *Checkers is not a difficult game to learn.*
2. *Mark Twain is a noted novelist.* He also has written many outstanding short stories.
3. *Caesar had a cruel manner.* He was greatly disliked.
4. Ann discovered the gasoline tank was leaking. *We had traveled many hours.*
5. Two bears arrived on the scene. *We cleared the picnic area.*

Samuel Clemens *(Mark Twain)*

Activity C

Reverse the position of the adverbial clause in each sentence of Activity B. If the clause was introductory, make it final; if final, make it introductory.

More to Explore

Write original complex sentences showing the following relationships: cause and effect, comparison, time, manner, and condition. Vary the positions of the adverbial clauses to create variety.

Lesson 4 Expanding Sentences

Expanding sentences involves adding extra words, phrases, or clauses in order to make the sentences more interesting.

One way to make a sentence more interesting is to add extra information to it, or to expand it. This can be done by inserting words, phrases, or clauses in appropriate places in the sentence.

This added information can tell:
where   why
when   how

It can also describe:
nouns   adjectives
verbs   adverbs

Notice the following sentence:
    The woman walked to the store.
The arrows indicate several places where information can be added to expand the sentence. One possible result could be:
    The *tired old* woman walked *slowly up the block* to the *corner* store.
If other words were used to expand the sentence, an entirely different picture might emerge:
    The *tall, dark-haired* woman walked *briskly across the mall* to the *discount clothing* store.

Activity A

Expand the following sentences by adding words, phrases, or clauses where the arrows indicate.

1. Karen ∧ decorated for the ∧ party ∧ .
2. ∧ John ∧ finished his ∧ homework.
3. The ∧ television broke ∧ .
4. The ∧ train ∧ screeched to a ∧ stop.
5. ∧ The ∧ bell ∧ rang to begin ∧ class.

Activity B

Expand the following sentences by adding words, phrases, or clauses where you think they would fit.

1. The doctor examined the patient.
2. The beach chair collapsed.
3. The rock broke the window.
4. Herve's bike was stolen.
5. Nicole received a stereo.
6. The fire burned the house.
7. The bus moved along.
8. The pioneers traveled west.
9. Charles Dickens wrote novels.
10. The athlete made the team.

The Quilting Party,
American folk art

55

Activity C

Use words, phrases, and clauses to expand each of the following sentences, and then combine the sentences to make an interesting, creative paragraph.

1. The room was wallpapered.
2. There was a rug on the floor.
3. There was furniture scattered about.
4. White curtains framed the windows.

More to Explore

The paragraph below needs revision. Use any of the skills you have learned for expanding and combining sentences to make the paragraph more interesting. Rewrite the paragraph on a sheet of paper and create a title for it.

We went hiking on the trail. The sun was shining. The air was cool. It felt good. The leaves were already changing. Many had fallen. They smelled wonderful. We tramped through them. We saw squirrels foraging for nuts. A flock of geese flew over. Fall was here. The signs were everywhere. Winter was around the corner.

Lesson 5 Word Substitution

Word substitution involves the choosing of vivid, colorful vocabulary to convey your message in an interesting manner.

Look at the sentence below and note the colorless way in which it is written; then look at all the possible substitutions that can be made to enliven the sentence. The important thing is not just to *tell* your reader what happened, but to let your reader *experience* the event.

Feeling quite scared, I sat in the colorful roller coaster waiting for it to go up the first hill.

A colorful
gaudily painted
brightly-hued
gleaming
riotously colored
silver-toned

roller coaster
chariot
coach
Thunderbolt
rocket car
express train

What can a roller coaster do?
swoop   soar   glide   crawl
careen   zip   plunge   lurch

What response do you give?
gasp   tremble   stiffen   cling
huddle   slide   cringe   jerk
slouch   grasp   squirm   shudder

What was the ride like?
downward plunge
breathtaking descent
mad rush through time and space
crawling ascent
perilous curves

How did you feel?
soaring spirits
wildly pounding heart
mounting terror
breathless joy
fear and trepidation
excitement

Your new sentence might look like this:

(Feeling quite scared)

(I sat in the colorful roller coaster)

With a wildly pounding heart, I huddled in the silver-toned chariot, anxiously awaiting its crawl up the mountain for the initial downward plunge.

(waiting for it to go up the first hill)

What does a paragraph look like when there is a vivid, colorful vocabulary replacing worn-out, drab words?

Eventful Journey

Mingled emotions of fear and regret clashed within me as I settled myself in the Thunderbolt that July afternoon. The strident shouts of the operator cut across the air as the screeching of released brakes noisily announced the initial ascent. With a racing heart, I stiffened myself against the back of the brightly gleaming car. For one thrill-packed second I was conscious of being unwillingly poised on a gigantic hill. Then down, down I plunged at breathtaking speed. Before I had even a slim chance of retrieving my composure, this mad rush was repeated with terrifying rapidity. Desperately I clung to the steel bar of the chariot as it careened and whizzed around each perilous curve. Suddenly, as I shuddered and cringed in my place, the rocket car gave a wild, uncontrolled lurch, then with an asthmatic cough wheezed to a full stop. Head reeling, I staggered out of the coach, relieved and grateful for the feeling of solid ground under my feet. I am sure that even a trip around the world would not be so thrilling as that five-minute ride on the roller coaster.

How do you come up with a phrase that paints a picture? One way is to use words that describe as accurately as possible the experiences of your senses: *sight, sound, taste, smell*, and *touch*. To say, for instance, that music *came* from the speakers might not describe your experience of the sound as accurately as saying that music *blasted* from the speakers.

Activity A

SIGHT is the sense through which we collect the most images. Think of five words that could be substituted for each word in italics in order to make the action come alive. Write the words on a sheet of paper. A few have already been given to get you started.

People *walk*, saunter, hike, _____
Animals *walk*, trot, _____
Leaves *drop*, whirl, _____
Waves *fall*, _____
Lights *shine*, _____

SOUND is the second most common way in which we gather experiences. List five words that could be substituted for each word in italics.

Voices *talk*, _____   Birds *sing*, _____
Water *flows*, _____   Bells *ring*, _____
Animals *talk*, _____

Many images come through TASTE. Give five words for how

food *tastes*, _____
beverages *taste*, _____

Other images come to us through the sense of SMELL. Give five words that describe how

flowers *smell*, _____   air *smells*, _____
forests *smell*, _____

The last way you receive impressions or images is through TOUCH. Give five words to describe how

water *feels*, _____   fruit *feels*, _____
cloth *feels*, _____   wind *feels*, _____

Activity B

Find substitutes for the words in italics, and then write one new sentence. Use your imagination and expand your ideas wherever you can. The first one has been done for you.

1. The *car went* down the road.

   The red sportscar roared down the country road.
2. Amy made a *beverage* that *tasted good*.
3. Her perfume *smelled good*.
4. The *cat walked* through the tall grass.
5. Hamburgers *were frying in the pan*.
6. The water *in the shower* was *hot and relaxing*.
7. The *horse trotted* along.

More to Explore

How many new words can you substitute for *nice*? Read the following paragraph and try to provide more specific adjectives. On a sheet of paper, write the more precise adjective and the word that follows it. After you have finished this exercise, reread the paragraph to make certain that every substitute for *nice* is as exact as possible.

Ringing in the New Year

The school added a *nice* affair to the social calendar this year: the New Year's Eve dance. The dance committee aroused our interest by planning a *nice* theme and hiring a *nice* band. With its colored lights, swinging silver bells, and plump snowmen, the gym presented a *nice* sight. The Satellites, a local group, played *nice* dance music. Best of all, the brightly decorated table offered a tempting variety of *nice* food, donated by *nice* sponsors. As the striking clock ushered in the New Year, everyone agreed that the dance had brought the holidays to a very *nice* close.

Lesson 6 Sentence Modeling

Modeling is the imitation of a given pattern.

When you read good books, you will notice that authors use a variety of sentence patterns and combinations of patterns. This adds interest to the writing and forms part of what is called an author's "style." As you discover different ways of structuring sentences, you will want to try them out in your own writing. Such experimentation will help you grow as a writer, and eventually you will develop a writing style of your own. A good way to learn a new sentence pattern is to analyze the structure of the sentence and then try modeling a sentence after it. Here are some examples of sentence modeling.

Model: He is the player who led the team to victory.

                                                 adjectival clause
Analysis: He is the player ⌐who led the team to victory.⌐

New Sentence: Joan is the runner who won the women's marathon.

Model: We saw them when we were in San Francisco.

                                                 adverbial clause
Analysis: We saw them ⌐when we were in San Francisco.⌐

New Sentence: I will give you the money when you need it.

Model: That the earthquake was severe was noted on the seismograph.

                         noun clause (subject)
Analysis: ⌐That the earthquake was severe⌐ was noted on the seismograph.

New Sentence: That you are determined to go is obvious to me.

Model: Learning a new word every day increases one's vocabulary.

                         gerund phrase (subject)
Analysis: ⌐Learning a new word every day⌐ increases one's vocabulary.

New Sentence: Controlling your weight requires willpower.

Model:	My father's chief delight is to read mystery novels.
Analysis:	**infinitive phrase (subj. comp.)** My father's chief delight is ⌐to read mystery novels.⌐
New Sentence:	The duty of the governor is to enforce the laws of the state.
Model:	They watched the boats sailing down the river.
Analysis:	**participial phrase** They watched the boats ⌐sailing down the river.⌐
New Sentence:	The lifeguard watched the children swimming in the pool.

Activity A

Label the pattern in each sentence below. Compose an original sentence using that pattern. Refer to the model examples for help.

1. Did you hear the children singing in the street?

2. Solving crossword puzzles is fun for me.

3. That Michaelangelo painted the Sistine Chapel is well known.

4. Darlene learned the value of exercise when she lived in the mountains.

5. Leonardo da Vinci, who was a great painter, was also an accomplished architect.

6. Your best plan is to go by airplane.

Activity B

The next six sentences are variations of the patterns used in the examples. Identify and label these patterns and compose original sentences using them.

1. Paula related what happened yesterday on the trip.

2. We should try to reach camp before dark.

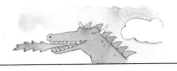

3. Lucia did not know when the check would arrive.

4. Having tried liver before, Sara refused to eat it.

5. His job was grooming the horses.

6. Since I had my tonsils removed, I have been free of sore throats.

More to Explore

Model an original sentence after each one listed below. Change the topic, but keep the basic parts of speech.

1. Apparently he didn't notice the new building. Why would he?
2. Trudging and stomping along, the youth finally reached his destination.
3. Excited? Me? Never!
4. I wonder—although I think I know the answer—why the coach never puts me in the game.
5. When the moment arrived, I stood frozen in my tracks, but something inside urged me to approach this awesome, horrifying creature.

Word Study 3

Root Words

A root word is a base word from which other words are built.

As you learned in Word Study 2, the majority of our root words come from either the Latin or Greek language.

Activity A

Here is a new list of five roots that will help you create other related words. Copy the chart onto a sheet of paper and look up each root word in your dictionary. Write the meaning of the root and its origin, Latin or Greek.

Root	Meaning		Language
cosmo	_____	<	_____
vert	_____	<	_____
scope	_____	<	_____
astro	_____	<	_____
audio	_____	<	_____

Activity B

Use the chart in Activity A as a guide. Consult your dictionary and find three words based on each root. Write the meaning of each new word.

Root	New Words	Meanings
cosmo	_____	_____
	_____	_____
	_____	_____
vert	_____	_____
	_____	_____
	_____	_____

(Continue in same manner with remaining roots.)

Activity C

Complete each of the following sentences by using a word based on the root shown in parentheses.

1. The nurse used an (audio) to test our hearing.
2. Because there was so much noise outside, the directions were barely (audio).
3. All submarines are equipped with a (scope).
4. The beat of the heart can be heard through a (scope).
5. Because Seth was an (vert), he really looked forward to meeting new people.
6. The work was so intense, I took a walk just for a (vert).
7. (cosmo) rays penetrate the earth's atmosphere.
8. A Russian space traveler is called a (cosmo).
9. The (astro) used her telescope to track the path of the comet.
10. Sally Ride was the first American woman (astro).

Chapter 4

Types of Paragraphs

Lesson 1 Writing Descriptive Paragraphs

A descriptive paragraph uses words to vividly portray a person, place, or thing.

In descriptive writing, vivid, colorful language and sensory images are used to present a picture. A writer chooses words that will appeal to the reader's senses: sight, hearing, taste, touch, and smell. Often a writer will use figures of speech, such as simile, metaphor, or personification, to better communicate the image he or she has in mind.

Read the paragraph below and answer the questions on the next page.

Twilight of Evening

Big flakes of wet snow are whirling lazily about the street lamps, which have just been lighted, and lying in a thin soft layer on roofs, horses' backs, shoulders, caps. Iona Potapov, the sledge-driver, is all white like a ghost. He sits on the box without stirring, bent as double as the living body can be bent. If a regular snowdrift fell on him, it seems as though even then he would not think it necessary to shake it off....His little mare is white and motionless too. Her stillness, the angularity of her lines, and the sticklike straightness of her legs make her look like a halfpenny gingerbread horse. She is probably lost in thought. Anyone who has been torn away from the plough, from the familiar gray landscapes, and cast into this slough, full of monstrous lights, of unceasing uproar and hurrying people, is bound to think.

Share some sensory impressions suggested by this painting.

1. This paragraph is a description of
   a. a snow scene in the country   b. a snow scene in a town
   c. a snow scene on the road between the country and a town
2. The description of this place leads us to believe that it is
   a. quiet   b. noisy   c. lonely
3. The sense which the author appeals to the most is
   a. sight   b. hearing   c. taste   d. touch   e. smell
4. Find as many words as you can that tell about people, places, or things with which you are not familiar. Look up these words in the dictionary and define them.
5. Find two similes in the paragraph. What do they compare? Why do you think that it was better to use a simile than to use other descriptive words?
6. Can you find any words in the paragraph that refer to the sense of touch?
7. If you were an artist and wanted to paint this picture, would you have enough information? Describe your picture. What colors would you use?

Now that you have investigated how writers use description, you can begin to develop your own descriptive writing skills.

Activity A

Point out the vivid words in each sentence.

1. Nervously, the young man entered the bustling office for his job interview.
2. The deep blue sky was dotted with clouds that resembled fleecy cotton.
3. White-capped waves glistened in the sun as they surged toward the shore.
4. As we descended the ancient cellar stairs, a damp, musty odor enveloped us.
5. Weather-beaten and dirty, the old bag lady shuffled toward the park bench.
6. She had a joyous, free kind of laugh that was impossible to resist.
7. The blazing sun beat down mercilessly on the exhausted hiker.
8. The aroma of sizzling bacon filled the house and tickled the nostrils of the groggy sleepers.
9. Hanging from an invisible thread, the spider labored to spin its majestic web.
10. As the misguided hammer smashed the unsuspecting thumb, the boy recoiled with pain.

Activity B

Improve the sentences by substituting vivid words for plain words.

1. We were surprised that the building was so large.
2. The happy child ran to his mother.
3. The ruler gave nice gifts to her loyal servants.
4. In the distance stood a dark mountain, plainly outlined against the sky.
5. The horse ran quietly along the curved path.
6. All day, we worked in the small office.
7. I could not do a difficult puzzle like that.
8. Sea gulls flew back and forth as the waves flowed onto the beach.
9. The eagle flew down from the high cliff.
10. Our friend told us about funny happenings at school.

Activity C

List ten details that could describe each of the scenes below. Be sure to appeal to as many of the senses as you can, and include your own feelings.

1. a stray dog that wandered up to your house
2. a deserted street late at night
3. the kitchen at your house just before dinner
4. a large concert hall where a rock star is performing
5. being awakened at night by the sound of a siren
6. an abandoned car in a junkyard
7. a pair of old sneakers in the school gym

More to Explore

Choose one idea to develop into a descriptive paragraph of your own.

1. You saw the crime. At the police station, you give your description of the criminal to the composite artist. Write your exact description of the criminal. When your paragraph is finished, ask a friend to draw a picture from your description.

2. You have just received a brand new stereo for your birthday. You call your friend on the phone and describe its appearance and all of its features.

3. The party has ended. Your last friend just went home. Now you have to clean up. The place looks like a disaster area! Describe it.

4. You lost your shoes during gym class. They were really different from anyone else's in school. Write a description of them for the Lost and Found bulletin board.

5. You are a creature from another planet. Your spacecraft just landed at a busy intersection in a big city. This is your first encounter with human beings. When you write your entry in your travel log, this is how you describe them.

6. You gave two million dollars to a contractor to build you a mansion. Your limousine pulls up in the driveway, and for the first time you see your magnificent new home. You had no idea it would look like this! Describe it.

Revising a Descriptive Paragraph

Reread the paragraph and underline all the sensory details.

Ask yourself the following questions:

—Which senses predominate in my piece of writing?

—Can I picture the characters or scenes in my mind? Could they be drawn on a piece of paper?

—Did I use a creative beginning sentence?

—Does my title attract attention?

—Did I use strong action verbs? Avoid verbs of being?

—Is there a blend of simple, compound, and complex sentences?

—Was I able to use simile, metaphor, or personification?

—Does my paragraph make sense?

Now is the time to add, delete, or re-arrange ideas. Discuss these changes with another student or your teacher. Rewrite the paragraph and then go on to proofreading.

Proofreading a Descriptive Paragraph

¶	New paragraph
⌒	Close up space
∧	Insert
℘	Delete
/	Lowercase
∿	Reverse letters
≡	Capitalize

As you look over your paragraph, ask yourself these questions:

—Is the correct mark of punctuation used at the end of each sentence?

—Have I used commas after introductory phrases and clauses? Can I explain the other marks of punctuation?

—Did I capitalize the important words in the title?

Start at the last word of the paragraph and check for correct spelling. Rewrite the paragraph if necessary.

Lesson 2 Writing Narrative Paragraphs

A narrative paragraph tells a story.

Narrative writing tells a story. The writer must relate the events in the order in which they happen, name the characters, tell where the events happen, and give the story an ending. There are different types of narrative writing.

Personal Experience
A short piece of writing that tells a single incident in the life of the author

Biography
The life of a person written by someone else

Autobiography
A personally written account of one's life

Log
A written record of daily progress—usually of a ship's voyage

Journal
A regularly kept record of experiences, ideas, or reflections for private use

Diary
A record of events or observations kept daily or at frequent intervals—usually intended for private use
It is similar to a journal.

Legend
A story that comes from the past and is thought to be historical, although it cannot be verified

Fantasy
A fictional story that often contains strange settings and unusual characters

Myth
A story that uses fantasy to explain people's beliefs or some phenomenon in nature

Fable
A fictitious story intended to stress a useful truth, often by giving animals the power of speech

News Story
The report of an incident told in the order in which the events occurred It contains the *who, what, where,* and *when* of the event, and sometimes the *why*.

Many narrative paragraphs contain transition words to help readers understand the order of events. Some of these words are: *first, then, later, before, during, while, next, finally, after, at last, when,* and *at once.*

Read the paragraph below and answer the questions that follow.

One evening my mother told me that I was old enough to help with the grocery shopping. She took me to the corner store to show me the way. I was proud; I felt like a grownup. The next afternoon, I looped the basket over my arm and went down the pavement toward the store. When I reached the corner, a gang of boys snatched the basket, took the money, and sent me running home in a panic. That evening I told my mother what had happened, but she made no comment; instead she sat down at once, wrote another note, gave me more money, and sent me to the grocery store again. I crept down the steps and saw the same gang of boys playing down the street. I ran back into the house.

1. Where does this story take place? What words indicate this?
   a. farm   b town   c. mountains
2. Recount three events from the story in the order in which they happened.
3. List any transition words the author used in the paragraph.
4. In what span of time do you think the story took place? What words show this?
5. Would you call this paragraph
   a. a biography   b. a personal experience   c. a diary? Why?

Two things are important in narrative writing: having the events in the order in which they take place and having each event flow smoothly into the next.

Activity A

Below are two personal experiences. The sentences were taken out of order and placed in a list. On a sheet of paper, write the first two words of each sentence in a column and then number the sentences in the order in which they should be. Finally, rewrite them as an entire paragraph.

The Giant Fish

_____ Although it looked as if a storm were heading our way, we stayed another hour.

_____ People around us wondered if it was a giant flounder or even a shark.

_____ Finally, my father got a bite!

_____ The wind was getting stronger, and the water was becoming choppy.

_____ I waited with the net while my brother and uncle stood by to see if they should bring in the fish or cut the line.

_____ The tug of war rocked the boat furiously, and Dad almost fell overboard.

_____ By now, the wind had picked up speed, but Dad continued to struggle.

_____ Looking over the side of the boat, I began to laugh.

_____ Just as Dad pulled in the line, we all noticed that he had hooked the boat's anchor.

Changing Times

_____ After all these years, the old school was being torn down.

_____ I wondered what had happened to the friends with whom I had lost touch.

_____ I stood in the doorway of Room 335 and felt a wave of sadness.

_____ Then I remembered Mr. Jenkins, my biology teacher in sophomore year.

———— As I gazed down at its scarred surface, the room suddenly became filled with sounds and faces.

———— This was a great place, and it will live on in my memories.

———— School did a lot for me, even though I didn't always realize it at the time.

———— Looking around, I spotted my old school desk, and carefully crossed the torn-up floor to stand beside it.

———— I had never studied so hard for a class as I did for his, but that was the year I developed my love of science.

Activity B

Choose one of the following topics and imagine what might have happened. List specific details for the event; then, using the list as a guide, write a narrative paragraph.

1. You are on the Ferris wheel at an amusement park. On the seat next to you is a total stranger about your own age. When you get to the top, the amusement breaks down. You then begin to realize that this was the biggest mistake you ever made.

2. All you and your friends were doing was clowning in an old museum. How were you supposed to know that the Time Machine actually worked?

3. An accident occurred one evening and you were the only witness. You are now giving your story to the police.

4. It is Halloween night, and everyone is dressed up. When you see *this* creature, though, something tells you that it is not a costume.

5. You have fallen asleep. The dream begins. It is the most unusual dream you have ever had.

6. It is only an initiation, but it is terrifying. You have to spend the night alone in the old abandoned mansion, and rumors say that it is really haunted.

More to Explore

Write a narrative paragraph about a personal experience of your own. Select some event or special day in your life: an unexpected school holiday, something you did on vacation or on a school trip, an accident or other misfortune you had, or an ordinary Saturday you would like to share. Make a list of the events as they happened to use as a guide when you write your first draft. Revise and proofread your paragraph.

Revising a Narrative Paragraph

In your mind, list the events of the story as they happened. Check that they are *written* in the same order.

Ask yourself the following questions:

— Have I used effective transition words to connect sentences?

— Are my characters well described? Can the setting (if one was used) be pictured in my mind?

— Do I have an effective beginning and ending?

— Does my title attract attention?

— Have I used a blend of simple, compound, and complex sentences?

— Did I use strong action verbs? Avoid verbs of being?

— Was I able to use simile, metaphor, or personification?

— Does my paragraph make sense?

Now is the time to add, delete, or re-arrange ideas. Discuss these changes with another student or your teacher. Rewrite the paragraph and go on to proofreading.

Proofreading a Narrative Paragraph

As you look over your paragraph, ask yourself these questions:

¶	New paragraph
⌒	Close up space
ʌ	Insert
℘	Delete
/	Lowercase
∿	Reverse letters
≡	Capitalize

— Is the correct mark of punctuation used at the end of each sentence?

— Have I used commas after introductory phrases and clauses? Was any dialogue I used punctuated correctly? Can I explain all other marks of punctuation?

— Did I capitalize the important words in the title?

Start at the last word of the paragraph and check for correct spelling.

Rewrite the paragraph if necessary.

Lesson 3 Writing Expository Paragraphs

An expository paragraph explains something or informs the reader.

Expository writing must be clear and simple, with details in the right order. This kind of writing can be used to give information, directions, or definitions.

Writing Informative Paragraphs

An informative paragraph communicates knowledge to the reader. It should be written in a clear and interesting manner, with effective topic, beginning, and ending sentences. All middle sentences should relate to the narrowed topic, and any terms the reader is not likely to recognize should be explained.

Activity

Read the paragraph below and answer the questions that follow.

All poisonous snakes are dangerous, but the king cobra, or hamadryad, is especially lethal. Whereas a common cobra is rarely more than five feet long, a king cobra may reach a length of eighteen feet. It has enough venom in its poison glands to kill five hundred human beings. That isn't all. The hamadryad is the only snake known to attack without any provocation. These fearful creatures have been reported to trail a man through the jungle for the express purpose of biting him. They are so aggressive that they have closed roads in India by driving away all traffic. This is probably because the hamadryads, unlike other snakes, guard their eggs and young, and if a pair sets up housekeeping in a district, every other living thing must get out—including elephants. When a king cobra rears up, it stands higher than the head of a kneeling man. It is unquestionably the most dangerous animal in the world today.

King cobra

King cobra

1. The general topic of this paragraph is
   a. snakes   b. cobras   c. king cobras
2. The specific topic of this paragraph is
   a. how king cobras care for their young
   b. that king cobras are the most dangerous animals in the world
   c. how king cobras are different from other snakes
3. What is the topic sentence in this paragraph?
4. Make a list of all the words the author uses as a substitute for *king cobra.*
5. List all the facts about the king cobra that you find in this paragraph.
6. In what way is the king cobra unlike other snakes?

Writing Directions

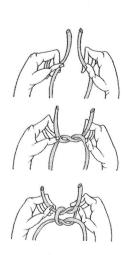

Besides providing information, the expository paragraph can be used to give directions or recipes. In all expository writing, it is important to list the details or steps in the proper order. For directions and recipes, the order is that which will produce the desired results in the most efficient way.

Directions for tying a square knot would be:
1. Take two ends of cord and hold one in each hand.
2. Take the cord in the right hand and place it over and under the cord in the left hand. Pull both ends slightly.
3. Take the cord that is now in the left hand and place it over and under the cord in the right hand.
4. Pull both ends in order to tighten into a square knot.

Activity

Write paragraphs giving directions for three of the topics in the following list. Don't forget to make a list of the steps involved before you begin to write your first draft.

Explain how to

1. make French toast
2. brush one's teeth
3. tie a shoe
4. make a milkshake
5. braid something
6. wash and wax a car
7. make popcorn
8. iron a shirt
9. make *your* favorite sandwich
10. wash a load of laundry
11. plan a party
12. make a Halloween costume
13. fly a kite
14. carve a pumpkin
15. _____ (your own idea)

Writing Definitions

Writing definitions is similar to writing directions. You must first make a list of all the details in the proper order. For definitions the order proceeds from the general characteristics of the object or term to the specific characteristics.

If you had to write a composition explaining what an *orange* is to someone who had never seen one, here is how you would begin.

Orange

1. citrus fruit
2. grown in tropical climate
3. grown on a tree
4. round
5. about the size of a baseball
6. red-yellow color
7. juicy
8. sweet-tangy taste
9. juice is a common breakfast drink

Activity A

Using the list of details on page 79, write a composition defining an orange.

Activity B

Try defining these words. Remember your list of details.
1. wristwatch   4. pencil
2. shoe   5. paper clip
3. snake   6. _____ (your own idea)

More to Explore

Below is a list of topics for expository writing. Choose one and develop it into a well-organized paragraph.
1. You are preparing a booklet to be used by all the new employees of a well-known fast food chain. Write an explanation of how to make
   a. a super hamburger   c. French-fried potatoes
   b. a special breakfast
2. I'm new in this country. What exactly is this food called "pizza"?
3. You are a computer whiz-kid. You are being paid a million dollars to invent a new game. Design it and write a composition explaining how it works.
4. You have hidden a treasure in a secret place in school. In case you don't return, you want to leave a note explaining where to find it.
5. I am lost. You are outside your house, and I stop to ask directions on how to get to the public library. Write what you would tell me.
6. Look up "vampire bats" in an encyclopedia and write a composition that gives some interesting facts about them.

Revising an Expository Paragraph

As you reread your paragraph, ask yourself the following questions:

—Are all the details in the correct order?

—Was I able to use transition words to connect sentences? (Try to use at least two.)

—If I wrote a definition, did I start with the most general idea and end with the most specific?

—Does my beginning or ending sentence state what I am explaining or defining?

—Have I used a blend of simple, compound, and complex sentences?

—Are my sentences clear and precise? Have I used specific vocabulary?

—Does my paragraph make sense?

Now is the time to add, delete, or re-arrange your ideas. Talk over these changes with another student or your teacher. Rewrite the paragraph and go on to proofreading.

Proofreading an Expository Paragraph

As you look over your paragraph, ask yourself these questions:

¶	New paragraph
⌒	Close up space
ʌ	Insert
ℒ	Delete
/	Lowercase
∿	Reverse letters
≡	Capitalize

—Have I used the correct marks of punctuation at the ends of my sentences?

—Can I explain all other marks of punctuation?

—Are all appropriate words capitalized?

Start at the last word of the paragraph and check for correct spelling. Rewrite the paragraph if necessary.

Lesson 4 Writing Persuasive Paragraphs

 A persuasive paragraph states an opinion and supports it in a convincing way.

Persuasive writing attempts to convince the reader that the point of view expressed is the right one. This is done by logically presenting evidence to support the ideas. In some cases, references to the work or statements of well-known authorities on the subject are included.

The area of persuasive writing is broad. It includes such things as advertisements and commercials, letters to the editor and editorials, and campaign speeches.

Read the paragraph below; then discuss or write the answers to the questions that follow.

> If everyone eligible to vote in the United States actually cast a ballot on election day, then we would have a representative government. As it stands now, when the turnout for a national election is over fifty percent, news reports comment on the high percentage of participation. And that's only half of the *registered* voters! What about all of those people who never registered? Who are they, where are they, and why don't they vote? Many of them are black, Hispanic, or poor. Many have been discouraged from voting and encouraged to believe they are powerless. The truth is that as long as they don't vote, they *are* powerless. They are invisible. If we want to be fairly governed, we have to make ourselves visible, every one of us.

1. According to the author, the United States
   a. has a fair system of government as it now operates
   b. has the potential to have a fair system of government
   c. needs to change its system of government completely
2. What does the author think people should do?
   a. only vote when they are sure the people they will vote for will win
   b. accept the fact that they are unimportant
   c. vote every time they get a chance and encourage others to do so

3. What is the general tone of the paragraph? (Is the author angry, sad, hopeless, hopeful?) What makes you think that?

4. Discuss those sections of the paragraph that try to convince the reader through logic or reasoning. Discuss those sections that are intended to appeal mainly to emotions.

5. Read this paragraph orally in class. Use your voice to convey the meaning you think the author intends.

Persuasive writing must sound convincing. Your arguments should be presented in a way that stresses your point of view, and any facts you include should clearly support your arguments. You can press your case by using statements that appeal to reason or emotion or both.

Activity A

Below are some topics about which people have different opinions. Make a list of all the reasons *for* and *against* each of the topics.

1. capital punishment
2. giving in to the demands of terrorists who hold innocent people captive
3. nuclear power
4. United States involvement in the political affairs of underdeveloped countries

Activity B

There may be issues on a more personal level about which you would like to state your opinion. Select any topic below and decide your point of view. Make a list of your supporting statements and write a paragraph to explain how you feel about the issue.

1. having school all year, with one month off during Christmas time, Easter time, and summer time
2. taking a competency test before being able to graduate from high school
3. trying juveniles in adult court when they are guilty of a felony
4. raising the driving age to eighteen
5. earning your own spending money
6. having school only in the morning
7. giving homework only to those students who fail a test
8. giving report cards to parents instead of the student

Activity C

Write a commercial or design an advertisement to sell
1. tickets to a rock concert
2. submarine sandwiches for a team's fund raising campaign
3. tickets for a neighborhood car wash

More to Explore

Below are topics for persuasive writing. Choose one and develop it into a well-organized paragraph, using the guidelines presented in this lesson.

1. You are running for class president. Write your campaign speech. You may want to deliver it to the class.
2. You are trying to sell your old bike in order to raise money to buy a new one. You clean it and buy ornaments to make it attractive. Write the advertisement that you will post on the bulletin board in school.
3. Do you think that professional athletes are overpaid? Write a convincing paragraph to defend your point of view.
4. You are the editor of the school newspaper. Write an editorial giving the reasons why there should be school only four days a week.
5. You want to get a Siberian husky for a pet, but your parents say no. Write a paragraph that might help to change their mind.
6. You are applying for a part-time job as a baby-sitter. Write a paragraph giving all your qualifications and stating why you would be good for the job.

Revising a Persuasive Paragraph

As you reread your paragraph, ask yourself the following questions:
— Did the opening sentence state my opinion?
— How many facts support my opinion?
— Have I appealed to my audience through reason, emotion, or both? (Read over the sentences that make these appeals.)
— Is my most convincing idea last?
— Does my ending sentence restate my opinion, but in a different way?
— Have I used interrogative sentences to get my reader's attention?
— Have I used a blend of simple, compound, and complex sentences?
— Does the paragraph make sense?

Now is the time to add, delete, or re-arrange ideas. Talk over these changes with another student or your teacher. Rewrite the paragraph and go on to proofreading.

Proofreading a Persuasive Paragraph

Ask yourself the following questions as you look over your paragraph:

¶	New paragraph
⊂	Close up space
⋀	Insert
℘	Delete
/	Lowercase
∼	Reverse letters
=	Capitalize

— Have I used the correct mark of punctuation at the end of each sentence?
— Are capital letters used for proper nouns?

Start at the last word of the paragraph and check for correct spelling. Rewrite the paragraph if necessary.

Optional Activities for Chapter 4

1. Rewrite a famous fairy tale. Tell it from the point of view of the "villain"; e.g., the wolf's version of "Little Red Riding Hood."
2. Write a narrative story that could be entitled "Trapped."
3. Take a story from your reader and rewrite it as a newspaper article.
4. Write a story about your favorite picture or photograph.
5. Select an event in history and place yourself in that setting. Write an account of the event from your point of view.
6. Keep a journal of your daily activities for a period of two weeks.
7. Choose an animal or an event in nature. Write your own legend on how it came into being.
8. Rewrite a famous fairy tale so that it has a modern day setting.
9. Select a famous person who is deceased. Read about the person's life and write a eulogy that could have been given at his or her funeral.
10. Write a short fantasy in which the magic world is entered by means of a dream, a magic potion, or some ordinary object that turns out to have unusual properties.
11. Select an event in the life of an historic figure. Begin your story: "If I had been in your shoes, _____, I would have/not have...."
12. Choose an inanimate object and write the biography of its life.

Word Study 4

Suffixes (verb endings)

A suffix is a syllable added to the end of a word to make a new word.

A suffix often changes the part of speech of a word, as in the case of the suffixes in Activity A. These suffixes change the words to verbs.

Activity A

Add the suffix to the word in order to create a verb. In some cases you will have to drop the original ending of the word and use the suffix in its place. Do this work on a separate sheet of paper.

Word	Suffix	Verb
legal	ize	_____
hesitant	ate	_____
identity	ify	_____
failure	s, ing, ed	_____
deep	en	_____

Activity B

Change each word below to a verb by using one of the suffixes listed in Activity A.

departure   height

mortification   analysis

personal   captive

sharp   terror

commentator   crystal

dedication   considerable

Activity C

Choose an appropriate verb from Activity B to complete each of the following sentences.

1. Campers should _____ all their clothing by sewing on name tags.
2. The roving band of thieves _____ the countryside.
3. If you want to be a poet, you must _____ your senses to the world around you.
4. The owner is _____ opening a new store in this area.
5. The mayor _____ the statue in honor of the war veterans.
6. When fudge is put in the refrigerator, it tends to _____ .
7. I was _____ when I realized what I'd said.
8. The teacher _____ about the upcoming humanities fair.
9. The novel was so good, I was _____ for the whole day.
10. My anxiety _____ when I discovered that the report was due a week earlier than I'd thought.
11. The train is _____ at 8:58 A.M.
12. The chemist tried to _____ the mixture.

Chapter 5

Writing Across the Curriculum

Lesson 1 Answering Essay Questions

Essay questions must be answered in paragraph form.

Essay questions require you to really *think* about the material you have been studying, and they are often the best evaluation of how well you understand it. This is why teachers put them on tests. Answers to essay questions are always written in paragraph form, so that you must give more than a one-word answer. Sometimes an essay question will ask for facts; other times it will ask for your interpretation of facts. The key to knowing exactly what type of answer you should give is to look at the *verb* used in the question.

Below are some verbs commonly used in essay questions.
1. *Compare*: Show how two things are alike.
2. *Contrast*: Show how two things are different.
3. *Discuss*: Give the facts and tell how they relate to one another.
4. *Define*: Give the meaning of a term.
5. *Explain*: Tell how or why something is done.
6. *Describe*: Give a word picture of something.
7. *Trace*: Give all the events in sequential order and tell how they are related.
8. *Prove*: Give evidence to show that something is true.

It is important to analyze each essay question that you are given in order to determine what kind of information is being asked of you. Study this sample question:

> Give three major concepts presented in Abraham Lincoln's Gettysburg Address and explain why these ideas are particularly relevant to our society today.

Presidents are people, too. What personal qualities of Abraham Lincoln are captured in this painting? What qualities do you think leaders need?

89

The two key words in this question are *give* and *explain*. *Give* is a sign that factual information is being requested. *Explain* indicates that a personal interpretation is also required.

Facts: three concepts in Abraham Lincoln's Gettysburg Address

Interpretation: How are they relevant today?

Activity A

Listed below are some essay questions that require only factual information, and some that ask for facts plus interpretation. Divide a piece of paper in half from top to bottom. On one side, write "facts," on the other "interpretation." Analyze the questions and place the appropriate part of each sentence in the correct column.

1. Contrast the military strategy of the Allied powers and the Axis powers in World War II.
2. In John Steinbeck's story *The Red Pony*, Jody admires the hired hand Billy Buck. Give two reasons why Jody likes Billy, and what effect this has on Jody's life.
3. Give the effects of a volcanic eruption upon the atmosphere.
4. Compare the Sahara Desert with the Mojave Desert.
5. In your opinion, what are the benefits of the space shuttle as a form of modern transportation?

Once you have analyzed your question, you are ready to compose the answer. Since your question is an essay type, you must write a well-constructed paragraph. An excellent way to provide a topic sentence for your answer is to *restate the question*. Look at the following example:

Question: Explain why so many Europeans came to America between 1607 and 1733.

Topic sentence: Between 1607 and 1733, many Europeans came to America in search of religious freedom, economic opportunities, and land ownership.

Folk art figure
of Abraham Lincoln

Activity B

Below are five topic sentences. They belong to the five questions in Activity A. On a separate sheet of paper, write each question from Activity A and, under it, the topic sentence that belongs to it.

1. The space shuttle has many possibilities as a modern day means of transportation.
2. A volcanic eruption can have varied effects upon the atmosphere.
3. The military strategy of the Allied powers and the Axis powers in World War II differed greatly.
4. Although the Sahara Desert and the Mojave Desert are on different continents, they have many points in common.
5. In John Steinbeck's novel *The Red Pony*, Jody admires the hired hand Billy Buck for two specific reasons, and their relationship has a strong impact on Jody's development.

After you have written your topic sentence, you are ready to compose the rest of the answer. When your answer is complete, read through it to be sure that you have given the information that was asked of you and have composed a well-worded paragraph with appropriate transitions.

Activity C

Analyze the following essay questions from various subject areas. Tell what kind of answer the verb indicates and whether the answer will be factual, interpretive, or both. Then write topic sentences for any five of the essay questions.

1. Discuss the relationship between poverty and crime.
2. Explain the stages of the water cycle.
3. Prove that Franklin Delano Roosevelt increased the power of the presidency during his administration.
4. Describe the characteristics of the Ice Age.
5. Explain why the piano is considered both a string and a percussion instrument.
6. Define what is meant by the *commutative property of multiplication*.
7. Trace the advancements made in the civil rights movement from the time of the Emancipation Proclamation to the present.
8. Define *sedimentary rock*.

9. Contrast the orchestra with the band.
10. Compare the Atlantic Ocean with the Pacific Ocean.
11. Contrast the foreign policy of Franklin Delano Roosevelt with the foreign policy of John Fitzgerald Kennedy.
12. Discuss the impact the Russian satellite Sputnik I had on educational priorities in the United States.
13. Compare the oboe and the clarinet.
14. Define the *baroque period*. How did music and art reflect the trends of that time?
15. Discuss the effects of the Industrial Revolution on small businesses, child labor, and the national economy.

Remember, when answering an essay question,
1. study the question to find out what it asks you to do.
2. decide if the answer is factual, interpretive, or both.
3. map or outline your answer, making sure all information is related to the question.
4. restate what is asked in the question and make it the opening sentence.
5. give your information in a well-constructed paragraph.
6. reread your paragraph to make sure you have given the information that the question requires.

More to Explore

Use the questions provided in any of your textbooks to perform the following activities:
1. Locate and copy
   five questions that ask for factual information
   five questions that ask for your interpretation
   five questions that ask for facts and interpretation
2. Select one question from each of the three groups above and write a topic sentence by rewording the question.
3. Select any *one* question from the above and write a complete answer in paragraph form.

Lesson 2 Outlining and Writing a Report

An outline is an organized plan for a report, essay, or term paper.

If a report or essay is going to be two, three, or more paragraphs in length, it is worthwhile making an outline, or plan, to give direction to your writing. An outline has a specific format.

  I. Paragraph topic
    A. Subtopic
      1. Detail
      2. Detail
      3. Detail
    B. Subtopic
      1. Detail
      2. Detail
      3. Detail

Answer the following questions about this outline:
1. What indicates a paragraph topic?
2. How many subtopics does this report have?
3. What indicates a subtopic?
4. How many details support each subtopic?
5. How is a detail indicated?
6. Why is capital letter B under capital letter A?
7. What happens in the design of the outline every time it changes from a numeral to a letter?

93

Suppose you have been assigned to write a paper about deserts. The narrowed topic is "how the desert can support life." After going to the library to use the encyclopedia and other sources, a map of your ideas might look like this:

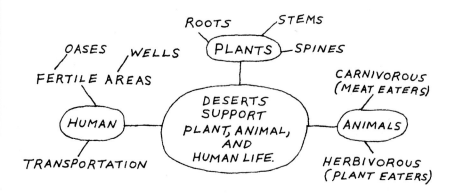

The ideas can easily be put into outline form.

Subject: Desert life

Narrowed topic: How plant, animal, and human life can exist in the desert

I. Introductory paragraph
II. Plant life
    A. Roots
    B. Stems
    C. Flowers
III. Animal life
    A. Carnivorous animals (meat eaters)
    B. Herbivorous animals (plant eaters)
IV. Human life
    A. Fertile areas
        1. Oases
        2. Wells
    B. Transportation
        1. Automobile
        2. Train
        3. Airplane
V. Concluding paragraph

Once the outline is completed, you can begin the writing stage of the process. A first draft and revisions, along with peer and teacher conferences, will be necessary. Below is a final draft of the report on desert life, showing how the elements of the outline were incorporated.

The first paragraph includes the narrowed topic, either expressed in the same words or in a different way. This paragraph tells the reader what will be in the report.

> The desert has a unique terrain. Because it tends to appear dry and flat, many people conclude that there is no life at all on its shifting sands. Contrary to popular belief, however, a desert is rarely barren, but instead supports a substantial amount of plant, animal, and human life.

The second paragraph includes the expanded ideas contained under roman numeral II of the outline. The first sentence should state the topic of the paragraph.

> Plants are the most obvious form of life in the desert. Although this vegetation may be sparse, what does exist is both hardy and colorful. Succulents, such as the cactus plant, have shallow roots that absorb water quickly from light rainfalls and flash floods. The water is then stored for long periods of time in the plants' thick, waxy stems and leaves and used as needed. In addition to being rugged survivors, desert plants bring beauty to their surroundings by producing brilliant orange, red, and violet flowers.

The third and fourth paragraphs include expanded ideas contained under roman numerals III and IV. Again, the first sentence for each should state the topic. Note that each of these topic sentences begins with a transition word.

> Besides plants, many animals have adapted well to the desert environment. Some obtain their needed moisture from the meat of the animals they prey upon. Others get their water from the juicy leaves and stems of succulents. Certain animals, such as the camel and burro, who have long accompanied humans through the desert, sustain life both from what the desert has to offer and from what people can supply.

Finally, humankind has now come to inhabit this vast territory. Because of island-like areas called oases, people can survive the brutal heat and dryness. Some oases are natural, developing from the desert's own underground springs, and others have been created by the re-routing of rivers and streams, or by other artificial means. Highways and railroads have made travel to oases easier, and many former watering holes have blossomed into large cities. Today visitors can even travel by air to areas that were once inaccessible to all but the most adventurous.

The concluding paragraph pulls together in one or two sentences all the ideas from II, III, and IV. It often contains a personal observation on what has been written, and should reflect the comments made in the first paragraph.

All forms of life, then, flourish in the desert. No longer must people fear this formerly inhospitable area. We are free to share its richness with the plants and animals, as long as we are careful not to destroy its wonders in the process.

Activity A

Use the words on the right to complete the outline on the left.

Subject: Bread

Narrowed topic: Some kinds of bread, their food value, and the process involved in making bread

I. Kinds
  A. _____
       1. White
       2. _____
       3. Rye
       4. _____
  B. Special
       1. _____
       2. Zucchini
       3. _____
II. _____
  A. _____
  B. _____
  C. Thiamine
III. _____
  A. Mix flour
  B. Add water, yeast, minerals
  C. _____
  D. Cut dough
  E. _____

Dough begins to rise
Raisin and nut
Iron
Whole wheat
Process
Common
Place in pans to bake
Protein
Pumpernickel
Applesauce
Food value

Activity B

Put the following information in outline form. The subject, narrowed topic, and two paragraph topics are indicated. All others are subtopics and details.

Subject: Poems
Narrowed topic: How to appreciate a poem
Paragraph topics:

I. Careful oral reading
II. Careful listening

Subtopics and details:

Watch punctuation
Personification
Pronounce words carefully
Listen for figures of speech
Simile
Onomatopoeia

Notice rhyme scheme
Metaphor
Feel the rhythm
Alliteration
Read slowly
Listen for sound devices

More to Explore

From the list below, choose two topics to outline. Then choose one of the two outlines and develop it into a written report following the guidelines given in the lesson.

1. Define the three types of rocks and explain how they are formed.
2. Explain complementary, analogous, and triadic color harmonies.
3. Contrast plane and solid geometric figures.
4. Compare the violin, cello, and bass.
5. Discuss how cloud formations help in the prediction of weather.
6. Name and explain the elements of art.
7. Discuss the causes of the Great Depression.
8. Explain the uses of three different types of aircraft.
9. Explain the value of two current television shows.

Revising an Essay or Report

Ask yourself the following questions:

— Does the opening paragraph express the main idea of the essay or report?

— Does each paragraph open with a topic sentence that tells the main idea of the paragraph?

— Does the concluding paragraph restate the main idea of the entire essay or report and draw everything to a close?

— What transition words connect the paragraphs?

— Does the essay or report make sense?

Now is the time to add, delete, or re-arrange your ideas. Talk over these changes with another student or your teacher. Rewrite the composition and go on to proofreading.

Proofreading an Essay or Report

As you look over your composition, ask yourself these questions:

¶	New paragraph
⌒	Close up space
⋏	Insert
ℒ	Delete
/	Lowercase
∿	Reverse letters
≡	Capitalize

— Did I use the correct mark of punctuation at the end of each sentence?

— Are proper nouns capitalized?

— Is each new paragraph indented?

Start at the last word of the composition and check for correct spelling. Rewrite the composition if necessary.

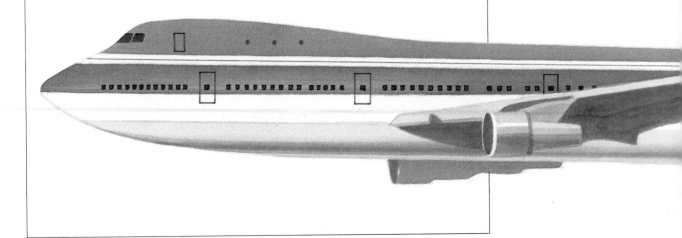

Lesson 3 Writing a Lab Report

 Scientific writing is the type of writing used to communicate scientific information.

There is a special form of writing called *scientific writing*. Its main purpose is to explain scientific information. For this reason, the facts, directions, and descriptions are stated in a straightforward manner. Concise words are chosen, and any picturesque language, imagery, or personal opinions are avoided. This type of language is used in most science books, scientific magazine articles, science fair projects, and lab reports.

The Lab Report

A lab report gives information about a scientific experiment that has been done. Ordinarily it is organized into five parts:

1. *Purpose*: This section tells why the experiment was done. Often the purpose of an experiment is to test a scientific hypothesis or theory. Sometimes it is simply to measure or observe something. A well designed experiment should have a clear and specific purpose.

     Examples:
     A. to observe the crystal structure of table salt.
     B. to measure the melting point of an unknown liquid.

2. *Materials*: This is a complete list of the supplies and equipment used in the experiment.

     Examples:
     A. —light microscope
        —glass microscope slide
        —NaCl (table salt)
     B. —75 ml of the unknown liquid
        —100 ml beaker
        —1000 ml beaker
        —mercury thermometer (-40 to $+45$ degrees Celsius range)
        —stopwatch
        —dry ice

3. *Procedures*: This section gives the steps used in the experiment. The procedures should be clearly explained, so that another person could repeat the experiment exactly as it was done originally. It is important to explain just how the materials were used and to describe any special techniques that were employed.

Examples:

A. 1. NaCl crystals were spread in a sparse single layer on a microscope slide.
    2. The crystals were observed under the light microscope with a magnification of 100 times normal.

B. 1. A dry ice bath was prepared by filling a 1000 ml beaker two-thirds full with crushed dry ice.
    2. 75 ml of the unknown liquid at room temperature was placed in a 100 ml beaker.
    3. The 100 ml beaker containing the sample was placed in the dry ice bath with a mercury thermometer submersed in the liquid.
    4. The temperature of the sample was recorded every 60 seconds until the sample was completely frozen.

Microphotograph of table salt crystals

4. *Results*: This is where all the measurements and observations taken during the experiment are presented. No interpretations are given at this point. Note that there are two types of data: *qualitative* observations describe what happened; *quantitative* observations describe what happened by giving numerical measurements. Results should be clearly presented, using tables and graphs where possible.

Examples:

A. At 100X, the crystals appeared large enough for easy viewing. They varied in size by approximately a factor of two. They all had smooth definite faces. Most of them appeared to be perfect cubes.

B.

Time (sec.)	Temp. (°C)	Time (sec.)	Temp. (°C)
0	+30	241	−18
61	+10	301	−18
122	−10	359	−18
178	−18	425	−25

At time equal to 160 seconds, the first crystals of solid appeared. At time equal to 380 seconds, the sample appeared completely frozen.

5. *Conclusions*: This is the section in which the results are interpreted. The conclusions should always be supported with facts from the data, and they should be written without the use of personal pronouns.

     Examples:

    A. The crystal structure of NaCl (table salt), as evidenced by observation under a microscope, is cubic.

    B. The melting point can be defined as the temperature at which a liquid and its solid coexist. In this experiment the sample was present in both its liquid and solid form from an elapsed time of 160 sec. to 380 sec. Within this range, four temperature readings of $-18°$ C were taken. The melting point of the unknown liquid is therefore $-18°$ C.

The following is a sample of a completed lab report.

Lab Report

Purpose:

    To test the hypothesis that water expands when it freezes

Materials:

    75 ml beaker
    freezer (not self-defrosting) set at 0 degrees Celsius
    wax pencil
    50 ml distilled water
    ruler (with mm markings)

Procedures:

1. 50 ml of distilled water was placed in the 75 ml beaker.
2. The beaker was placed in the freezer until ice just began to form.
3. The beaker was allowed to stand outside the freezer until the newly formed ice just melted (careful stirring was used to speed this process).
4. The level of the liquid was marked on the outside of the beaker with the wax pencil. An *l* (liquid) was placed next to this mark.
5. The beaker was returned to the freezer, and the water was allowed to completely freeze (5 hrs.).
6. The level of the solid water was marked on the outside of the beaker with the wax pencil. An *s* (solid) was placed by this mark.
7. The difference in mm between the two levels was measured.

Results:

The solid mark was 4.5 mm above the liquid mark.

Conclusions:

The hypothesis that water expands when it freezes is supported by the results of this experiment.

Activity

Here is an account of a scientific experiment. It contains all the information needed, but is not written in formal, scientific language. Rewrite it in the format of a lab report.

My cousin and I were interested in performing an experiment to see if sunlight is really necessary for plant growth. We found two plants exactly alike in type and size, and decided that we would check the color and number of leaves on each plant at the beginning and end of our experiment. First, we examined the plants. Plant #1 had 30 green leaves; plant #2 had 28 green leaves. Then we fed each plant 200 ml of a standard plant nutrient solution. Next we placed plant #1 on a windowsill in a room with a southern exposure. We placed plant #2 in a room with no windows or lights. The following week, we fed each plant again with 200 ml of nutrient solution.

After two weeks, both plants were brought to another room and the number of leaves and color were again compared. Plant #1 had 33 green leaves; plant #2 had 6 leaves, which were yellow. Our experiment had proven that plants require sunlight in order to remain healthy and to grow.

More to Explore

Now that you have practiced writing a lab report, try this one on your own.

My brother and I were interested in learning what things conduct electricity. We built a testing device using a 1.5 volt flashlight battery, a flashlight bulb, a thick rubber band, and three 18″ pieces of copper wire. The rubber band was placed around the battery to hold a wire against each terminal. This gave the battery two leads. Then we connected the third wire to one terminal of the light bulb. The last connection was to hook up one lead of the battery to the remaining lightbulb terminal. This left two leads free, one from the battery and one from the test lamp (lightbulb).

We tried to close this circuit, and therefore light the lamp, with a piece of glass, a piece of pencil lead, a paper clip, a piece of paper, a solution of water with as much table salt dissolved in it as would dissolve, and a piece of plastic wrap. The second, third, and fifth items lighted the lamp. They are conductors. The first, fourth, and sixth items did not. They are insulators.

Lesson 4 Writing about Books

You can be a stowaway in the pages of a book. You can journey into chapters of some far-off land or lift the curtain of fantasy within an imaginary tale. The biography of a great man or woman or a story of adventure can hold you spellbound. You can dream of matching the noble deeds of heroes and heroines. Books and the interesting characters they bring to life can stir you deeply and influence you tremendously. To discover the many values hidden within the pages of a book, you must be ready to exert yourself in the treasure hunt. That means you must choose your books wisely and read them intelligently. In the company of great books, you will experience a rewarding and exciting life.

Advertising Books

A book advertisement is meant to arouse your interest in a particular novel or factual work. You can find such advertisements in newspapers, magazines, or bookstore catalogs. Some newspapers and magazines have regular columns in which they mention a number of books they think might be of interest to their readers. Libraries advertise books, too, by making up booklists that describe recommended books in certain categories, such as mysteries or cookbooks. Since a book advertisement is meant to capture a reader's attention, it is usually short, lively, and to the point. It reveals just enough of the book's contents to promote the sale or reading of the book.

Here is a sample book advertisement:

Model: A Book Advertisement

What was it like to be a black person in the South in the late 1950s? John Griffin, a white man, decided to find out. How he changed the color of his skin, shaved his head, and posed as an educated black man makes a moving and dramatic story. Discover the hardships of life for blacks under the Jim Crow rules; see from an inside-outside view the unity of the Southern black community. Read *Black Like Me* by John Griffin.

Activity A

Read the following book advertisement and then answer the questions:

The White House Gang was the terror of every Washington official. Led by Quentin, President Roosevelt's son, the gang managed to make life exciting for themselves and for everyone they encountered. Needless to say, they were brought to justice more than once. The presiding officer at the court was none other than Theodore Roosevelt. Kindly and understanding, he dealt with the boys in a manner that won their everlasting admiration. Earle Looker reveals many daring adventures in *White House Gang*, for he was once a member. This is a book that demands a place on the bookshelf.

1. What type of book would you expect *White House Gang* to be?
2. Does this advertisement make you want to read it? Why or why not?

Activity B

Try writing your own book advertisement. The book you enjoyed the most will probably be the best and the easiest to write about.

Book Reports

A book report summarizes a book, gives a personal reaction to it, and usually follows a set format.

Book reports are longer than book advertisements and contain more information. They give the contents in greater detail, name the principal characters, and tell how the reader felt about the book. Often they are requested as class assignments to show what books a student has read and to provide practice in thinking about books. Writing a summary of a book and your reaction to it can lead to a better understanding of the author's message. It is also a way to keep a record of the books you have read so that you can renew your acquaintance with them at a later time or share them with a friend.

When preparing a book report, there is a specific format you can follow to make sure you include the essential information.
1. Title (underlined)
2. Author
3. Type of book (fiction, science fiction, historical fiction, fantasy, nonfiction, biography, play, etc.)
4. Principal characters
5. Brief summary
6. Personal reaction

Read the following book report and note how it follows the format.

<u>Model: A Book Report</u>

TITLE: *The Member of the Wedding*

AUTHOR: Carson McCullers

TYPE: Novel

CHARACTERS: Frankie Addams, Berenice Sadie Brown, John Henry West, Royal Quincy Addams (Frankie's father), Jarvis Addams, Janice Evans, Honey Brown, T. T. Williams, the red-headed soldier, the monkey man, Aunt Pet, Uncle Charles, Mary Littlejohn

SUMMARY: *The Member of the Wedding* is the story of one summer in the life of Frankie—F. Jasmine—Addams, who is going on thirteen. The summer is long and hot, the impossible Southern kind. It is a summer when Frankie feels "unjoined." Her best friend has moved away, and she spends her time with her five-year-old cousin John Henry and the family cook Berenice. But Berenice has friends of her own: her brother Honey and her boyfriend T. T. Williams. F. Jasmine feels alone and bored. She has a strong need to find her place in the world, but doesn't know how. Finally she decides the answer to her problems lies in the upcoming marriage of her brother Jarvis to Janice Evans. She will join them as a "member of the wedding," and the three of them will go off and live together forever.

MY REACTION: This story shows the loneliness felt by many people in our society. The particular awkwardness Frankie feels is part of being a teenager—no longer a child and not yet an adult. McCullers makes it clear that this is just one kind of isolation.

Activity

Prepare a book report for your class, following the format of the model book report.

Book Reviews

A book review is a critical evalution of a book.

A book *review* tells in detail what the reviewer liked and disliked about the book, and whether or not it is recommended to other readers. A book *report* is a *summary* of a book, whereas a book *review* is an *evaluation*. Many newspapers and magazines contain reviews of new books along with book advertisements.

Reviews differ from advertisements in that they are longer, more thorough, and not necessarily favorable. A book advertisement is always a very positive recommendation of a book and mentions only the book's good points, while a review might tell what is wrong with a book as well. A book review is also different in that the points the reviewer brings up have to be supported. In other words, a reviewer has to tell *why* he or she liked or did not like what the author wrote. It is always good when reading an unfavorable review to remember that the reviewer is giving a *personal* impression.

The format of a review is not as structured as that of a report, but it usually contains a few standard items.

The *introductory paragraph* gives the reader a general impression of how the reviewer responded to the book and an idea of what the book is about.

The *concluding paragraph* contains a summary of the reviewer's evaluation and tells whether or not he or she recommends the book (or other books by the same author).

In the *middle paragraphs*, the reviewer discusses the plot, setting, and characters of the book. How many middle paragraphs there are depends on how much the reviewer has to say and how much space he or she is given in which to say it. Often there is only one middle paragraph containing brief comments on each of the three elements.

Here are some questions to consider when evaluating a fiction book:

Plot: Do the events seem to follow in logical order? Does the author make the story believable? Is there enough suspense to make you want to read to the end? Do you feel satisfied with the way the story ends?

Setting: Is the setting well described? Can you picture it in your mind? Should the author have given more details? Why or why not? If there are illustrations, are they good representations of the characters and setting?

Characters: Are the characters interesting? Can you relate to how they think or feel? Would you like to know them? Are you able to picture how they look? Is each character's behavior consistent with the type of personality he or she has been given? Do the characters grow or learn through their experiences?

Following is a review of *The Incredible Journey* by Sheila Burnford. As you read it, look for the elements that have been discussed.

Model: A Book Review

Sheila Burnford's *The Incredible Journey* is an exciting and heartwarming story of three heroic animals who must cross the Canadian wilderness in order to be reunited with the people they love. Although the two dogs and a cat never speak, or in any other way behave like humans, their characters are so beautifully drawn that they are each inspiring and unforgettable in their own way.

It is the young Labrador retriever, with his excellent sense of direction, who initiates the journey and starts off first. He is quickly joined by the gentle old bull terrier, and then, with some hesitation, by the Siamese cat. The cat turns out to be the most resourceful of the group and pulls them out of several rough spots. Yet it is obvious that not one of the three could have made the journey alone, and their reliance on one another is one of the most inspiring parts of the book.

There is constant tension as the travelers face the problem of finding food and shelter in the vast wilderness, and of fending off wild animals. In describing the rugged country through which they travel and the natural obstacles they encounter, the author never wastes a word; yet, she manages to fully convey how each scene looks, feels, and smells.

This is not a story for animal lovers alone, but for anyone who enjoys an exciting tale of determination and courage. It is highly recommended to readers young and old.

Activity

Write a review of a novel or play that you have read recently.

More to Explore

Take the book report you wrote earlier and rewrite it as a book review.

Suffixes (noun endings)

Besides changing words to verbs, suffixes can also change words to nouns.

In seventh grade you studied the following noun-forming suffixes: ity, ion, ment, ship, ness. Now you will learn six new suffixes.

Activity A

On a sheet of paper, write the nouns that are formed when the suffixes in the second column are added to the words in the first column. Some words will have to have their endings changed before the suffixes can be added.

Word	Suffix	Noun
criticize	ism	_____
act	or	_____
teach	er	_____
attend	ance	_____
motherly	hood	_____
responsive	ility	_____

Activity B

Use a suffix from Activity A to change each word to a noun.

irritable	invent
speak	patriotic
guide	drive
childish	reliable
profess	perform
terrorize	neighborly

Activity C

Choose an appropriate noun from Activity B to complete each sentence.

1. Because of Pauline's _____ , I always trust her to feed my cat when I'm away.
2. Carlos spent his _____ in Ecuador.
3. Even though she was suffering from the flu, the actress put on an excellent _____ .
4. When my brother is facing a deadline, his _____ keeps everyone away from him.
5. Acts of _____ result in the loss of many innocent lives.
6. Guglielmo Marconi was the _____ of the radio.
7. On the Fourth of July, Americans show their _____ by displaying the flag.
8. I received _____ from my dance instructor on how to stay loose for the performance.
9. Most of the people in our _____ live in apartment buildings.
10. Tonight's guest _____ is a professional basketball player.
11. The bus _____ made sure the little girl got off at the right stop.
12. My mother is a college _____ .

Chapter 6

Creative Tools For Writing

Lesson 1 Simile

A simile is a figure of speech that compares two unlike things. It usually contains the word "like" or "as."

Wordsworth, who recognized the greatness of Milton as a man and a poet, wrote this simile about him:

> Thy soul was like a Star, and dwelt apart;
> Thou hadst a voice whose sound was like the sea.
>
> ("London, 1802")

How many similes are used?

To what does Wordsworth compare Milton's soul?

When Wordsworth says, "and dwelt apart," do you think he is speaking of Milton as a man, a poet, or both? Why?

To what is Wordsworth referring when he uses the word "voice"?
To what does Wordsworth compare Milton's voice? Why does he use this comparison?

You probably use similes in speaking more often than you realize. A simile helps to convey an idea by giving your listeners "double vision." They can see in their minds both the actual object and the one to which it is being compared. With their "double vision," they gain a clear understanding of what you are trying to express. Writers use similes for the same reason.

William Wordsworth

Big Ben in London makes people think about times past and wonder about times to come. Do you think about the passing of time in your own life? When?

Activity A

In each sentence there are two objects being compared.

First, name the two objects that are being compared.

Second, note what specific quality or idea about these objects is being compared (point of comparison).

Third, list as many ideas as possible that are similar about these two objects.

Fourth, set up a diagram like the one below for the other five sentences.

1. My brother's brain works like a computer.

   Brain is compared to a *computer.*

   ⌐works⌐

   (point of comparison)

memory	memory *(Same)*
calculates	calculates *(Same)*
creative	programmed *(Different)*
generates output	generates output *(Same)*
works quickly	works quickly *(Same)*

2. The tree shook its branches as a girl shakes her raindrenched hair.
3. The barbell fell from Jeff's hands like a ton of bricks.
4. Upon hearing the news, the woman turned as pale as a ghost.
5. Seeing the dog, the thief darted like a streak of lightning.
6. Having completed her performance, the ballerina collapsed like a wilting flower.

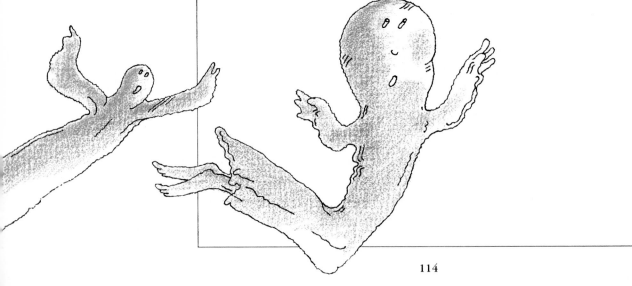

Activity B

Read the following poem and notice the many similes the poet uses to describe a face without a smile.

Smile

Like a bread without the spreadin',
    Like a puddin' without sauce,
Like a mattress without beddin'
    Like a cart without a hoss
Like a door without a latchstring,
    Like a fence without a stile,
Like a dry an' barren creek bed—
    Is the face without a smile.

Like a house without a dooryard,
    Like a yard without a flower,
Like a clock without a mainspring,
    That will never tell the hour;
A thing that sort o' makes yo' feel
    A hunger all the while—
Oh, the saddest sight that ever was
    Is a face without a smile!

Take out a sheet of paper and answer the following questions:
1. To how many objects is a face compared?
2. To how many objects is a smile compared?
3. Explain some of the comparisons; for example, why is the face without a smile like "bread without the spreadin'"? What does the smile do for one's face that a flower might do for a yard?

More to Explore

1. Create your own simile poem by imitating the first stanza of the poem in Activity B. Write seven lines beginning with *like*. For the eighth line, begin with the word *is*, but use a different ending from the one in "Smile." For example:

   > Is life without a friend, pet, sports, cheerleading, etc.
   > Is a day without music, clouds, sun, etc.

2. Create two original similes for each of the qualities listed below. The first one is done for you.

   Height:

   > The mountain peaks loomed above us like skyscrapers in the sky.
   > The basketball players were like giants stomping across the court.

Fear	Nervousness
Beauty	Speed
Loneliness	

Lesson 2 Metaphor

A metaphor is an implied comparison between two things. It is almost like a simile except that "like" and "as" are not used.

Read the following poem:

Dreams

Hold fast to dreams
For if dreams die
Life is a broken-winged bird
That cannot fly.
Hold fast to dreams
For when dreams go
Life is a barren field
Frozen with snow.

Langston Hughes

Find two lines that give examples of metaphor.
How are these two lines different from a simile?
What are the two things being compared in both lines?
Why is life a broken-winged bird if dreams die?
Why is life a barren field if dreams leave?
How does the metaphor of broken-winged bird and barren field help you "picture" life?

Read the next two examples of a metaphor and answer the questions that follow.

All the world's a stage.
And all the men and women merely players:
They have their exits and their entrances;
And one man in his time plays many parts…

William Shakespeare,
As You Like It,
Act ii, sc.7, l.139

What line has the metaphor?
What do you think Shakespeare meant when he implied that the world is a stage?

…we are caterpillars born to form
the angelic butterfly.

Dante Alighieri,
Purgatory, Canto X

What is the metaphor?
What do you think Dante means?

In a simile, you see the two objects, but in a metaphor you see only one object. It's as if the two have merged into one. The world is really a stage, and we are genuinely caterpillars.

Activity A

Following are ten similes. Change each one to a metaphor by making the two objects become one.

1. The supple trees swayed like graceful dancers.
2. His tongue was as sharp as a knife.
3. The fan swirled the air like a small tornado.
4. The old man rambled on like a babbling brook.

5. Having no sense of direction is like being in a ship without a rudder.
6. The track star ran like a gazelle in the forest.
7. Like the parched earth, the little boy longed for a drink.
8. The aged lady's face was like a delicate etching.
9. Like an angry sea, the youth's temper flared out of control.
10. The monster's mouth was as wide as a cave.

Activity B

The following poem, "Southbound on the Freeway," contains two special types of metaphors called *implied* metaphor and *extended* metaphor. Read the poem two or three times before you answer the questions following it.

Southbound on the Freeway

A tourist came in from Orbitville,
parked in the air, and said:

The creatures of this star
are made of metal and glass.

Through the transparent parts
you can see their guts.

Their feet are round and roll
on diagrams or long

measuring tapes, dark
with white lines.

They have four eyes.
The two in back are red.

Sometimes you can see a five-eyed
one, with a red eye turning

on the top of his head.
He must be special—

the others respect him
and go slow

when he passes, winding
among them from behind.

They all hiss as they glide,
like inches, down the marked

tapes. Those soft shapes,
shadowy inside

the hard bodies—are they
their guts or their brains?

May Swenson

Implied Metaphor

1. What are the two objects being compared?
2. Which object is actually stated by the poet?
3. The second object is described but never stated. What is the implied object?

From the description given, the poet expects the reader to be able to identify the second half of the metaphor. This is why it is called an *implied metaphor.*

Extended Metaphor

You already know that the basic metaphor is that the intelligent inhabitants of earth are automobiles.

1. Divide a sheet of paper into two columns.
2. In the first column list all the parts in the poem that belong under human being. In the second column list all the parts of the automobile that are compared to a part of a human being.

Because the poet uses so many comparisons based on the original metaphor, and extends the comparison from beginning to end, it is called an *extended metaphor.*

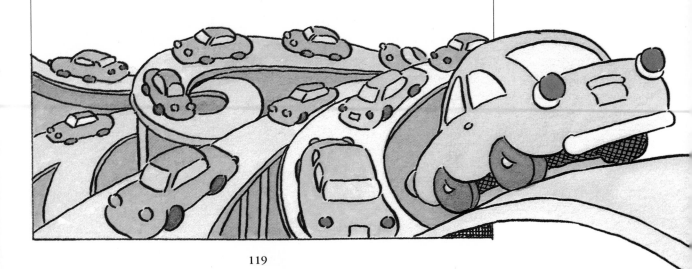

More to Explore

1. Listed below are ten nouns. Write each one as a metaphor, and underline the two objects being compared. The first one is done for you.

   Hair: On a windy day, Jan's <u>hair</u> is a <u>knotted mass of string.</u>

Bee	Turtle	Moon	Waves
Ship	Clouds	Book	Face

2. Follow the pattern below to create your own poem using a metaphor.

   Begin by thinking of a metaphor:

   The sun is a fiery chariot.

   Line 1: Use the second object in the metaphor as the first line in the poem.

   The fiery chariot

   Line 2: Add a verb (action word).

   descends

   Lines 3, 4, and 5: Add three adverbs of manner.

   gradually
   gracefully
   gently

   Line 6: Add an adverbial phrase.

   into the placid glass.

   Line 7: Name the first part of the metaphor (sun) in a creative way.

   Earthbound traveler.

Lesson 3 Personification

Personification is a figure of speech that allows an idea, inanimate object, or animal to take on the qualities of a person.

The Sea-Gull

Hark to the whimper of the sea-gull
He weeps because he's not an ea-gull.
Suppose you were, you silly sea-gull,
Could you explain it to your she-gull?
Ogden Nash

What is being personified in the poem by Ogden Nash?
What words give it the quality of a person?
Which line reveals an attitude?
Do you agree with this attitude? Why or why not?
Because the sea gull is behaving like a person, it is being personified.

Activity A

Discuss what lifelike qualities you see and hear in each of the
following poems. Tell what is being personified.

A silver-scaled Dragon with jaws flaming red
Sits at my elbow and toasts my bread.
I hand him fat slices, and then, one by one,
He hands them back when he sees they are done.

William Jay Smith

In the gray evening
I see a long green serpent
with its tail in the dahlias.

It lies in loops across the grass
And drinks softly at the faucet.

I can hear it swallow.

Beatrice Janosco

The dinosaurs are not all dead.
I saw one raise its iron head
To watch me walking down the road
Beyond our house today.
Its jaws were dripping with a load
Of earth and grass that it had cropped.
It must have heard me where I stopped.
Snorted white steam my way,
And stretched its long neck out to see.
And chewed, and grinned quite amiably.

Charles Malam

Activity B

Read the two sentences. Tell what is being personified in each, and what specific words give it human qualities.

1. Summer, brightly dressed, danced throughout the town.

2. The arms of the ocean opened wide for all the summer residents.

Complete each sentence by supplying one or more words to personify the nouns in italics.

1. The discarded *toy* _____ as it was thrown into the trash heap.
2. When it was batted into the outfield, the *baseball* _____.
3. My *school desk* _____ out, "_____."
4. The *daffodils* _____ the breeze.
5. The *wind* _____ a savage cry.
6. The *car's engine* _____ as it came to a sudden stop.
7. The rickety *elevator* _____ its way to the 11th floor.
8. *Poverty* _____ millions of people.

More to Explore

1. The following two poems were written by students. Use them as a springboard for bringing your own inanimate object or animal to life in a poem.

The Train

Steam flowed
and fire raged
from the belly
of the ferocious monster.
The roar echoed for miles
around as the one-eyed
dragon entered the town.

Robert Slinkard

Teakettle

The teakettle
Letting off steam
Impatiently waiting
Screaming for attention
Gargles
Gasps
And then dies out.

Janise Stankiewicz

2. Listed below are six nouns that can be personified. Write a creative sentence for each, showing your ability to use personification effectively.

   time   happiness   bulldozer
   moon   morning   mirror

3. Television commercials use personification to appeal to the audience, and there are often personified objects in children's stories: trains, animals, houses, and even decks of cards. Draw an object and write a sentence about it using personification.

Lesson 4 Hyperbole

Hyperbole is a figure of speech that exaggerates. It usually exaggerates the truth about something in order to emphasize an idea.

The following line is taken from "Concord Hymn" by Ralph Waldo Emerson:

> . . . And fired the shot heard round the world.

Emerson refers to the battles of Lexington and Concord, where the first shot of the American Revolution was fired on April 19, 1775.
Was the shot really heard around the world?
What does Emerson mean when he says the shot was heard around the world?

> Tears too are useful; with tears you can melt iron.
>
> Ovid, *Ars Amatoria*,
> Bk. i, l.659

Can tears really melt iron?
What does the writer mean?
What is meant by "tears too are useful"?

Sometimes exaggerations are humorous. Read "Hungry Mungry" by Shel Silverstein for many examples of hyperbole.

Hungry Mungry sat at supper,
Took his knife and spoon and fork,
Ate a bowl of mushroom soup,
ate a slice of roasted pork,
Ate a dozen stewed tomatoes, twenty-seven deviled eggs.
Fifteen shrimps, nine baked potatoes,
Thirty-two fried chicken legs,
A shank of lamb, a boiled ham,
Two bowls of grits, some black-eye peas,
Four chocolate shakes, eight angel cakes,
Nine custard pies with Muenster cheese
Ten pots of tea, and after he
Had eaten all that he was able,
He poured some broth on the tablecloth
And ate the kitchen table.

His parents said, "Oh Hungry Mungry, stop these silly jokes."
Mungry opened up his mouth, and "Gulp," he ate his folks.
And then he went and ate his house, all the bricks and wood,
And then he ate up all the people in the neighborhood.
Up came twenty angry policemen shouting, "Stop and cease."
Mungry opened up his mouth and "Gulp," he ate the police.
Soldiers came with tanks and guns,
Said Mungry, "They can't harm me."
He just smiled and licked his lips and ate the U.S. Army.

The President sent all his bombers—Mungry still was calm,
Put his head back, gulped the planes, and gobbled up the bomb.
He ate his town and ate the city—ate and ate and ate—
And then he said, "I think I'll eat the whole United States."

And so he ate Chicago first and munched the Water Tower,
And then he chewed on Pittsburgh but he found it rather sour,
He ate New York and Tennessee, and all of Boston town,
Then drank the Mississippi River just to wash it down.
And when he'd eaten every state, each puppy, boy and girl
He wiped his mouth upon his sleeve and went to eat the world.

He ate the Egypt pyramids and every church in Rome,
And all the grass in Africa and all the ice in Nome.
He ate each hill in Green Brazil and then to make things worse
He decided for dessert he'd eat the universe.

He started with the moon and stars and soon as he was done
He gulped the clouds, he sipped the wind and gobbled up
   the sun.
Then sitting there in the cold dark air,
He started to nibble his feet,
Then his legs, then his hips
Then his neck, then his lips
Till he sat there just gnashin' his teeth
'Cause nothin' was nothin' was
Nothin' was nothin' was
Nothin' was left to eat.

Activity A

Complete each statement by giving an exaggerated response.

1. I'm so hungry _____.
2. Frank talked so long _____.
3. The grumpy man was so mean _____.
4. The ship was so tall _____.
5. The auditorium was so crowded _____.
6. I'll love you until _____.
7. There must have been a _____ people waiting for the bus.
8. The gong on the grandfather clock was so loud _____.
9. The plains are so flat _____.
10. An eighty-year-old woman drove so slowly _____.

Activity B

Shel Silverstein exaggerated being hungry when he created "Hungry Mungry." See if you can exaggerate one of the following ideas. Write a short poem or paragraph.

Tall Paul
Loud crowd
Strong Wong

More to Explore

1. Write a poem or paragraph that exaggerates a talent you or a friend may have.

   soccer   fishing
   dancing   spelling
   drawing   weight lifting
   horseback riding cooking

2. Write a poem or paragraph that exaggerates an experience you or someone else has undergone.

   first day in a new school
   receiving your report
   attending a rock concert
   your first job babysitting
   being alone
   tryouts for a sport
   a watchdog who failed
   keeping a surprise party a secret

Lesson 5 Alliteration

Alliteration is the repetition of initial consonant sounds. It is a sound device that helps to create melody or mood.

Read "Foul Shot," looking and listening for words or phrases that begin with the same sound.

Foul Shot

With two 60's stuck on the scoreboard
And two seconds hanging on the clock,
The solemn boy in the center of eyes,
Squeezed by silence,
Seeks out the line with his feet,
Soothes his hands along his uniform,
Gently drums the ball against the floor,
Then measures the waiting net,
Raises the ball on his right hand,
Balances it with his left,
Calms it with fingertips,
Breathes,
Crouches,
Waits,
And then through a stretching of stillness,
Nudges it upward.

The ball
Slides up and out,
Lands,
Leans,
Wobbles,
Wavers,
Hesitates,
Exasperates,
Plays it coy
Until every face begs with unsounding screams—

And then

    And then

       And then,

Right before ROAR-UP,
Dives down and through.

Edwin A. Hoey

1. How many different examples of alliteration can you find in the poem?
2. Can you hear the same sounds in the middle and at the end of words? Give examples.
3. Because the author uses a predominance of certain sounds, he establishes a particular mood or tension. What is the mood of "Foul Shot"? What tension seems to be created?

Activity A

Try creating your own poem using alliteration. Choose a sound that you like to hear, then answer the questions *Who? Did what? When? Where? Why?*

Example:

Who?	Paul and Peggy
Did what?	Planned to go
When?	Promptly at 1P.M.
Where?	To the Vet in Philadelphia
Why?	To see the Phillies pitcher prepare to play the Pirates.

Activity B

Write five poetic sentences using alliteration.

Example:

The waves, wandering whitecaps of the sea, washed against the shore.

More to Explore

Create some tongue twisters. Try them out on another student.

Example:

Cookies crumbled crazily on kitchen cabinets and corner cupboards.

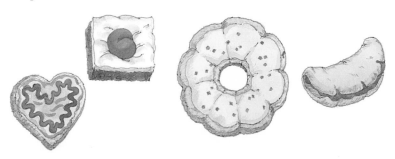

Lesson 6 Onomatopoeia

Onomatopoeia is a sound device. Onomatopoetic words imitate the sound of a person, animal, or thing.

Hark, hark!
  Bow-wow
The watch-dogs bark!
  Bow-wow
Hark, hark! I hear
The strain of strutting chanticleer
Cry, "Cock-a-diddle-dow!"

  William Shakespeare
  The Tempest
  Act i, sc. 2,l.382

What words in the above poem are onomatopoetic?
Why do you think Shakespeare compares dogs with a rooster?

While some figures of speech may help you to *see* better, onomatopoeia helps you to *hear* better. Instead of writing,

  The baseball flew by.

you can actually hear the sound when you write,

  The baseball *whizzed* by.

Activity A

On a piece of paper, write the sounds that are listed below. Opposite each sound, give the person, animal, or object that could make that sound.

swish   varoom
splat   crackle
gulp   sizzle
clackity-clack ra-pa-pa-pum

Activity B

Write down the objects listed below, and then give the sound each one might make.

lightning   wind
snoring   laughing
book hitting the ground   telephone
snake   thunder

More to Explore

1. Read the following poem to yourself and then orally as a class. Pronounce the onomatopoetic words carefully so that you can enjoy the sounds.

Cheers

The frogs and the serpents each had a football team,
and I heard their cheer leaders in my dream:

"Bilgewater, bilgewater," called the frog,
"Bilgewater, bilgewater,
Sis, boom, bog!
Roll 'em off the log,
Slog 'em in the sog,
Swamp 'em, swamp 'em,
Muck mire quash!"

"Sisyphus, Sisyphus," hissed the snake,
"Sibilant, syllabub,
Syllable-loo-ba-lay.
Scylla and Charybdis,
Sumac, asphodel,
How do you spell Success?
With an S-S-S!"

    Eve Merriam

2. Read the poem "Jabberwocky." Practice it silently a few times before reading it aloud. Choose three onomatopoetic words that Lewis Carroll used. Write your definition of each of the three words. Draw the Jabberwock doing or saying the three onomatopoetic words.

Jabberwocky

'Twas brillig, and the slithy toves
    Did gyre and gimble in the wabe:
All mimsy were the borogoves,
    And the mome raths outgrabe.

"Beware the Jabberwock, my son!
    The jaws that bite, the claws that catch!
Beware the Jubjub bird, and shun
    The frumious Bandersnatch!"

He took his vorpal sword in hand:
    Long time the manxome foe he sought—
So rested he by the Tumtum tree.
    And stood awhile in thought.

And, as in uffish thought he stood,
    The Jabberwock, with eyes of flame,
Came whiffling through the tulgey wood,
    And burbled as it came!

One, two! One, two! And through and through
    The vorpal blade went snicker-snack!
He left it dead, and with its head
    He went galumphing back.

"And hast thou slain the Jabberwock?
    Come to my arms, my beamish boy!"
Lewis Carroll

Idioms

An idiom is an expression that has a meaning different from that indicated by its words.

Sometimes phrases cannot be understood word by word. They often have an entirely different meaning. For example:

When giving your speech, put your *best foot forward*.

Does this mean: a. make sure your best foot is in front of you
b. be the best you can be

If you interpret the words *best foot forward* by what each word means, then you have to choose *a*. But the words together are just an *idiom* (a way of writing or speaking) that means to be the best you can be.

When searching for the meaning of an idiom in a dictionary, look under the most important word in the phrase. In the example above, you would look under *foot*. Your dictionary may also give you other idioms that use the same word, such as *put your foot down* or *put your foot in your mouth*.

Activity A

Write each idiom on a sheet of paper, underline the most important word, and then look for the meaning in a good dictionary.

1. right up my alley
2. my cup of tea
3. pulling my leg
4. go bananas
5. cream of the crop
6. eat your words
7. see eye to eye
8. go jump in the lake

Activity B

Choose any four idioms from the list in Activity A. Write an original sentence for each one showing that you understand the meaning of the expression. Try to add more idioms to the list. Share them with the class.

Chapter 7

Letter Writing

Lesson 1 Writing Social Letters

A social letter is an informal letter written to friends and relatives.

A social letter is a very personal piece of writing. In it, you reveal yourself: your likes and dislikes, your feelings and attitudes. It is a reflection of your uniqueness.

Although the telephone has replaced much of today's letter writing, there are still times when a thank-you, sympathy, or congratulatory note must be written. And for friends and relatives who live at a distance, there is nothing better than a long, chatty letter arriving in the mail.

This painting is entitled *Letters in a Doorway.*
In what sense are letters doorways?

The Parts of a Social Letter

There are five parts to a social letter:

1. Heading

The heading includes the address of the writer and the date. It is usually written on three lines and in block form. If you are writing to a person who knows you very well, you may omit the address, but not the date.

6312 South Oakley Street
Chicago, Illinois 60626
September 20, 19____

2. Salutation

The salutation is the greeting at the beginning of the letter. It is written at the left-hand margin of the paper, below the heading, and is followed by a comma. The first word and the person's name are capitalized. *Dear* and *dearest* are not capitalized unless they are the first words.

Dear Dave,

(Dear Aunt Sally,)
(Dear Grandpa,)
(My dear Joan,)

3. Body or Message

Your message is delivered in the body of the letter. This may take the form of a friendly conversation, an invitation, a request for information, an expression of gratitude, or a combination of all of these. Whenever you introduce a new subject, you must begin a new paragraph. The first word of every paragraph is indented.

You certainly are missed back here on Oakley Street. When I start out for school, I always want to stop by your house to see if you're ready. What a strange feeling!

How do you like your new school? It must seem funny to be in a place half the size of Lawnwood. I'll bet you know everyone from grades 1 to 8 by now. I think I might just like that family spirit.

Remember the overgrown field behind the school? Mr. Wilkinson has decided to turn it into a ball field. On Saturdays, some of us go over to help the men clear away the brush, but the bulldozer is really doing all the work. It should be ready by next spring.

Let me hear from you soon, Dave. I'm anxious to know about life in your new town.

4. Complimentary Close

The complimentary close is your word of farewell. The first word of the closing is written directly under the first word of the heading. Only the first word is capitalized. It is always followed by a comma. The words you use depend upon the degree of intimacy between you and the receiver of your letter.

Your old pal,
(Your friend,)
(Love,)
(Your loving niece,)
(As always,)
(Fondly,)

5. Signature

The signature is begun under the first word of the complimentary close and should line up with it. When writing to a familiar person, you sign only your first name. When writing to someone unfamiliar, you give your full name.

Mike
Michael Brenner

When you put all the parts together, your letter should look like this:

6312 South Oakley
Chicago, Illinois 60626
September 20, 19—

Dear Dave,

    You certainly are missed back here on Oakley Street. When I start out for school, I always want to stop by your house to see if you're ready. It's a strange feeling!

    How do you like your new school? It must seem funny to be in a place half the size of Lawnwood. I'll bet you know everyone from grades 1 to 8 by now. I think I might just like that family spirit.

    Remember the overgrown field behind the school? Mr. Wilkinson has decided to turn it into a ball field. On Saturdays, some of us go over to help the men clear away the brush, but the bulldozer is really doing all the work. It should be ready by next spring.

    Let me hear from you soon, Dave. I'm anxious to know about life in your new town.

Your pal,
Mike

Since your letters represent you, you may frequently be judged by them. It is important, therefore, to be careful of their appearance as well as their contents. If a letter is handwritten, the writing should be clear and legible. If a letter is typed, it should be as perfect as possible, with errors erased and the corrections carefully typed in.

Activity A

Write each of the addresses and dates in the proper form for the heading of a letter.

1. Portsmouth, New Hampshire 03801, 171 Saratoga Way, September 12, 19____
2. June 27, 19____, 6333 Herbert Street, Detroit, Michigan 48210.
3. Shamrock Hotel, May 3, 19____, Houston, Texas 77023
4. 252 East Twelfth Street, February 10, 19____, St. Paul, Minnesota 55111
5. May 22, 19____, Winston-Salem, North Carolina 27101, 44 Mozart Street
6. 2219 Forest Avenue, October 26, 19____, Cleveland, Ohio 44123

Activity B

Write a salutation for a letter addressed to each of the following persons:

1. your father
2. a classmate
3. your teacher
4. your cousin
5. a dear friend
6. your pen pal
7. your aunt
8. your grandparents
9. Mrs. Lopez
10. your sister or brother

Activity C

Write the following sentences in the form of a letter. Supply the missing parts, use capital letters as they are needed, and paragraph the letter properly.

i was so happy to see a letter from you on my desk when i got home from school. it was a rather dull day, so i was glad for a friendly note. thanks for sending your school picture. i especially liked the background of the library shelves. is that to make everyone believe you've read all those books? we are getting ready for a Christmas play, too, and i have a speaking part. i have to practice at a microphone, and you know how nervous i get when i read in front of others. here's hoping i don't lose my voice. if you have any ideas for a science project, let me know because i can't think of anything interesting to do. my mom won't let me work with chemicals, so that's out. science is your favorite subject, so you must have some suggestions. keep in touch. it's nice to hear about what you're doing on the other coast.

Activity D

Choose one of the following ideas and create an interesting letter. Make sure that the *heading, salutation, complimentary close,* and *signature* are properly written.

1. Write a letter to a pen pal telling him or her about some of the interesting things to see and do in your hometown.
2. Write to a cousin or some other relative and tell about a recent trip you took.
3. Write a letter to someone you especially admire. Tell why you think so highly of the person.

Finishing Touches for Letters

Folding the Letter

Some paper only has to be folded in half in order to fit into the envelope. The creased edge should be placed at the bottom of the envelope.

 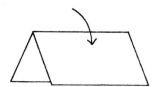

Sometimes you might want to write your letter on larger paper. In order for it to fit in a regular size envelope (6½″ by 3¾″), you must first fold the paper in half, then fold the right side over a third of the way. Finally, fold the left side over. The letter should be inserted in the envelope with the last fold at the bottom.

 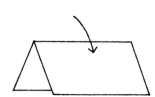 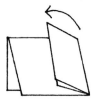

If you use a legal size envelope (9½" x 4"), large paper needs only to be folded in thirds to fit neatly into the envelope. The way to do this is to fold the bottom third of the paper a little past the halfway mark, then fold the top third over within an eighth of an inch of the bottom fold. Insert the letter in the envelope with the last fold at the bottom.

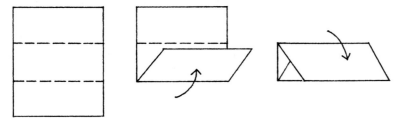

Addressing the Envelope

The envelope should contain the full name and address of the person to whom the letter is being sent. The first line contains the person's name, and is begun just above the middle of the envelope and slightly to the left of center. The second line contains the street address, and the third line the city, state, and zip code. It is customary to write your own address in the upper left-hand corner. This is called the *return address*.

Adam Smith
8641 Winchester
Chicago, Illinois 60626

Tom Mesh
130 Sunset Ridge
Shokie, Illinois 60076

Activity

Write the following names and addresses as they should be written on envelopes. Use your own return address.

1. Mr. Robert Lowell, 2820 West Fourth Street, Phoenix, Arizona 85000
2. Mr. John Vivaqua, 4823 Webster Street, Omaha, Nebraska 68100
3. Mrs. Thomas Campbell, 4218 North Hermitage Avenue, Chicago, Illinois 60600
4. Ms. Sheila Brocke, 903 East Woodlin Road, Dallas, Texas 75200
5. Dr. Sharon Klein, 2510 Maple Avenue, Baltimore, Maryland 21200

Lesson 2 Special Types of Social Letters

A Letter of Invitation

Keep invitations short, but be sure to include the time, the place, and the nature of the party or gathering.

1714 Ritner Street
Ogden, Utah 84400
April 28, 19—

Dear Ron,

Are you in the mood for a few days in the mountains? Mom said that I may invite four friends to our cottage at Arrowhead for the weekend of May fifth, and I want you to be one of them.

There will be lots of things for us to do. We can ride the trails and swim in the lake during the day, and on Saturday night we can go to the roller-skating rink in town.

Dad is driving up on Friday evening, and there will be plenty of room in the car for all of us. Let me know if you can join us, and I'll tell you what time we'll pick you up.

Your friend,
Gary

143

A Letter of Acceptance

A letter accepting an invitation should be brief and enthusiastic.

5601 Moulton Street
Ogden, Utah 84400
April 30, 19—

Dear Gary,

I wouldn't miss this trip for anything. I've never been to the mountains, so everything we do will be new and different.

I'll be waiting with my bag packed at the front door. Just let me know the time.

Your friend,
Ron

A Thank-You Letter

Name the gift you have received and make the person feel that the present is quite special.

July 27, 19 —

Dear Grandmom,

You always buy me the most unique things for my birthday. The skating passes are great, and the gift certificates to The Hamburger Shack will probably be used this weekend.

My friends think I have the best grandmom, and I agree. Thanks for everything.

Love,
Kim

Activity

Try the following ideas for letters. Be sure that each letter contains the five essential parts: heading, salutation, message, complimentary close, and signature.

1. *Invitation*

    You are planning a Halloween party. Create your own original invitation. Be sure to include time, date, and place. Decorate the invitation appropriately.

2. *Acceptance*

    Your aunt (or friend) asks you to volunteer to be a clown at the Children's Hospital bazaar. Accept the challenge.

3. *Thank You*

    Thank someone for providing a wonderful weekend for you.

More to Explore

Choose two of the following ideas and write polished, courteous social letters.

1. The Christmas play at your school is December 18th. You have a special part and would like your grandparents (or other relative) to come to see you. Write them an invitation they can't refuse.
2. A gift for you from a special relative has arrived damaged. How would you respond to the sender?
3. Your basketball team has made the playoffs for the district championship. Invite a former student (or someone else) to the series.
4. You have just won a food processor (something you don't want or need). Accept the prize graciously.
5. A student in your class has just received an award: scholarship, athletic trophy, essay contest, recital, speech contest, science contest, etc. Write a note of congratulations.
6. A relative who lives at a distance and hasn't seen you for awhile sends a gift that is too young for you. Write a gracious thank you for the gift.
7. Think of the events and activities of the last few weeks. Write to a friend and give an account of your adventures.
8. At a country fair, you took a chance on a pony. A letter just arrived indicating that you are now the proud owner. You live in the city. Handle the situation courteously.
9. Send a thank-you letter to your local newspaper editor, who has awarded you a $500 savings bond for being "Outstanding Paperboy/girl of the Year."
10. You have just had a new member added to your family. Describe your baby brother or sister to a friend or relative who lives at a distance.

Lesson 3 Writing Business Letters

A business letter is a formal letter written to a company in order to obtain or give information, or to request specific merchandise.

Business letters should always be brief, courteous, and clear. The form of a business letter is very similar to that of a social letter. It does, however, contain one part that is not found in a social letter. This part is called the *inside address*.

The Parts of a Business Letter

1. Heading

This is the same as the heading of any social letter.

607 Lincoln Drive
Dubuque, Iowa 52001
January 20, 19____

2. Inside Address

The inside address is not found in a social letter. It contains the complete name and address of the firm or the person to whom the letter is written. It is placed at the left-hand margin above the salutation.

E.M. Lohmann Company
314 Sibley Street
St. Paul, Minnesota 55100

3. Salutation

The salutation, or greeting, is very formal. It is best to use the person's name if it is known. The salutation is always followed by a colon.

Dear Sir or Madam:

(Dear Mr. Jones:)
(Dear Ms. Callahan:)
(Dear Mrs. Sommers:)
(Dear Miss Clifford:)

4. Body or Message

The body of the letter contains the message. The message must be courteous, clear, accurate, and brief. Since a letter represents you before a business firm, you should endeavor to be courteous in your manner, and to be clear and accurate in your statements. The letter must be brief so that the reader can pick out the necessary information as quickly as possible.

> Please send, as soon as possible, the ivory and gold trophy listed in your catalogue as S-214. Enclosed is a check for fifteen dollars ($15.00), as specified in your current price list.

5. Complimentary Close

The complimentary close is also more formal in a business letter. It consists of a short phrase indicating respect for the person addressed in the letter and is followed by a comma.

Sincerely,
(Sincerely yours,)
(Respectfully,)
(Respectfully yours,)
(Very truly yours,)

6. Signature

The signature of a business letter contains the full name of the writer. It is always written, never typed.

Sarah J. Meier

(Miss) Margaret Jones

Jonathan C. Pearson

Here is how a business letter should look:

Activity A

Put the following inside addresses in correct order:

1. 189 Prospect Avenue, Soup to Nuts, Inc., Buffalo, New York 14214
2. Homer, Louisiana 71040, 2922 Carlton Drive, Picture Perfect, Mr. Alfred Snyder
3. Creative Christmas Gifts, Los Altos, California 94022, Ms. I. M. Merry, 18 North Second Avenue

Activity B

Draw three 9½″ by 4″ rectangles on a piece of paper. Address three envelopes using the information from Activity A.

Activity C

Put the following sentences in business letter form. The punctuation and capitalization must be added. Use your own name and address and the present date.

ms. terese platzer librarian of childrens department goshen public library goshen, indiana 46526 dear ms. platzer: please consider me an applicant for the position of assistant library aide advertised in today's sentinel. i am fourteen years old and attend powell school. i have held a library card for five years. for references, i have permission to name the principal of our school, mrs. susan jardine, and my teacher, mr. marlon niven. very truly yours,

Lesson 4 Special Types of Business Letters

A Letter Placing an Order

This type of business letter should contain the following information:
1. names of items to be purchased
2. catalogue numbers, if provided
3. where the items were advertised
4. the prices of the items
5. how payment for the merchandise will be handled: cash, check, money order, COD (cash on delivery)

1269 Asbury Street
Stone Harbor, New Jersey 08247
February 3, 19—

Junior High Book Club
110 Chestnut Street
Rockville, Maryland 20850

Dear Sir or Madam:

Please send to the above address the following novels listed in your catalog:

1	The Sea-Wolf by Jack London	(9046)	$1.95
1	Little Women by L. Alcott	(9085)	2.25
1	Lisa, Bright and Dark by J. Neufeld	(9010)	.95
			$5.15
		shipping	1.00
			$6.15

A check for $6.15 is enclosed.

Respectfully yours,
Karen L. James

A Letter of Request

In this type of business letter, you are usually requesting information, catalogues, pamphlets, or samples. Be clear, brief, and polite.

Whitemarsh School
Dayton, Ohio 45400
November 6, 19—

Daily Local Times
1060 Morgan Avenue
Dayton, Ohio 45400

Dear Sir or Madam:

In our language arts class, we have been studying news and editorial writing. A friend and I thought it would be helpful if our class could see a real newspaper at work. Would it be possible for us to have a tour of the *Daily Local Times* within the next two weeks? If so, please tell us what day and time would be convenient for you.

Very truly yours,
Scott Bannon

A Letter of Complaint or Adjustment

Give a clear and courteous explanation of your position on the matter. Be sure to include the following information:
1. Mention the error by stating the name of the product and the date and place of purchase.
2. Explain the action you are planning to take and the action you would like the business firm to take.

Bryn Mawr School
137 Locust Avenue
Spokane, Washington 99200
September 24, 19 —

Enley Sport Shop
932 North Tacoma Street
Tacoma, Washington 98400

Dear Sir or Madam:

On September 9th, we ordered one dozen blue-and-white football jerseys. The blue-and-gold ones that arrived today are not satisfactory substitutes since our school colors are blue and white.

I am returning these jerseys collect. Kindly send the colors ordered as soon as possible.

Very truly yours,
William Armstrong

Activity A

Number a piece of paper from 1 to 10. Next to each number write the letter *a, b,* or *c* to tell whether the item refers to

    a. a business letter   b. a social letter   c. both

1. letter of invitation
2. heading
3. Dear Ms. McCole:
4. inside address
5. Your faithful friend,
6. letter of request
7. Sandy
8. Respectfully,
9. letter of acceptance
10. salutation

Activity B

Write the following business letters. Use your home address as the heading and your own name for the signature.

1. *Placing an Order*

    You would like a subscription to *Popular Computer.* The cost is $8.98 for six issues. The magazine is published at 8219 Lindberg Boulevard, Seattle, Washington 98124.

2. *Letter of Request*

    You have written a marvelous short story, and your teacher suggests that you try to publish it. Write to a student publication called *Creative Corner*, 6019 Penn Avenue, Santa Monica, California 90404

3. *Letter of Complaint or Adjustment*

    You ordered a baseball mitt from SPORTING GOODS UNLIMITED, 19 Peterson Drive, Boise, Idaho 83742. Instead, you received a pair of mittens. Make known your problem.

More to Explore

Here are some business letters for you to write. If a company and address are not supplied, create an original one. Use your own address for the heading and your own name for the signature.

1. You have thought up a new computer game and would like a local company to see your program. Write to them requesting an interview. Create your own company.

2. In the newspaper, there is an advertisement for ordering a small exotic pet. Write to The Zoo-y Zoo, 100 Kangaroo Lane, Tampa, Florida 33684 and ask for a brochure listing the various animals and prices.

3. You ordered a poster of your favorite actor (actress). Instead you received a picture of a not-so-popular actress (actor). Write to Picture Pin-ups, 1666 Cresent Road, Chicago, Illinois 60657.

4. Your local paper states that by ordering two cassette tapes within the next week, you will get a third one free. Decide which ones you want and take advantage of the offer. Write to

   Tons of Tapes
   3099 Market Street
   Philadelphia, PA 19101

   Check page 150 for a list of what is included in an order.

5. You hosted a party at your home last week. The pretzels you bought were stale, even though the expiration date on the package was several months away. Write a letter of complaint to the company.

6. Write a letter to Montgomery Ward and Company, 618 West Chicago Avenue, Chicago, Illinois 60652, ordering any three of the following articles:

   1 tennis racket, No. 6H 1229, $24.00
   1 tennis cap, No. 6H 1259, Size 7, $6.95
   3 tennis balls, No. 6H 1231, $5.95
   1 basketball, No. 6H 1607, $21.95
   1 soccer ball, No. 6H 01740, $16.95

   Add shipping charges and tell the method of payment. Use your own address and signature.

7. Your order of 100 personalized pencils arrived. Your name is misspelled. Create a company and render your complaint.

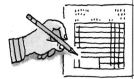

Lesson 5 Completing Forms

Completing a form is an orderly way of requesting information or materials.

Many companies, schools, clubs, and organizations ask that you fill out a form when requesting information or material. When businesses receive numerous requests, a form makes it easier for them to compile and process the information. Before you complete a form, you should do the following:

1. Read the entire form to find out what is being asked.
2. List on a piece of paper the information you must look up or ask about.
3. Collect the information needed to answer what you don't know.
4. Check how you will complete the form: write? print? type?
5. Complete the form carefully and neatly.
6. Reread the form to see that all the information you have given is accurate and in the correct place.

Activity A

Study the form opposite; then answer the questions.

1. How was the form to be completed? Written? Printed? Typed?
2. What is the difference between "price each" and "total price"?
3. Why are there four columns under "Item No."?
4. Why does the company request a page number?
5. What is meant by a subtotal?
6. How did Karen know to add $3.50 for shipping charges?
7. Why did she not include sales tax?
8. What does the statement "no cash or C.O.D." mean?

THE PERFECT GIFT
1039 Bryant Lane
Seattle, WA 98103

Please print or type all information.

Page No.	Name of Item	Item No.				QTY	Price Each	Total Price
18	White Porcelain Candlesticks	9	0	1	6	1	4.98	4.98
22	Cookie Jar	7	7	7	6	2	8.98	17.96
29	Hand Puppets	3	9	5	0	1	12.98	12.98

Shipping Instructions

Up to $20.00............................$1.50
$20.01 to $30.00.........................$2.50
$30.01 to $40.00.........................$3.50
$40.01 to $50.00.........................$4.50
Over $50.00 ....$5.50

Subtotal	**$35.92**
Shipping Charges	3.50
NY sales tax (residents only)	——
Total	**$39.42**

(No cash or C.O.D.)

Ship to

Karen   L.   Dalesandro

first name   middle initial   last name

1659 Wellington Avenue

street address (apt. no.)

Ann Arbor, Michigan 48107

city, state, zip code

Activity B

Make a copy of the savings deposit form, and then complete it by using the information in the paragraph.

Keith Turner has savings account #00016767123. He wants to deposit $60.50 from his paper route earnings, and a check for $25.00 he received on his birthday. He feels he should keep out $15.00 for expenditures for the coming week. Keith lives at 89 Marydell Lane in Mobile, Alabama (36604).

UNIVERSAL BANK

DATE_____

NAME_____
              (PRINT)

ADDRESS_____

_____

_____
              SIGNATURE

ACCOUNT NUMBER ☐☐☐☐☐–☐☐☐☐☐–☐☐☐

SAVINGS DEPOSIT

Dollars	Cents	
		Cash
		Checks
		Total
		Less cash received
		Total deposit

More to Explore

Copy the form for this check onto a piece of paper. Make out a check to cover the cost of the items purchased in Activity A. Your signature should be *one* of the names that is printed at the top of the check.

Sam A. Sample
Sally O. Sample
20 Ross Lane
West Chester, PA 19380

139

_____ 19 _____ 2-7/310

PAY TO THE
ORDER OF _____ $_____

_____ Dollars

UNIVERSAL BANK
FRAZER, PA **19345**

For_____   _____
Account: 000 111122   333 444 5   666

Word Study 7

Etymology

Etymology is the study of the history of a word: where it came from, how it was originally spelled, and what it originally meant.

Many English words developed from other languages, such as Greek, Latin, French, and Old English. In most dictionaries, the history of a word, or *etymology*, is found in brackets either at the end or the beginning of the definition. Following are some symbols you should know in order to understand the information that is given in the etymology. Check the front of your dictionary for other abbreviations.

      <   means "derived from or comes from"
      <L   means "comes from the Latin language"
      <Gk means "comes from the Greek language"
      <F   means "comes from the French language"
      <OE means "comes from the Old English language"
      <ME means "comes from the Middle English language"

Sometimes words come from two or more languages; for example, *anchor*. In some dictionaries, the etymology for *anchor* will look like this:

    [<OE ancor <L ancora <Gk ankyra]

Our word *anchor* originally came to us from the Old English word. The Old English word came from the Latin, and the Latin from the Greek word. Some dictionaries will only indicate that the word came from the Greek, since that is the earliest known form.

Activity A

Write each word on a piece of paper. Using the correct symbols, give the etymology of the word. If the word came from more than one language, indicate by symbol the various languages.

ranch	papoose	juvenile
rotate	cool	pizza
wharf	hypnosis	monster
pepper	chocolate	plastic

Activity B

Copy the words in column A onto a sheet of paper. Next to each word write the letter from column B that indicates the correct etymology of the word.

Column A	Column B
nightingale	a. Spanish
stomach	b. Old English
siesta	c. American Indian
school (of fish)	d. Latin
chauffeur	e. Italian
liberty	f. Dutch
piano	g. French
moccasin	h. Greek

161

Chapter 8

Speaking and Listening Skills

Speaking skills enable us to give effective oral expression to ideas, while listening skills lead to the proper perception and interpretation of spoken material.

In this chapter you will learn how to speak effectively when you are
—a member or leader of a group discussion
—giving a talk
—reading poetry aloud
You will also learn how to concentrate when someone else is speaking so that you can fully grasp the message that is being transmitted.

Lesson 1 Speaking in Groups

Much of your happiness in life will depend on your ability to work with others. No matter what your occupation may be, you will be a member of some group, club, association, or union. Decisions will be made that will affect your welfare. Will you be silent while questions are being discussed, or will you present your own ideas in such a way as to command respect?

It is important to practice interacting in a group—to learn to pool your bit of knowledge with that of others for the common good, to sift differences of opinion, to change your own opinion gracefully when you see that the arguments on the other side are stronger, and to defend your own view if you are certain that you are right. School offers many opportunities for practicing this kind of interaction.

Is the atmosphere of this illumination formal or informal? Can you think of some situations that call for a more formal tone in speaking or writing?

Informal Class Discussions

Informal class discussions are those held when the class is not organized with elected officers. The teacher, or someone appointed by the teacher, presides as chairperson or leader. A day in advance of the time set for the discussion, the teacher may make an announcement like this: "Tomorrow during our English period we shall hold an informal discussion on the qualities of good sportsmanship. I should like the members of the class to come prepared to take part in the discussion by offering helpful suggestions. Nancy Stein, will you please act as leader of the discussion?"

Model: An Informal Discussion

(The English period is in progress. Nancy Stein is the discussion leader, or chairperson.)

NANCY: We are here to discuss the qualities of good sportsmanship. Which do you think is the most important trait a person who practices good sportsmanship should possess?

FRED: I think dedication heads the list. Good sportsmanship involves putting forth your best efforts at all times and under all circumstances, however trying they may be. You should never let the other members of a team down — nor yourself, for that matter.

GERALDINE: Don't you want to put being a good loser high on this list? I like to see defeat acknowledged with a smile.

NANCY: Of course, Geraldine. Everyone likes to see the loser sincerely congratulate the winner.

STANLEY: I think being a gracious winner is equally important. When a person is arrogant about having won, he or she is insulting the loser. And if the loser really wasn't very good, then it didn't mean much to win, did it? So what is there to be arrogant about?

MICHELLE: I agree, and I think we should add that *how* a person wins is part of good sportsmanship, too. In other words, winning through fair play is the only way to win. It would be better to lose every time than to try anything underhanded.

JAMES: That's a good point, Michelle. All the truly great athletes detest cheating. And if someone cheats at sports, it is likely to carry over into other parts of life. My grandfather had a favorite quote he used to repeat when he heard of someone cheating in a game: "He that will cheat at play will cheat you any way."

NANCY: Will someone else express an opinion?

GEORGE: Being courteous is certainly part of good sportsmanlike conduct. There is no place in a game for a person who can't treat the other players with the respect he or she would like to receive personally.

NANCY: That's a good thing to remember, George. It seems to me that we could sum up this discussion by condensing all these qualities under one heading: courage. If a person has the courage to do the right thing, he or she will find that all these traits follow. Everything we mentioned calls for courage in some degree. Let's hope that from this talk we will all determine to possess these qualities when we are involved in competitive sports.

It is the duty of the discussion leader

—to see that the discussion is brief and orderly

—to keep the discussion to the topic

—to summarize the points discussed

Notice that it is the leader's duty to keep the discussion moving in an orderly fashion and to sum up the suggestions at the end. Think about the discussion you just read. Was it lively? Did a number of persons participate and express their ideas? Did the leader state any conclusion arrived at by the group?

Activity

Choose a leader and hold a group discussion. Select from the following list the topic you would like to discuss in class.

1. How does television influence us?
2. Why should we care about what we eat?
3. Do you think that UFOs are really visitors from other planets?
4. Do Americans depend too much on their cars?
5. Would you like to have lived in another time?
6. What kind of person would you like to see be president of the United States?
7. If you won the lottery, what would you do with the money?
8. What dangers are involved in the use of drugs?

More to Explore

Try holding an informal book discussion with several other students. Decide on a book you would all like to read, or one you have already read. Choose one person to be the chairperson and discuss the characters, plot, setting, and your general reactions to the book.

Illustration by
Norman Rockwell for
*The Adventures of
Tom Sawyer*
by Mark Twain

Lesson 2 Speaking to Groups

It is only a step from group discussions to reports and formal talks to groups. Talks before an audience are more interesting if the speaker plans in advance what he or she is going to say. Having a good opening sentence prepared is important because it captures an audience's attention. The details that follow this good beginning sentence must likewise be carefully chosen. The best way to organize a talk so that it keeps to the topic and covers all the essential points is to make an outline.

Mary Garcia decided to give a class talk on student councils, but this subject was too general. She therefore limited her talk to one topic: why we should form an eighth-grade student council. The following outline aided her in making the talk:

Why We Should Form an Eighth-Grade Student Council
  I. Structure
      A. Officers elected from the entire grade
      B. Representatives elected from each classroom
      C. Faculty advisor appointed by the principal
      D. Meetings held each month
      E. Agenda discussed each meeting
 II. Advantages
      A. Mediator between faculty and students
      B. Aid to teachers in certain activities
      C. Student participation in school policy
      D. Development of individual responsibility and initiative
III. Results
      A. Increase in faculty-student rapport
      B. Reduction of discipline problems
      C. Preparation for service in higher levels of education
      D. Greater student contribution to school community

Model:

Why We Should Form an Eighth-Grade Student Council

A profitable activity that is enjoying greater popularity with students is the formation of a student council. The principal officers — president, vice president, secretary, and treasurer — are usually elected from the entire grade. They and the representatives from each classroom meet monthly with their faculty advisor. The agenda regularly includes the organization of school activities for the coming month, the discussion of suggestions

submitted by the student body, and the resolution of any disciplinary problems that have arisen since the previous meeting.

A student oriented group such as this one offers many advantages to both faculty and students. Because the council serves as a mediator between these two groups, the teachers are made more aware of student needs and are better able to share their own problems. Faculty members also appreciate the assistance given them by student representatives who organize sports and social activities. Students welcome the chance to take an active role in implementing school policies. Perhaps the primary advantage of a student council is that it offers students an opportunity to learn to handle responsibilities similar to those they will have in later life. By allowing students to act on their own initiative, the program aids in the growth of their self-confidence and gives them a realistic sense of achievement.

Furthermore, the interaction that a student council promotes results in a greater rapport between the faculty and students. This understanding helps reduce disciplinary problems arising from poor communication. In addition, the students become better prepared to participate in student government as they continue their education. Thus, the entire school community benefits from such a program.

Did the speaker explain why we should have a student council? Did she follow her outline? Was the beginning sentence interesting? Was it evident that the speaker had given some thought to her subject?

The Elements of Good Speech

The good speaker has both mental and physical control. There are four elements to consider in preparing a talk, and each will play a role in how well your message is received by the audience.

1. **Ideas**: *What* is said is of the most importance. Ideas are acquired from four sources: observation of life; conversation with experienced speakers; reading; and personal reflections on what is seen, heard, and read.

2. **Style**: *How* ideas are presented also requires attention. The speech should be grammatically correct, with the words carefully chosen and the sentence structure varied.

3. **Voice**: Let it be low in pitch and flexible. Speak distinctly, so that everyone understands what is said.

4. **Position**: Stand with body straight, head not too high, eyes focused on the audience, and hands relaxed.

Activity A

Prepare a short talk on any one of the following topics. You may use the beginning sentence, the details to be developed, and the ending sentence suggested for each topic, or you may alter them to suit your own speech.

1. **Space Exploration**

   Beginning sentence: In the early 1950s, few people could have dreamed that space exploration would achieve so much so quickly.

   Details: Sputnik, weather and communication satellites, exploration of Mars and Venus, manned space flights, moon landings, space stations, space shuttles

   Ending: Today, the fact that vehicles travel to and from various points in space is an accepted part of life, and many of the former secrets of space are well known to us all.

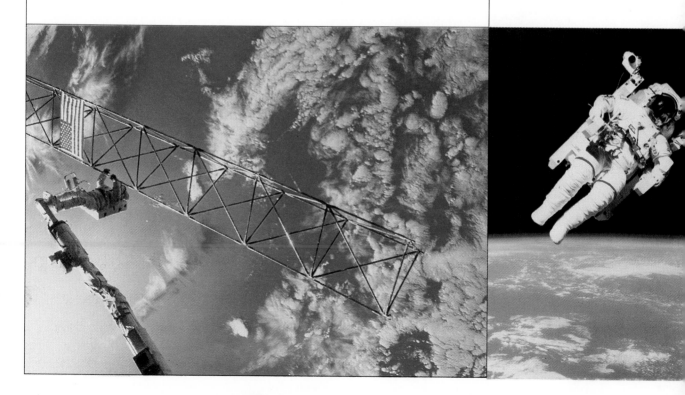

2. How Baseball Is Played

Beginning: Because baseball is such a popular sport, we should have more than a superficial knowledge of the game.

Details: playing field, position of players, object of game, method of scoring

Ending: Whether you are a player or a spectator of this great game, accurate knowledge should help you to enjoy it more.

3. Jane Addams

Beginning: Jane Addams, winner of the Nobel Peace Prize, social reformer, and humanitarian, dedicated her life to helping the underprivileged of Chicago.

Details: founded Hull House, advocated the eight-hour working day and other labor reforms, supported woman suffrage, wrote several books on her experiences

Ending: This courageous individual is an inspiration and model for all persons.

Jane Addams

Activity B

Prepare an original talk to be given in your classroom. These are the important steps to be followed:

1. Choose a subject.
2. Limit the subject to one topic that can be covered in a short speech.
3. Make an outline.
4. Prepare an interesting beginning sentence.
5. Follow the outline in developing the topic.
6. Think of a strong ending sentence. (The content of the speech and its desired effect will help you compose this final thought.)

More to Explore

Think of something you've always been curious about, and that might be of interest to your fellow students, and then research it in the library. Narrow the topic and prepare a brief class talk according to the steps given in Activity B.

Lesson 3 Reading Poetry Aloud

Rhythm

Often we become aware of a particular mood or attitude when we read a poem. This mood may be one of joy or sorrow, excitement or humor. We can determine the mood of a poem by the words and thoughts contained in it, and also by its *rhythm*. The rhythm often matches or harmonizes with the mood. Light, quick-moving rhythm usually conveys a whimsical thought and creates a joyous mood. Slower rhythm generally suggests a more thoughtful theme, or it may communicate a feeling of sadness. Note how the rhythm in the following poem changes: it is slow when the poet talks about the city, and light and joyful when he reminisces about his island home.

When Dawn Comes to the City

The tired cars go grumbling by,
The moaning, groaning cars,
And the old milk carts go rumbling by
Under the same dull stars.
Out of the tenements, cold as stone,
Dark figures start for work;
I watch them sadly shuffle on,
'Tis dawn, dawn in New York.

But I would be on the island of the sea,
In the heart of the island of the sea,
Where the cocks are crowing, crowing, crowing,
And the hens are cackling in the rose-apple tree,
Where the old draft horse is neighing, neighing, neighing
Out on the brown, dew-silvered lawn,
And the tethered cow is lowing, lowing, lowing,
And dear old Ned is braying, braying, braying,
And the shaggy Nannie goat is calling, calling, calling
From her little trampled corner of the long wide lea
That stretches to the waters of the hill stream falling
Sheer upon the flat rocks joyously!
There, oh there! on the island of the sea,
There I would be at dawn.

The tired cars go grumbling by,
The crazy, lazy cars,
And the same milk carts go rumbling by
Under the dying stars.
A lonely newsboy hurries by,
Humming a recent ditty;
Red streaks strike through the gray of the sky,
The dawn comes to the city.

But I would be on the island of the sea,
In the heart of the island of the sea,
Where the cocks are crowing, crowing, crowing,
And the hens are cackling in the rose-apple tree,
Where the old draft horse is neighing, neighing, neighing
Out on the brown dew-silvered lawn,
And the tethered cow is lowing, lowing, lowing,
And dear old Ned is braying, braying, braying,
And the shaggy Nannie goat is calling, calling, calling
From her little trampled corner of the long wide lea
That stretches to the waters of the hill stream falling
Sheer upon the flat rocks joyously!
There, oh there! on the island of the sea,
There I would be at dawn.

Claude McKay

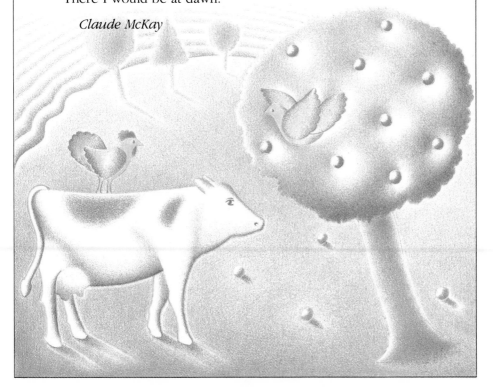

The following piece of writing looks like a paragraph, but it is actually a poem! Read it aloud and discover the rhythm.

Football

The Game was ended and the noise at last had died away, and now they gathered up the boys where they in pieces lay. And one was hammered in the ground by many a jolt and jar; some fragments never have been found, they flew away so far. They found a stack of tawny hair, some fourteen cubits high; it was the half-back, lying there, where he had crawled to die. They placed the pieces on a door, and from the crimson field, that hero then they gently bore, like a soldier on his shield. The surgeon toiled the livelong night above the gory wreck; he got the ribs adjusted right, the wishbone and the neck. He soldered on the ears and toes, and got the spine in place, and fixed a gutta-percha nose upon the mangled face. And then he washed his hands and said: "I'm glad that task is done!" The half-back raised his fractured head, and cried: "I call this fun!"

Walt Mason

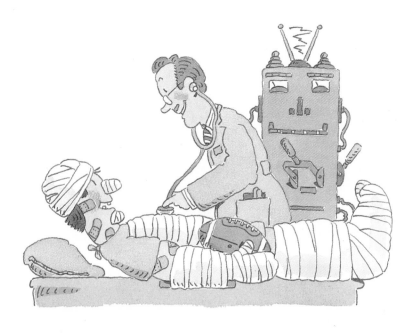

The Structure of a Poem

Just as prose is divided into paragraphs, so poetry is usually divided into stanzas. The number of lines in a stanza may vary. The poem "Some People" by Rachel Field has two stanzas, which are composed of four lines each.

Some People

Isn't it strange some people make
   You feel so tired inside,
Your thoughts begin to shrivel up
   Like leaves all brown and dried!

But when you're with some other ones,
   It's stranger still to find
Your thoughts as thick as fireflies
   All shiny in your mind!

Rachel Field

Note that the second and fourth lines of each stanza in this poem *rhyme*. That means that the poem has a "rhyme scheme" of a-b-c-b. Note also that there are four *beats*, or stressed syllables (´), in the first line, three in the second, four in the third, three in the fourth, and so on. These beats give the poem a definite rhythm. Determine the number of beats in each of these two lines.

Mary had a little lamb.

I wrote a letter to my friend today.

Activity

Read aloud several poems. Discuss the following points in relation to each work:
1. Tell what experience the poet is sharing.
2. Describe the mood he or she conveys. Does it stay the same or change?
3. Give the number of lines in a stanza and the number of beats in a line.
4. Explain the rhyme scheme, if any.

Windshield Wiper

fog smog   fog smog
tissue paper   tissue paper
clear the blear   clear the smear

fog more   fog more
splat splat   downpour
rubber scraper   rubber scraper
overshoes   macintosh
bumbershoot   muddle on
slosh through   slosh through

drying up   drying up
sky lighter   sky lighter
nearly clear   nearly clear
clearing clearing veer
clear here clear

Eve Merriam

The Sidewalk Racer

Or, On the Skateboard

Skimming
an asphalt sea
I swerve, I curve, I
sway; I speed to whirring
sound an inch above the
ground; I'm the sailor
and the sail, I'm the
driver and the wheel
I'm the one and only
single engine
human auto
mobile

Lillian Morrison

Foghorns

The foghorns moaned
  in the bay last night
  so sad
  so deep
I thought I heard the city
  crying in its sleep.

Lilian Moore

War

Dawn came slowly,
almost not at all.
The sun crept over the hill
cautiously
fearful of being hit
by mortar fire.

Dan Roth

Ancient History

I hope the old Romans
Had painful abdomens.

I hope that the Greeks
Had toothache for weeks.

I hope the Egyptians
Had chronic conniptions.

I hope that the Arabs
Were bitten by scarabs.

I hope that the Vandals
Had thorns in their sandals.

I hope that the Persians
Had gout in all versions.

I hope that the Medes
Were kicked by their steeds.

They started the fuss
And left it to us!

Arthur Guiterman

Whispers

Whispers
   tickle through your ear
   telling you things you like to hear.

Whispers
   are as soft as skin
   letting little words curl in.

Whispers
   come so they can blow
   secrets others never know.

Myra Cohn Livingston

Swift Things are Beautiful

Swift things are beautiful:
Swallows and deer,
And lightning that falls
Bright-veined and clear,
Rivers and meteors,
Wind in the wheat,
The strong-withered horse,
The runner's sure feet.

And slow things are beautiful:
The closing of day,
The pause of the wave
That curves downward to spray,
The ember that crumbles,
The opening flower,
And the ox that moves on
In the quiet of power.

Elizabeth Coatsworth

Poor

I heard of poor.
It means hungry, no food,
No shoes, no place to live.
Nothing good.

It means winter nights
And being cold.
It is lonely, alone,
Feeling old.

Poor is a tired face.
Poor is thin.
Poor is standing outside
Looking in.

Myra Cohn Livingston

Winter Poem

once a snowflake fell
on my brow and i loved
it so much and i kissed
it and it was happy and called its cousins
and brothers and a web
of snow engulfed me then
i reached to love them all
and i squeezed them and they became
a spring rain and i stood perfectly
still and was a flower

Nikki Giovanni

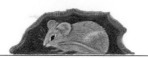

The Bird of Night

A shadow is floating through the moonlight.
Its wings don't make a sound.
Its claws are long, its beak is bright.
Its eyes try all the corners of the night.

It calls and calls: all the air swells and heaves
And washes up and down like water.
The ear that listens to the owl believes
In death. The bat beneath the eaves,

The mouse beneath the stone are still as death.
The owl's air washes them like water.
The owl goes back and forth inside the night.
And the night holds its breath.

Randall Jarrell

Lone Dog

I'm a lean dog, a keen dog, a wild dog, and lone;
I'm a rough dog, a tough dog, hunting on my own!
I'm a bad dog, a mad dog, teasing silly sheep;
I love to sit and bay the moon, to keep the fat souls from sleep.

I'll never be a lap dog, licking dirty feet,
A sleek dog, a meek dog, cringing for my meat,
Not for me the fireside, the well-filled plate,
But shut door, and sharp stone, and cuff and kick and hate.

Not for me the other dogs, running by my side,
Some have run a short while, but none of them would bide.
O mine is still the one trail, the hard trail, the best
Wide wind, and wild stars, and hunger of the quest!

Irene Rutherford McLeod

Lewis Has a Trumpet

A trumpet
A trumpet
Lewis has a trumpet
A bright one that's yellow
A loud proud horn.
He blows it in the evening
When the moon is newly rising
He blows it when it's raining
In the cold and misty morn
It honks and it whistles
It roars like a lion
It rumbles like a lion
With a wheezing huffing hum
His parents say it's awful
Oh really simply awful
But
Lewis says he loves it
It's such a handsome trumpet
And when he's through with trumpets
He's going to buy a drum.

Karla Kuskin

Earth

"A planet doesn't explode of itself," said drily
The Martian astronomer, gazing off into the air —
"That they were able to do it is proof that highly
Intelligent beings must have been living there."

John Hall Wheelock

More to Explore

1. Here is a poet's expression of how a perfect day by the sea made him feel. Practice reading it aloud until you think you have captured the feeling, and then recite it for the class. (*Spume* is the sea's spray or foam. It is pronounced SPŪM.)

How instant joy, how clang
And whang the sun, how
Whoop the sea, and oh,
Sun, sing, as whiter than
Rage of snow, let sea the spume
Fling.

Let sea the spume, white, fling,
White on blue wild
With wind, let sun
Sing, while the world
Scuds, clouds boom and belly,
Creak like sails, whiter than,
Brighter than,
Spume in sun-song, oho!
The wind is bright.

Robert Penn Warren
(from "Mediterranean Beach, Day after Storm")

2. Choose one poem for memorization from the selection in this lesson's activity. Practice saying it in front of a mirror or recording it on tape. Deliver your poem to the class, expressing the feeling you think the poet wishes to convey.

Lesson 4 Learning to Listen

It is very important to develop your listening skills. *Listening* means more than just *hearing*. *Hearing* simply involves the ability of the ear to pick up and transmit sound waves to the brain. *Listening*, though, is a conscious activity. It involves your ability to concentrate on what you hear and get meaning from it.

Your teacher is going to read a selection to you. Focus your attention on what is being said and shut out all distracting noises or thoughts. Be prepared to answer these questions:

1. What is happening?
2. Where is it taking place?
3. Who is the most important person in the story?

Listen carefully!

Now that you have heard the story, answer these questions:

1. What is the story about?
   a. an operation
   b. an attack
   c. a routine drill

2. Where does the action take place?
   a. Atlantic Ocean
   b. Pacific Ocean
   c. Mediterranean Sea

3. Who is the most important person in the story?
   a. George Weller
   b. Dean Rector
   c. Wheeler B. Lipes

Activity A

Like all other skills, the ability to listen requires practice. This activity and the following ones will improve your listening ability. Before you begin, it is important to remember two things:
1. You must have a *purpose* for listening.
2. You must shut out all distracting thoughts and sounds and concentrate on what is being said.

Distinguishing Hearing from Listening

In this exercise you are going to name the sound or word that you hear. Your teacher will ask you either to write your answer on paper or give it orally.

—Listen carefully for the sound and write/say what it is.
—Make a list of ten sounds or words and be prepared to take a turn leading the exercise for the class.

Activity B

Listener–Speaker Interaction

In this exercise you are going to demonstrate whatever you are told to do. You will be told three things. Ignore all but the one that is specified.

> *For example*: Snap your fingers; clap your hands; pull your right ear — second.
>
> In this instance you would *clap your hands*.

—Listen carefully and demonstrate what you are told to do.
—Make a list of ten actions and be prepared to lead the class in this exercise.

Activity C

Facts and Details

In this exercise you will pick out the *incorrect* word in each sentence and give the *correct* word.

> *For example*: The day was so cold I went for a swim.
> *Answer*: incorrect–cold, correct–hot

—Listen carefully and decide. Write/say the incorrect and correct words.
—Make a list of ten sentences that contain a wrong word. Be prepared to take a turn leading the exercises for the class.

Activity D

Sequence

In this activity you will decide what word should come next.

> *For example*: one–three–five–_____
> *Answer*: seven

—Listen carefully and decide. Write/say the correct word.
—Make a list of ten sequences that are missing the last item. Be prepared to lead the exercises for the class.

Activity E

Main Idea

In this activity you will decide what the main idea, or classification, of each selection is.

> *For example*: Charles–Jim–Betty
> *Answer*: names (or people)

—Listen carefully and decide the classification. Write/say it.
—Make a list of ten sets of items that have the same classification. Be prepared to lead the class in doing the exercises.

Activity F

Summarizing

In this exercise you will write/say one sentence that will summarize the selection read to you.

> *Sample answer*: This paragraph tells about a boy's close call
> with a shark.

—Listen carefully. Think. Write/say the summarizing sentence.
—Find two paragraphs in your social studies, science, or reading texts. Be prepared to lead the exercises in class.

Activity G

Relationships

In this exercise you will complete the analogies by determining the relationship that exists between the first two words.

> *For example*: Door is to wood, as window is to _____
> *Answer*: glass

—Listen carefully. Think. Write/say the analogy.
—Make a list of ten analogies. Be prepared to lead the exercises in class.

Activity H

Inferences

In this exercise you will infer meaning through the intonation of the speaker.

> *For example*: "Call the doctor" can be said calmly when it is simply an answer to a question. However, when there is an emergency, it would be said with a much different intonation.

—Listen carefully and determine what is *inferred* by the way the sentences are read. Write/say your answer.

—Make a list of ten sentences that could be said in different ways. Be prepared to lead the exercise for the class.

Word Study 8

Discovering Meaning through Context

By looking at words, phrases, or sentences that surround an unfamiliar word, you can often determine the meaning of that word.

You don't always have to consult a dictionary to discover the meaning of a new word. Many times the words that come *before* or *after* the unfamiliar word give you a clue as to what it means. This is called *finding the meaning from context*.

Activity A

Sometimes the context gives a *synonym* for the unfamiliar word. Find the meaning of each italicized word by discovering the synonym in the sentence.

1. Rose rarely makes a *conjecture* because her guesses are usually wrong.
2. The judge *exonerated* the alleged criminal and sent him home a free man.
3. Dottie's enthusiasm and excitement for acting made me wish that I had her *zeal*.
4. Since Jed is a *novice* at skiing, he registered for the beginner's course.
5. Worn thin by hunger and disease, the *emaciated* children of our world need help.

Activity B

Sometimes the context gives an *antonym* for the unfamiliar word.
Find the meaning of each italicized word by discovering the antonym
in the sentence.

1. The teacher thought the young girl was *diffident*, but she
   displayed all the confidence in the world when she stood on the
   stage.
2. After the robbery, the whole house was *askew*, but with everyone's
   help it was soon straightened.
3. My sister never used her real name when she wrote a poem, but
   used the *pseudonym* I.C. Ewe.
4. Melanie was an *avid* reader compared to Brian, who rarely picked
   up a book.
5. Skip came to school looking *immaculate*, but by recess he had
   accumulated a pound of dirt.

Activity C

Find the meaning of each italicized word by searching the context.
Choose the correct definition from the choices below the sentence.

1. I *concurred* with her decision. I would never disagree.
   a. disliked   b. agreed   c. appreciated
2. Eric really minded staying in his room *isolated* from the others.
   a. a part of   b. unaware   c. separated
3. Trying to resist with all her might, Natty *succumbed* to a third
   piece of pizza.
   a. gave in   b. bought   c. saved
4. Hector's army was *invincible*. No enemy had overcome his forces.
   a. unconquerable   b. strong   c. well supplied
5. Even the most *callous* person had to feel compassion for the
   victims of the tragedy.
   a. sensitive   b. hardened   c. casual

Chapter 9

Dramatizing Poems

Lesson 1 Choral Speaking

There is no better way to experiment with the voice than through choral speaking. Choral speaking is not a new discovery, but a revival of the old Greek manner of reading poetry. A choral-speaking group can give added dimension to a poem, intensifying both its music and its message.

A choral-speaking group may be likened to an orchestra. The human voices are the instruments that bring out the music, interpreting the thought. The deep or heavy voices are the brass; the light voices, the flutes and violins; and the medium voices, the oboes and clarinets. Separately and in chorus, these voices blend to interpret the measures of poetry in much the same fashion as the instruments interpret the measures of a sonata, a symphony, or a simple rondeau or chanson. Many of the principles of music may be applied to choral speaking.

Nineteenth-century botanical print

In this painting, what contrasts do you find between the beauty of the flower and the beauty of the mountain? Any similarities?

Time and Pitch

A choral-speaking group or choir is governed, as is the orchestra, by time and pitch. In lyric poetry, ringing with joy and gladness, the time is quick; in dirges or solemn poetry, slow and measured. Nonsense rhymes are read in quick time and in a higher pitch to indicate the joyfulness that is the basis of their rhythm. Elegies and songs that mourn the dead (a person or an ideal) are read in slow, measured time and low pitch. Descriptive poems are read in a conversational tone, time, and pitch. Such reading is faithful to the poet's expression, for he or she arranges stressed and unstressed syllables in a pattern that results in suitably quick or slow movement.

The Director

Just as every orchestra has its conductor, who blends the instruments into one beautiful whole, so every choral-speaking group has its director, who blends the different voices into one melody. The director should be a lover of poetry. He or she should possess a keen appreciation of rhythm, a delicate sensitivity to the effect of the pause and the inflections of the voice, and a definite awareness of the relation of these to the interpretation of the lines. For example, a simple, stressed word takes a *falling slide* or *inflection* of the voice:

Fallen cold and dead \

Words that ask a question take a *rising slide* or *inflection* of the voice.

How old are you, friend? /

Words used in pairs take a *rising* and *falling inflection* to avoid monotony of tone:

Come, / Death \

After a little practice, you will learn how to vary the inflection of your voice so as to produce the best possible effect.

Finally, just as a good orchestra conductor makes certain that all the instruments are in tune, so a good director in choral speaking sees to it that the human voices of the choir are in tune. For this purpose, the director gives tuning-up exercises.

Tuning-up Exercises #1

Breathing

Breathing is essential to the correct use of the voice. For this first exercise, inhale through the mouth or the nose, inflating the diaphragm, the chest wall, and the ribs; exhale through the sound box or larynx. Place the hands on the ribs just above the waistline. Feel the expansion and the recession of the ribs with the incoming and outgoing breath.

Enunciation

Correct vowel formation is essential to correct speech. The production of good tone depends upon the position of the mouth. Watch your teacher form the vowel sounds and try to imitate the position of his or her lips. The following suggestions will help you to pronounce each vowel correctly:
1. Form the vowels with the lips in the correct position.
2. Say the vowels first in low pitch, slow time; then repeat in quick time, high pitch; finally in conversational time and pitch.
3. Sing the vowels on different notes. Scale work is very valuable for acquiring a musical tone.

You may find it helpful to practice before a mirror until you feel that you are pronouncing the vowels correctly. Many prominent speakers began their training in this way. Exercises in enunciation are an excellent preparation for all speech work, and especially for choral speech.

Here is a nonsense jingle that will help you practice the vowel sounds *oo* and *woo*. First try making these sounds out loud a few times.

    oo oo oo   woo woo woo

Now read the poem aloud in unison.

    Coo, coo, coo,
    Turtle dove, coo
    Moo, moo, moo,
    Jersey cow, moo!
    Ow, ow, ow; bow, bow, bow
    How now, brown cow.
    Why do you moo down town?

Activity A

The poems that are read for choral speaking are paragraphs in verse. They might tell stories, paint pictures in words, or merely amuse. Reading poetry in unison helps to bring out more clearly the meanings of the verses.

Henry Wadsworth Longfellow (1807-1882) was one of the literary giants of the nineteenth century. His poems remain among the most familiar in American literature. Some of Longfellow's narrative poems that you may know are "Evangeline," "The Song of Hiawatha," and "The Courtship of Miles Standish." Favorites among his shorter works are "The Children's Hour" and "Paul Revere's Ride."

Longfellow's poems appeal to almost every taste and deal with a wide range of subjects. These characteristics coupled with the simplicity of his style undoubtedly account for his popularity.

1. Read "The Tide Rises" very carefully at least three times until you have made its beautiful pictures your own: the tide rising and falling, twilight along the sea, darkness covering the earth, and waves erasing all the footprints in the sand. Then picture the unfolding of a new day along the shore. Notice how the poet uses the refrain as an image of the passage of time.

2. Experience the phrasing as it is marked in the poem; feel the beat of the measure as you say the poem to yourself.
   \ is used to indicate a falling slide or inflection
   / is used to indicate a rising slide or inflection
   // is used to indicate a pause in the rhythm

3. Do you know the meaning of the last stanza? Keep a list of the words you do not know and find their meanings in the dictionary.

4. Decide on the time and pitch, and then read the poem in unison. Observe the pauses and inflections that are marked.

The Tide Rises

LIGHT VOICES: The tide rises, // the tide falls, //
The twilight darkens, // the curlew calls; //

SOLO 1: Along the sea-sands \ damp / and brown //
The traveler hastens \ toward the town, //

REFRAIN (unison): And the tide rises, // the tide falls. //

DEEP VOICES: Darkness settles \ on the roofs and walls, //
But the sea, \ the sea / in the darkness calls; //

SOLO 2: The little waves, \ with their soft, / white hands, //
Efface the footprints \ in the sands, //

REFRAIN (unison): And the tide rises, // the tide falls.

LIGHT VOICES: The morning breaks; // the steeds \ in their stalls /
Stamp \ and neigh \ as the hostler calls; //

SOLO 3: The day returns, // but nevermore \
Returns the traveler \ to the shore, //

REFRAIN (unison): And the tide rises, // the tide falls. //

Henry Wadsworth Longfellow

Meditation by the Sea

Tuning-up Exercises #2

Breathing

Inhale, hold breath for ten counts, then exhale, at first slowly, then all at once explosively.

Enunciation

Exercises for clean *t*:

tip of the tongue   tip of the tongue   tip of the tongue

Zinty Tinty, Two penny Bun!
The cat went out to have some fun,
He had some fun, he beat the drum—
Zinty Tinty, Two penny Bun!

Activity B

1. Before studying the poem, research the historical background of the Vietnam War. Have a short class discussion on your findings.
2. Read the poem over carefully three times, so that you will thoroughly understand its meaning.
3. According to the poem, what were the lives of the people of Viet Nam like before their land was torn apart by war?
4. What overall message do you think the poet is trying to communicate?
5. Are there any words you don't understand? Find out their meaning before you try to read the poem aloud.
6. Decide on the time and pitch, and then read the poem in unison. Observe the pauses and inflections that are marked.

What Were They Like?

DEEP VOICES   1   Did the people / of Viet Nam \
use lanterns / of stone? //

LIGHT VOICES   2   Did they hold ceremonies /
to reverence \ the opening of buds? //

DEEP VOICES   3   Were they inclined / to quiet laughter? //

LIGHT VOICES   4   Did they use bone \ and ivory, /
jade \ and silver, / for ornament? //

DEEP VOICES   5   Had they an epic poem? //

LIGHT VOICES   6   Did they distinguish / between speech \ and
singing? //

SOLO 1   1   Sir, / their light hearts \ turned to stone. //
It is not remembered \ whether in gardens \
stone lanterns \ illumined pleasant ways. //

SOLO 2   2   Perhaps they gathered \ once \ to delight in
blossom, //
but after the children \ were killed \
there were \ no more buds. //

SOLO 3   3   Sir, / laughter is bitter \ to the burned mouth. //

SOLO 4   4   A dream \ ago, perhaps.\ Ornament is for joy. //
All the bones were charred. //

SOLO 5   5   It is not remembered. // Remember, /
most were peasants; \ their life
was in rice \ and bamboo. //
When peaceful clouds \ were reflected in the
paddies /
and the water \ buffalo stepped surely / along
terraces, /
maybe fathers \ told their sons \ old tales. //
When bombs smashed \ those mirrors \
there was time \ only to scream. //

UNISON   6   There is an echo yet /
of their speech \ which was like a song. //
It was reported / their singing resembled
the flight of moths \ in moonlight. //
Who can say? / It is silent now. //

Denise Levertov

Tuning-up Exercises #3

Breathing

Inhale, hold breath for ten counts, exhale with *ah*, then with *hah*, then with *ou*, keeping the mouth very round as in *o*.

Enunciation

Exercises in the use of the long simple sounds *ah* and *er*:
> Laugh, clown, laugh, down the moonlit path
> Whir, whir, whir
> The earth whirs along—
> Work, world, work, mirth be your song!

Activity C

1. The following poem is a lyric poem. In it, the poet tells how she feels about the season of fall. Read over the poem silently in order to picture in your mind the scene the speaker is describing.
2. Note the portrayals of nature: the mist, the owl's call, the wailing wind, and the bare, dead branches—all suggesting a feeling of cold loneliness. Contrast these with the mood of the last seven lines. What ideas or attitudes is the speaker trying to convey?
4. Look up the meaning of any unfamiliar words in the dictionary.
5. Decide on the time and pitch, and then read the poem in unison. Observe the pauses and inflections that are marked.

The Mist and All

SOLO 1   I like \ the fall //
The mist \ and all. //

SOLO 2   I like \ the night owl's \
Lonely call — //

UNISON   And wailing \ sound /
Of wind around. //

SOLO 3   I like the \ gray
November day, //
And bare, \ dead boughs //
That coldly sway \
Against my pane. //

SOLO 4   I like / the rain. //

SOPRANO   I like to sit \
And laugh \ at it — //

ALTO   And tend \
My cozy fire \ a bit. //

UNISON   I like / the fall — //
The mist \ and all — //

Dixie Willson

199

Tuning-up Exercises #4

Breathing

Inhale, hold breath ten counts, exhale with *ou*, keeping mouth very round as in *o*.

Enunciation

Pronounce *ringing, singing* in medium, high, and low pitch. Say the following nonsense jingle in unison:

> Ding, dong, dell,
> Kitten's in the well,
> Ping, pong, pout,
> Who'll draw her out?

Activity D

Robert Frost (1874-1963) was the most popular American poet of his time. He won the Pulitzer Prize for poetry four times, and in 1960 Congress voted him a gold medal in recognition of his poetry and his contributions to culture. His public career reached its peak in January, 1961 when he read his poem "The Gift Outright" at the inauguration of President John F. Kennedy.

Frost is remembered for his plain language and his preference for New England scenes. In his lyrics, such as "The Road Not Taken," we often see people and nature side by side and note the poet's "homespun philosophy" at work.

1. Read the poem over carefully three times, so that you thoroughly understand its meaning.
2. Are there any lines that puzzle you? Find out their meaning before you try to read the poem aloud.
3. Decide on the time and pitch, and then read the poem in unison. Observe the pauses and inflections that are marked.

The Road Not Taken

MEDIUM
VOICES

Two roads diverged \ in a yellow wood, //
And sorry // I could not travel / both /
And be one traveler, // long I stood /
And looked down one // as far as I could /
To where it bent \ in the undergrowth; //

LIGHT
VOICES

Then took the other, // as just \ as fair, //
And having perhaps \ the better claim, //
Because it was grassy / and wanted wear; //
Though \ as for that, // the passing there \
Had worn them // really \ about the same, //

DEEP
VOICES

And both \ that morning / equally lay //
In leaves \ no step / had trodden black. //
Oh, / I kept \ the first / for another day! //
Yet \ knowing how way / leads on to way, //
I doubted \ if I should ever / come back. //

UNISON

I shall be telling \ this // with a sigh \
Somewhere \ ages and ages \ hence: //
Two roads \ diverged in a wood, // and I — //
I took the one / less traveled by, //
And that / has made all / the difference. //

Robert Frost

Tuning-up Exercises #5

Breathing

Repeat the breathing exercises studied in previous chapters. Inhale, hold breath for ten counts, exhale with *wh, wh*.

Enunciation

Exercises in the use of long *e*:

    bee bee bee   wee wee wee
    deep keep leap steep

Say the following nonsense rhyme in unison:

    Rock-a-bye, baby, thy cradle is green;
    Father's a nobleman, Mother's a queen;
    Sister's a lady, and wears a gold ring;
    And Brother's a drummer, and drums for the king.

More to Explore

With two other students, choose a poem you would like to present to the class. Decide which lines you will say individually and which ones you will say in unison as the chorus. Practice your presentation several times.

Lesson 2 Ballad Acting

A ballad is a poem that tells a story. Each stanza of a ballad consists of four lines, with the second and fourth lines rhyming. Many ballads were composed to be sung, and were passed along orally from singer to singer for generations. Each singer would give his or her own interpretation to the story, so it would change over the years. The singers were usually wandering minstrels, who traveled from court to court entertaining royalty. They accompanied themselves on stringed instruments, often a harp.

Ballad acting is the dramatic presentation of a ballad by a group, with individuals taking the parts of the characters, and a chorus giving the narration. Ballad acting is different from play acting in that there is no elaborate staging or lighting. There are simply the actors, with the chorus serving as an accompaniment. Ballad acting employs physical expression (action, movement) to reinforce verbal expression (the words). The verses of a ballad and the story they tell are important. Everything else serves as a background. The author of a ballad wastes no time in description or explanation, but instead tells the story in a simple and direct manner. The choral performance should be undertaken in the same fashion. Simplicity of presentation is necessary if the spirit of the ballad is to be preserved.

Steps in Ballad Acting

1. Individual speakers are chosen for the single parts, and the rest of the group is divided into left chorus and right chorus.
2. Different parts of the narrative are assigned to be said by the left and right choruses.
3. The scenes are planned, and the stage is set up. The different scenes may be managed with a traverse curtain; that is, a curtain traveling on a pulley across the middle of the stage. You may also use a chorus curtain; that is, a curtain formed by members of the chorus.
4. The ballad is acted, with the individual speakers as the principal actors, and the chorus serving as narrators and accompanists.

Tuning-up Exercises

Tuning-up exercises will improve your enunciation and enrich your tone of voice for ballad acting. Before you present your ballad, go through the tuning-up exercises you have already learned and add these for the *t* sound.

Breathing

Inhale, hold your breath for ten counts, exhale with the sound of *t*.

Enunciation

Strive for a clean *t*. Place the tip of the tongue back of the teeth. Use this phrase for practice in placing the voice in front of the mouth:

> Tat-tat-tattoo
> tat-tat-tattoo

Say this rhyme with special attention to crisp final *t*'s:

Night Blessing

Good night!
Sleep tight;
Wake up bright
In the morning light
To do what's right
With all your might.

Say these sentences with the lips only. Have other class members guess what is said.

The moo cow moos.
Spink, spank, spink.
Greedy gray gossoons.
Ding, dong dell.
Brown donkeys yawn "He, haw!"
Seashells shone on the seashore.

Activity

One of the most famous ballads is "The Singing Leaves," by James Russell Lowell. This is an old-world story written in verse form. Like many old ballads, "The Singing Leaves" gives special significance to a certain number—in this case, the number *three*. There are *three* daughters, the king rides for *three* days and *three* nights, and the Princess Anne brings her husband *three* earldoms.

The lesson in the story of "The Singing Leaves" is that material things, gems and silk and gold, do not satisfy hearts that are made for higher things. The Singing Leaves represent the love of Walter the Page for the Princess Anne. Love is the force behind all good. Love is greater than any material gift whatsoever, no matter how splendid or costly that gift may be.

1. Before studying the poem "The Singing Leaves," research the life and works of James Russell Lowell. Then have a short class discussion on your findings.

2. Read the poem over carefully and discuss the following questions:

   What is the eldest daughter's appearance? What color hair do the two younger daughters have?

   Why did the eldest daughter ask the king for pearls, diamonds, and gold rings?

   Was her sister like her when she asked for silks that "stand alone"?

   Why did the Princess Anne want only the Singing Leaves?

   Did the king remain angry with the Princess Anne for long? Why?

   How did the king obtain the gems and the silk?

   Explain the sentence "The trees all kept their counsel."

   Did Walter the Page expect a reward for giving the Singing Leaves?

   Did the leaves sing to the Princess Anne?

   What was the princess's marriage portion?

   What was the wealth of Walter the Page?

3. Follow the "Steps for Ballad Acting" to present this poem. The scenes are as follows:

   Scene 1 A room in the palace (*in front of the curtain*)

   Scene 2 The mart or market (*behind the curtain at right*)

   Scene 3 The forest (*behind the curtain at extreme left, actors walking left at the words, "Then deep in the greenwood"*)

   Scene 4 The gate (*again in front of the curtain, the princess coming from the left and the king and Walter from the right*)

The Singing Leaves

I

KING   "What fairings will ye that I bring?" //

RIGHT   Said the king \ to his daughters three: //

KING   "For I to Vanity Fair \ am bound, //
Now say \ what shall they be?" //

LEFT   Then up and spake the eldest daughter,
The lady tall and grand: //

ELDEST   "Oh, bring me pearls \ and diamonds / great, //

DAUGHTER   And gold rings \ for my hand." //

RIGHT   Thereafter spake the second daughter,
That was both white \ and red: //

SECOND   "For me \ bring silks \ that will stand alone, //

DAUGHTER   And a gold comb \ for my head." //

LEFT   Then came the turn of the least daughter,
That was whiter than thistle-down, //
And among the gold of her blithesome hair //
Dim \ shone the golden crown. //

ANNE   "There came a bird this morning, //
And sang \ 'neath my bower eaves, //
Till I dreamed, \ as his music \ made me,
'Ask thou for the Singing Leaves!'" //

RIGHT   Then the brow \ of the King swelled crimson
With a flush of angry scorn: //

KING   "Well \ have ye spoken, my two eldest,
And chosen \ as ye were born; //

KING   But she, \ like a thing of peasant \ race,
That is happy binding the sheaves." //

LEFT   Then he saw her dear mother in her face, //
And said, "Thou shalt have thy leaves." //

II

RIGHT He mounted \ and rode / three days \ and nights, //
Till he came to Vanity Fair, //
And 'twas easy \ to buy the gems \ and the silk, //
But no Singing Leaves \ were there. //

LEFT Then deep in the greenwood \ rode he,
And asked of every tree, //

KING "Oh, if you have ever a Singing Leaf, //
I pray you give \ it to me!" //

RIGHT But the trees all kept their counsel, //
And never a word \ said they, //
Only there sighed from the pine-tops
A music of seas \ far away. //

LEFT Only the pattering aspen \
Made a sound of growing rain, //
That fell ever faster \ and faster, //
Then faltered to silence \ again. //

KING "Oh, where shall I find a little foot-page
That would win both hose \ and shoon, //
And will bring to me the Singing Leaves //
If they grow under the moon?" //

RIGHT Then lightly turned him Walter the Page, //
By the stirrup as he ran: //

WALTER "Now pledge \ me the truesome word
Of a king \ and gentleman, //

WALTER That you will give the first, \ first / thing
You meet at your castle-gate, //
And the Princess shall get the Singing Leaves, //
Or mine \ be a traitor's \ fate." //

LEFT The King's head dropped upon his breast
A moment, \ as it might be; //

KING "'Twill be my dog," \

RIGHT   he thought, and said, //

KING "My faith I plight to thee." //

LEFT Then Walter took from next his heart
A packet small and thin, //

WALTER "Now give you this \ to the Princess Anne, //
The Singing Leaves \ are therein." //

III

RIGHT	As the king rode in at his castle-gate, //
	A maiden to meet him ran, //
ANNE	And "Welcome, father!" //
RIGHT	she laughed and cried
	Together, \ the Princess Anne. //

KING	"Lo, here \ the Singing Leaves," //
LEFT	quoth he, //
KING	"And woe, \ but they cost me dear!" //
LEFT	She took the packet, \ and the smile,
	Deepened down \ beneath the tear. //

RIGHT	It deepened down till it reached her heart, //
	And then gushed up / again, //
	And lighted her tears \ as the sudden sun
	Transfigures the summer rain. //

LEFT	And the first Leaf, when it was opened
	Sang: //
WALTER	"I am Walter the Page, //
	And the songs I sing 'neath thy window
	Are my only heritage." //

RIGHT	And the second / Leaf sang: //
WALTER	"But in the land
	That is neither on land \ nor sea, //
	My lute \ and I / are lords of more
	Than thrice \ this kingdom's fee." //

RIGHT	And the third Leaf \ sang, //
WALTER	"Be mine! Be mine!"
LEFT	And ever it sang, //
WALTER	"Be mine!"
LEFT	Then sweeter it sang and ever sweeter,
	And said:
WALTER	"I am thine, / thine, \ thine!" //

RIGHT	At the first \ Leaf she grew pale enough, //
	At the second \ she turned aside, //
	At the third, \ 'twas as if a lily \ flushed
	With a rose's \ red heart's tide. //

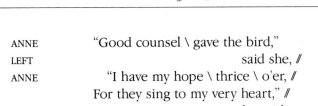

ANNE	"Good counsel \ gave the bird,"
LEFT	said she, //
ANNE	"I have my hope \ thrice \ o'er, //
	For they sing to my very heart," //
RIGHT	she said,
ANNE	"And it sings to them \ evermore." //
BOTH	She \ brought to him her beauty \ and truth, //
SIDES	But and broad earldoms \ three, //
	And he \ made her queen of the broader lands //
	He held of his lute \ in fee. //

James Russell Lowell

More to Explore

Dramatize other ballads that you find in your local library. Discuss
each ballad in class first so that your interpretation will be accurate.

Using the Thesaurus

A thesaurus is a book that contains synonyms and antonyms.

The thesaurus helps you choose just the right word to express what you want to say. Entry words are listed alphabetically for easy location.

Activity A

In your thesaurus, find
1. four synonyms and two antonyms for *danger.*
2. five synonyms and three antonyms for *enlarge.*
3. five entry words that have a cross-reference. (The words *see* and *see also* indicate a cross-reference. They direct you to other words that may help you.)

Activity B

Synonyms have different shades of meaning. They are not perfect substitutes for each other. On a separate piece of paper, write out the sentences below and decide which synonym for the word *instrument(s)* best fits each sentence.

  device(s) instrument(s) tool(s) appliance(s) utensil(s)

1. My dad bought some new _____ for his carpentry shop.
2. We left for the picnic in such a hurry that we forgot many of our eating _____ .
3. The summer home was just about ready except for hooking up the _____ .
4. A harpsicord is a musical _____ of the Middle Ages.
5. On most cars there is a _____ to control air pollution.

Activity C

Copy the paragraph below. Using your thesaurus, find substitutes for the words in italics.

The *big* mountain loomed before the nervous climbers. Each one *wondered* if they would conquer this *big, old* creature. They knew it would be a *big* task, *bigger* than any they had tackled before. Finally, the *big* day *came* and the expedition *headed up* the *big* mountain. Their *biggest* fear was their own inability to cope with the forces of nature.

Chapter 10

Using the Library

Lesson 1 Finding Your Way Around the Library

The General Layout

A library consists of various sections, each one containing specific information that can help you with your school projects and research reports.

When you enter a library, one of the first places you encounter is the *circulation desk*. This is where you check out your books, and where you might ask for information and help in locating needed reference materials. A large portion of the library contains *circulating books*. These are books that may be borrowed for a specified period of time.

The library also contains *reference books*, which give general, often-needed information to researchers. Because of their frequent use, these books usually are not loaned. Dictionaries, encyclopedias, and almanacs are examples of reference books.

Another section of the library contains films, filmstrips, tapes, records, slides, art prints, and miscellaneous audiovisual equipment. This section is known as the *media center*.

Still another section contains *periodicals*. The periodical section has the most recent copies of magazines that would be of general interest to the population the library serves. Therefore, a school library subscribes to magazines that would interest a school-age population.

Most libraries have a *vertical file*. This is a special cabinet that contains pictures, pamphlets, charts, and newspaper clippings about timely topics, arranged by subject for quick and easy reference. Ask your librarian if your library has a vertical file.

How can libraries become windows to the world? How many different kinds of worlds can be glimpsed through these windows?

Activity

Visit your school or local library. Draw a floor plan and label the following sections:

circulation desk   vertical file
media center   periodical section
reference books

Circulating Books

The books that you can check out of a library are called *circulating books*. Circulating books are classified into two groups: fiction and non-fiction.

Fiction Books

A fiction book is an invented story. The people and events have been imagined by an author. Even when real people and events are used, the story is largely imaginary. Most libraries group fiction books together in one area and arrange them in alphabetical order according to the author's last name. When there are a number of books by the same author, the books are often alphabetized by the first word in the title. Words such as *The, An,* or *A* are not used for alphabetizing. If an author's last name begins with *Mc,* it is alphabetized as if it were spelled *Mac. St.* would be considered *Saint.* In listing fiction books, you write the author's last name, followed by a comma, then the author's first name. The title of the book comes after the name of the author.

Illustration by Rockwell Kent
for *Moby Dick* by Herman Melville

Activity A

Arrange the following fiction books in alphabetical order:

Author	Title
Samuel L. Clemens	*Adventures of Huckleberry Finn*
S.E. Hinton	*The Outsiders*
Antoine St. Exupery	*The Little Prince*
Charlotte Brontë	*Jane Eyre*
S.E. Hinton	*That Was Then, This Is Now*
Robert Cormier	*I Am the Cheese*
Louisa May Alcott	*Little Women*
Herman Melville	*Moby Dick*
Carson McCullers	*Clock Without Hands*
John Steinbeck	*The Grapes of Wrath*

Nonfiction Books

Nonfiction books contain true facts and information. Because of the variety of subjects in the nonfiction area, some system of organization is necessary. Many libraries use the Dewey Decimal System. This system was invented by an American librarian named Melvil Dewey, who divided all nonfiction books into ten major subject areas. He gave each major area a range of numbers, so that all books on the same subject would be grouped together. Each book in an area is given a specific number, called a *call number.*

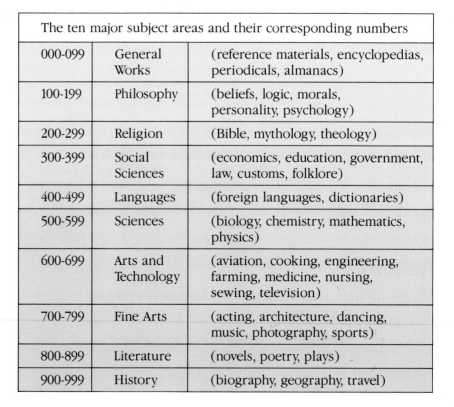

The ten major subject areas and their corresponding numbers		
000-099	General Works	(reference materials, encyclopedias, periodicals, almanacs)
100-199	Philosophy	(beliefs, logic, morals, personality, psychology)
200-299	Religion	(Bible, mythology, theology)
300-399	Social Sciences	(economics, education, government, law, customs, folklore)
400-499	Languages	(foreign languages, dictionaries)
500-599	Sciences	(biology, chemistry, mathematics, physics)
600-699	Arts and Technology	(aviation, cooking, engineering, farming, medicine, nursing, sewing, television)
700-799	Fine Arts	(acting, architecture, dancing, music, photography, sports)
800-899	Literature	(novels, poetry, plays)
900-999	History	(biography, geography, travel)

Activity B

Number your paper from 1 to 12. Think about the subjects of the following books. Within which number range would you place each title?

1. *Middle English Literature*
2. *World Book Encyclopedia*
3. *A Geography of Europe*
4. *Classic French Dictionary*
5. *Counseling Psychology*
6. *A Picture Salute to the Grand Canyon*
7. *Great Issues of American History*
8. *Learn Biology the Easy Way*
9. *Great Dishes of the World*
10. *Current Issues in Theology*
11. *Personality and Behavior*
12. *The Poetical Works of John Milton*

Here is an example of an author card.

If you know the title of the book, then locate the *title card*. Words such as *A, An*, and *The* are not used in alphabetizing the cards. The name of the book appears first on a title card. Here is an example of a title card.

If you need information on a particular subject, look for the subject card. The general subject area is the initial information on this card. Here is an example of a subject card.

Handicrafts

745.5
V394 **Van Zandt, Eleanor R**
      Crafts for fun and profit, by Eleanor Van Zandt.
      Garden City, N.Y., Doubleday, 1974 [c1973]

        144 p. illus. 27 cm. $6.95
        Bibliography: p. 143–144.

Each card contains the call number so that you can locate the book on your library shelves. All three cards contain the publisher and date of publication, the number of pages in the book, and, sometimes, cross references.

Activity A

Answer the following questions about the sample library cards:
1. What is the main subject area on the subject card?
2. What publishing company printed this book?
3. When was the latest printing of this book?
4. How many pages does this book contain?
5. Where would one find the bibliography?
6. Does the book contain illustrations?
7. What is the call number?

Activity B

Visit your library and find the following information in the card catalog:

1. Locate the author card for Cynthia Voigt. List two books written by this author.
2. Locate the title card for *The Case of the Baker Street Irregular*. Who is the author? What is the call number for this book?
3. Locate the subject cards for sports. Name two titles and authors found in this subject area.

More to Explore

Tell whether you would use a title, author, subject card, or combination to locate the information below. Give the general call number range (100-199, 600-699, etc.) for each item, using the chart on page 216, or write *fiction*.

1. books by Rosemary Sutcliff
2. books about the people of Japan
3. *Stories from Around the World*
4. book on the beginning of space exploration
5. Stephen Dunning's poetry
6. *The Reluctant Dragon*
7. *The World of the Greek Gods* by T.J. Rowan
8. a collection of Irish folktales
9. book on ballet by Marcia E. Ellis
10. information on climbers who have made it to the top of Mt. Everest

Lesson 2 Using the Dictionary

Alphabetical Order

A dictionary is one of the most frequently used reference books in the library. This book helps you with the spelling, pronunciation, and various meanings of words. However, in order to use your dictionary in the most beneficial way, certain basic skills need to be mastered. You already have mastered alphabetical order. But how quickly can you alphabetize words that begin with the same three, four, or five letters? The following activity gives you practice in doing this kind of alphabetizing. Time yourself and see how proficient you are.

Activity

Divide your paper into four columns. As quickly as possible, alphabetize each column.

3rd Letter	4th Letter
shovel	conjugation
sheath	conform
shuttle	consumer
shilling	coniferous
shaman	conquest
shrimp	contrast

5th Letter	6th Letter
repel	underfoot
repercussion	understand
repetition	underweight
repent	undertow
repeat	underline
repeople	underbrush

Guide Words

Guide words are the two words printed in heavy type at the top of each dictionary page. They name the first and last words on that particular page so that you can locate your word faster. Because guide words may have the same spelling up until the third, fourth, or fifth letters of a word, you will have to be careful to check that far into a word to be sure that it would appear before, on, or after that page.

Activity A

Above each column are possible guide words for a dictionary page. If a word in the column would appear *on* that page, write "on" next to the word; if the word would appear *before* the page, write "before" on the line; and if the word would appear *after* the page, write "after" on the line. Do this work on a separate sheet of paper.

cottage–counterblow	magnitude–maize	represent–reprove
counselor	majority	report
counterfeit	maid of honor	reprisal
countdown	magnificent	reproach
cotillion	maim	reprieve
cottage cheese	maharaja	rescind
countenance	magnetic	replenish

Activity B

1. Using your dictionary, copy the two guide words from the page where you would find the following words:

   blossom   polarity
   tenuous   clandestine
   frivolous   incognito
   stoic   ornithology

2. Give your dictionary and answers to your partner. Have him or her check your work for accuracy.

Reading Dictionary Entries

When you read a dictionary entry, you are able to learn a great deal about a word. The following information appears in most dictionary entries:

1 Ⓐ Ⓑ Ⓒ Ⓓ Ⓔ

show-er (shau̇´ər) *n.* [Old English scūr, Middle English shoure]Ⓕ1. a brief fall of rain, sleet, or hail:Ⓖ*The shower lasted five minutes.* 2. abundant flow resembling a rain shower: *A shower of letters followed the performance.* 3. a party at which gifts are presented to a guest of honor: *She enjoyed her bridal shower.* 4. a bath in which water is splashed on the body: *Take a shower daily.* Ⓗ Syn. rain, abundance, bath Ⓘ ⟨-y, adj.⟩

2

show-er (shau̇´ər) *v.* 1. to pour down copiously and rapidly; to bestow liberally: *She showered her dog with attention.* 2. to make wet with water or other liquid: *He showered after gym class.* Ⓗ Syn. pour, lavish, deluge Ⓘ ⟨-ed, -ing⟩

A. Syllabication
B. Pronunciation
C. Accent
D. Part of speech
E. Etymology
F. Definition of word
G. Sample phrase or sentence
H. Synonyms
I. Other forms of word

Some dictionaries choose to print all parts of speech under one dictionary entry. The following entry demonstrates this idea:

> **trans plant** (*v.* tran splant´; *n.* tran´splant), *v.t.* **1** plant again in a different place: *We grow the flowers indoors and then transplant them to the garden.* **2** remove from one place to another: *A group of farmers was transplanted to the island by the government.* **3** transfer (skin, an organ, etc.) from one person, animal, or part of the body to another: *transplant a kidney.* —*v.i.* bear moving to a different place. —*n.* **1** the transfer of skin, an organ, etc., from one person, animal, or part of the body to another: *a heart transplant.* **2** something that has been transplanted. —**trans plant´a ble**, *adj.* —**trans´plan ta´ tion**, *n.* —**trans plant´er.** *n.*

Etymology is the history of the development of a word. The etymological information given in the dictionary might appear at the beginning of an entry, right after the part of speech, or at the end of the entry. The order in which the entry information is presented varies slightly with each dictionary. Also, not every dictionary entry will include every item mentioned above.

Activity A

From the three sample entries given, answer the following questions on a sheet of paper:

1. How many definitions does *shower* have as a noun?
2. As a verb, *transplant* is accented on which syllable?
3. From which language does *shower* originate?
4. How can *shower* be used as an adjective?
5. Copy the sentence that uses *transplant* as "removing from one place to another."
6. Write the adjective form of *transplant*.
7. List three synonyms for *shower* as a verb.

Activity B

Try to find dictionary entries for the following words, which are phonetically spelled. Pronounce each word to yourself and think how it might be spelled. Then look up the word in the dictionary. On a separate sheet of paper, write the correctly spelled word and *one* of its definitions.

1. res´əl
2. kwil´ting
3. sī´kē
4. dis ker´ tə sē
5. shō´və nis´tik
6. ek´splə nā´shən
7. fō´nə graf
8. mis də mē´nər
9. ak´yə rə sē
10. pə thet´ik

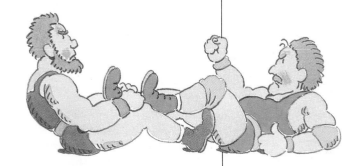

Choosing the Right Meaning

Many words in the English language have more than one meaning. Words also may have more than one part of speech. Once you locate the word in the dictionary, your next job is to find the part of speech and meaning that best corresponds to the sense of your sentence.

Suppose you read this sentence:

> To *rehabilitate* a person after an accident can be a long and tedious process.

In the following dictionary entry, *rehabilitate* has three meanings. Which of the three meanings best fits how *rehabilitate* is used?

> **re ha bil i tate** (rē´hə bil´ə tāt), *v.t.,* **-tat ed, -tat ing. 1** restore to a good condition; make over in a new form: *The old neighborhood is to be rehabilitated.* **2** restore to former standing, rank, rights, privileges, reputation, etc.: *The former criminal was rehabilitated and became a respected citizen.* **3** restore to a condition of good health, or to a level of useful activity, by means of medical treatment and therapy. [<Medieval latin *rehabilitatum* made fit again < Latin *re-* + *habilis* fit] —**re´ha bil´i ta´tion,** *n.*

Suppose you read this sentence in your history textbook:

> Nicholas II *reigned* over Russia for twenty-two years.

In this dictionary entry, *reign* has two parts of speech and two or three meanings for each part of speech. Which part of speech and which definition best fit the way *reign* is used in the sentence?

> **reign** (rān), *n.* **1** period of power of a ruler: *Queen Victoria's reign lasted sixty-four years.* **2** act of ruling; royal power; rule: *The reign of a wise ruler benefits a country.* **3** existence everywhere; prevalence. —*v.i.* **1** be a ruler; rule: *A monarch reigns over a kingdom.* **2** exist everywhere; prevail: *On a still night silence reigns.* [<Old French *reigne* < Latin *regnum* < *regem* king]

People use the dictionary most often to check the correct spelling of a word or to learn its meaning.

Activity

The following words have two parts of speech and several different meanings. For the italicized word in each sentence, give the part of speech and the number of the most accurate meaning.

> **ac claim** (ə klām´), *v.t.* **1** welcome with shouts or other signs of approval; praise highly; applaud: *The crowd acclaimed the winning team.* **2** proclaim or announce with approval: *The newspapers acclaimed the results of the election.* —*n.* a shout or show of approval; applause. [< Latin *acclamare* < *ad-* to + *clamare* cry out]—**ac claim´ er,** *n.*

> **al ien** (ā´lyən, ā´lē ən), *n.* **1** person who is not a citizen of the country in which he or she lives; a resident foreigner whose allegiance is owed to a foreign state. **2** person belonging to a different ethnic or social group; stranger; foreigner. —*adj.* **1** of or by another country; foreign: *an alien language, alien domination.* **2** having the legal status of an alien: *an alien resident.* **3** entirely different from one's own; strange: *alien customs.* **4** not in agreement; opposed, adverse, or repugnant: *Cruelty is alien to his nature.* [< Latin *alienus* < *alius* other]

com pli ment (*n.* kom′ plə mənt; *v.* kom′ plə ment), *n.* **1** something good said about one; something said in praise of one's work, etc. **2** a courteous act: *The town paid the old artist the compliment of a large attendance at his exhibit.* **3 compliments,** *pl.* greetings: *In the box of flowers was a card saying "With the compliments of a friend."* —*v.t.* **1** pay a compliment to; congratulate; praise: *The principal complimented me on my good grades.* **2** give something to (a person) in order to show one's regard. [< French < Italian *complimento* < Spanish *cumplimiento* < *cumplir* fulfill < Latin *complere* fill up, complete] ◆ See **complement** for usage note.

de lib er ate (*adj.* di lib′ ər it; *v.* di lib′ ə rāt′), *adj., v.,* **-at ed, -at ing.** —*adj.* **1** carefully thought out beforehand; made or done on purpose; intended: *a deliberate lie.* See synonym study below. **2** slow and careful in deciding what to do; thoughtful; cautious. **3** not hurried; slow: *walk with deliberate steps.* See **slow** for synonym study. —*v.i., v.t.* **1** think over carefully; consider. **2** discuss reasons for and against something; debate. [< Latin *deliberatum* carefully weighed < *de- + librare* weigh] —**de lib′ er ate ly,** *adv.* —**de lib′ er ate ness,** *n.* —**de lib′ e ra′ tor,** *n.*
Syn. *adj.* **1 Deliberate, intentional** mean done after thinking something over. **Deliberate** suggests full thought before acting: *The lawyer made a deliberate attempt to confuse the jury.* **Intentional** means done on purpose, with a definite end in mind: *His mean remark was intentional; he wanted to make you angry.*

e lab or ate (*adj.* i lab′ ər it, i lab′ rit; *v.* i lab′ ə rāt′), *adj., v.,* **-at ed, -at ing.** —*adj.* worked out with great care; having many details; complicated. See synonym study below. —*v.t.* **1** work out with great care; add details to: *She is elaborating her plans for the new addition to the house.* **2** make with labor; produce. —*v.i.* talk, write, etc., in great detail; give added details: *The witness was asked to elaborate upon one of his statements.* [< Latin *elaboratum* worked out < *ex- out + labor* work] —**e lab′ or ate ly,** *adv.* —**e lab′ or ate ness,** *n.* —**e lab′ o ra′ tive,** *adj.* —**e lab′ o ra′ tor,** *n.*
Syn. *adj.* **Elaborate, studied, labored** mean worked out in detail. **Elaborate** emphasizes the idea of many details worked out with great care and exactness: *The elaborate decorations were perfect in every detail.* **Studied** emphasizes care in planning and working out details beforehand: *Her studied unconcern offended me.* **Labored** emphasizes great and unnatural effort to work out details: *The boy gave a labored excuse for arriving late at school.*

1. Thoughtful and *deliberate* consideration preceded the important voting.
2. Visiting India exposed us to *alien* dress.
3. She *elaborated* the steps needed to paint the room.
4. The newscaster *acclaimed* the unexpected victory.
5. We received a *compliment* for our honesty.
6. The *aliens* studied industriously to obtain their citizenship.
7. The athlete was *complimented* on her excellent victory.
8. Congress will *deliberate* the repeal of the law in next week's session.
9. *Elaborate* preparations were made for the Fourth of July celebration.
10. The crowd demonstrated their *acclaim* with applause.

More to Explore

Here is a list of ten words for you to locate in your dictionary. After reading the definition, write a sentence using the word, give the guide words at the top of the page, name any other part of speech given for the word, and, finally, put all words in alphabetical order.

loathe (v)   scuttle (v)
characteristic (adj)   clangorous (adj)
resilience (n)   periwig (n)
bounteous (adj)   galleon (n)
decal (n)   expatiate (v)

Lesson 3 Using Other Reference Tools

Reference books are designed to give information on a wide variety of subjects. Probably the most frequently used and most familiar reference books in the library are dictionaries, encyclopedias, almanacs, and the *Readers' Guide to Periodical Literature*. You've already learned about the information contained in dictionaries, so it's time to see what these other resources have to offer.

Encyclopedias

An encyclopedia is a set of books giving information on many branches of knowledge. *Encyclopedia* is a Greek word that means a "well rounded education." Articles in an encyclopedia are arranged in alphabetical order. Guide letters on the spine of each encyclopedia volume indicate that articles beginning with those letters will be found in that particular volume. So an article on "Quebec," for instance, would be found in the "Q–R" volume.

Sometimes you might not be able to locate an article on the particular subject you desire. In that case, you need to think of similar topics and titles that might incorporate your idea. For example, if you want to obtain information about the summer solstice or the autumnal equinox, you might have to look under the broader title of "Seasons." Most encyclopedias have index volumes that can help you determine which broad subject to look under for your information

There are guide words at the tops of encyclopedia pages that are used in a similar manner as the guide words in a dictionary. Encyclopedias, however, have only *one* guide word per page. Any article that can be alphabetized between the guide words on two facing pages will be found on either of these pages. An example of guide words would be:

Whitney, Mount   Wichita State Univ.

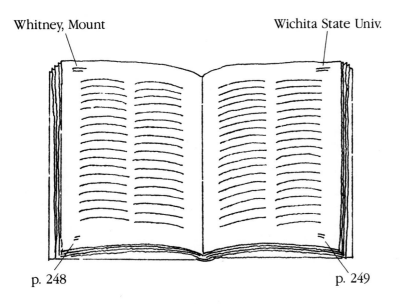

p. 248   p. 249

An article on "Whittier, John Greenleaf" would be located on one of these two pages.

To keep an encyclopedia up to date, a *yearbook* is added at the end of a calendar year. The yearbook includes important events, discoveries, changes, and developments of the past year. Yearbooks are usually shelved after all the other volumes of the encyclopedia.

Activity

Choose eight of the following fifteen topics. For each topic chosen, write the title of the encyclopedia article in which the topic is discussed, the name of the encyclopedia, and the volume and page numbers used. Then state two major ideas contained in the topic.

1. Groundhog or Woodchuck
2. Uses of water
3. Running
4. Tourist attractions of Rome
5. Space travel
6. Shelter around the world
7. Manufacturing of glass
8. Parts of a microscope
9. Red Cross
10. Seven wonders of the world
11. Florence Nightingale
12. Germany
13. Montana
14. History of the Olympic Games
15. Metabolism

Almanacs

An almanac is a reference book that contains current facts, data, and statistics of miscellaneous information. Some topics included in the almanac are:

government officials	historical records
current events	weather predictions
astronomical data	sports
entertainment	recent population figures
important people	holidays
information on states and foreign countries	

You must use the almanac's index or table of contents to locate the desired information, since the data is not alphabetically arranged. Two important almanacs are:

World Almanac and Book of Facts
Information Please Almanac

Activity

Using a recent almanac, answer the following questions:
1. What were two of the top ten stories in the year covered by the almanac?
2. Which state had the highest number of deaths due to automobile accidents in the last year reported? How many people died?
3. What was the population of the United States in 1980? 1970? What percent did it increase or decrease?
4. Name the five areas in which the Nobel Prize is given.
5. What is the origin of the name of the state of Colorado?
6. Where is the highest point in the world? How high? Where is the lowest point in the world? How low?
7. What is the creed of the Olympic contestants?
8. Which baseball team won the most World Series championships in the 1950s? How many championships did they win?

Atlases

An atlas is a reference book of maps. It gives information on population, rivers, mountains, climate, geography, and airline distances. Every atlas has an index to help you locate the appropriate continent, country, or state.

Activity

Consult your atlas to answer the following questions:
1. In what state would you find most of Yellowstone National Park?
2. What mountain range is in New Hampshire?
3. Which ten states have borders along the Mississippi River?
4. Name the north/south interstate highway that goes through Alabama.
5. What Canadian province borders both Montana and North Dakota?
6. Name the long, narrow country on the western coast of South America and give its capital.
7. What five countries border Switzerland?
8. In what country is the Tiber River, and through what capital city does it flow?
9. What countries border Lake Victoria in Africa?
10. Sumatra is one of the large islands contained in the Republic of _____.

Biographical References

A biographical reference is a book or set of books that gives a short biography of famous people—past and present. The most commonly known biographical reference books include:

Current Biography   *Who's Who in America*
International Who's Who   *Contemporary Authors*
American Men and Women of Science
Webster's New Biographical Dictionary

Activity

Look up these five people. On a separate sheet of paper, give a brief description of why they are famous.

History: Mahatma Gandhi   *Sports:* Roger Staubach
Science: Linus Pauling   *Art:* Georgia O'Keeffe
Government: Geraldine Ferraro

Mahatma Gandhi

Readers' Guide to Periodical Literature

One final reference source that can help you with your research reports is the *Readers' Guide to Periodical Literature*. This is a subject and author guide to magazine articles that have been published in a variety of popular magazines about many contemporary events. It comes out twice a month, so it is a good source for obtaining current information.

Since much of the information in this guide is reported in abbreviated form, it is important to check the abbreviation key in the front of the book in order to understand each entry. Here is a sample page from the *Readers' Guide* that shows the kind of information it contains.

Television industry
See also
American Broadcasting Companies, Inc.
CBS Inc.
Lorimar (Firm)
Television equipment industry
Women in the television industry
Now, sponsors do their own thing on TV [producing their own programs] G. Bronson. il *U S News World Rep* 98:74 My 6 '85

Acquisitions and mergers
Capital Cities' capital coup [takeover of ABC] S. P. Sherman. il *Fortune* 111:51-2 Ap 15 '85
Captain Outrageous opens fire [T. Turner's attempt to buy CBS] S. Koepp. il pors *Time* 125:60+ Ap 29 '85
CBS's cool commander in chief [T. Wyman] il por *U S News World Rep* 98:15 My 6 '85
The courtship of CBS has only just begun. G. G. Marcial. *Bus Week* p72 Ap 22 '85

Name of Magazine →

It's a David vs. Goliath battle for the control of CBS [T. Turner's bid] il por U S News World Rep 98:9 Ap 29 '85
It's prime time for Ted Turner [takeover battle for CBS] D. Pauly. il por *Newsweek* 105:54-5+ Ap 29 '85
A news king bids for CBS [T. Turner] I. Austen. *Macleans* 98:61 Ap 29 '85
Turner confronts a dug-in CBS and skeptical Street. G. Fabrikant and J. Wilke. il por *Bus Week* p44 My 6 '85
Television journalism *See* Television broadcasting—News
Television news *See* Television broadcasting—News
Television producers
See also ← *Cross Reference*
Friedman, Steve
Television production and direction
See also
Women in the television industry
Television program reviews
Single works
The Cosby show
Ebony 40:27-30+ Ap '85. L. Norment
Jet il 68:61 Ap 22 '85
Saturday Evening Post il 257:42-5 Ap '85 T. Gold
Time il 125:88 My 6 '85. R. Zoglin

Volume Number →

Dynasty
People Wkly 23:92-4 My 6 '85
End of Empire
Hist Today il 35:41-4 Ap '85. B. Lapping
Good morning America
People Wkly 23:107-9 My 6 '85. J. Hall
How wars end
Hist Today 35:58 Ap '85 D. W. R. Johnson
Miami Vice
Film Comment il 21:66-7 Mr/Ap '85. R. T. Jameson
Nightline
New Repub 192:42 Ap 15 '85. L. Wieseltier
The People's Court
Vogue il 175:104 Ap '85. C. Schine
Peyton Place: the next generation
People Wkly il 23:54-6+ My 6 '85. D. Donahue
Smithsonian world
Smithsonian il 16:30+ Ap '85. E. Park
Space
Time 125:77 Ap 22 '85. R. Zoglin
Vogue il 175:100 Ap '85. B. Handy

Title of Article →

The sporting life
Changing Times il 39:26 Ap '85.
Star search
Newsweek il 105:81 Ap 22 '85. C. McGuigan
Today
N Y il 18:28 My 6 '85. T. Schwartz
People Wkly 23:107-9 My 6 '85. J. Hall
Time 125:72 Ap 29 '85. T. Griffith

Page Numbers →

The Tony Orlando show
Jet 68:62-3 Ap 22 '85

See Television circuits
Safety devices and measures
Safe-TV. *Consum Res Mag* 68:2 Ap '85
Television reporters *See* Television broadcasting—News
Television sets *See* Television receivers
Television sound
The audio/video synergy. J. D. Hirsch. il *Stereo Rev* 50:19-20 Ap '85
Television transmission
Resolution. D. Ranada. il *Stereo Rev* 50:16 Ap '85
Televisions *See* Television receivers
Teleworking *See* Telecommuting
Temper
How to cope with your child's temper tantrums [excerpt from Raising a confident child] J. Oppenheim and others. il *Essence* 15:111 Ap '85
Temperature
See also
Atmospheric temperature
Temperature, Animal and human
See also
Fish, Effect of temperature on
Tennessee
See also
Great Smoky Mountains National Park (N.C. and Tenn.)
Tenney, Merrill Chapin, 1904-1985
about
Obituary
Christ Today por 29:54 Ap 19 '85
Tennis
Equipment
See also
Tennis rackets
It's not just a racket in the tennis market. D. Eskow. il *Pop Mech* 162:90 Ap '85
Tennis players
See also
Navratilova, Martina, 1956-
Tennis rackets
The new tennis racket. R. J. LaMarche. il *Pop Mech* 162:88-90 Ap '85

Author's Name →

A racket for the weekend warrior. B. Riggs il *Pop Mech* 162:91 Ap '85
Tension (Psychology) *See* Stress
Tension structures
The evolving design vocabulary of fabric structures. H. Berger. il *Archit Rec* 173:152-6 Mr '85
The nature of architectural fabrics; Fabric structure pioneers look back—and envision the future. J. B. Gardner. il *Archit Rec* 173:157-9 Mr '85
Tent structures *See* Tension structures
Terraces (Agriculture)
Ridges take to the hills. M. Holmberg. il *Success Farm* 83:26D Ap '85
Terraces (Outdoor living areas) *See* Decks, patios, terraces, etc.
Terrorism
Son of Brink's? [C. Chimerenge and the New York 8 to stand trial on alleged terrorist activities] J. Z. Larsen. il por *N Y* 18:50-7+ My 6 '85
A strange definition of terrorism [abortion clinics] P. Simpson. il *Work Woman* 10:44 Ap '85
Up in smoke [abortion clinic bombings] S. Baer. il por *Christ Today* 29:19 Ap 19 '85

Author Heading →

Tesconi, Charles A.
Multicultural education: a valued but problematic ideal. *Educ Dig* 50:21-3 Mr '85
A test of love [film] *See* Motion picture reviews—Single works
Test pilots *See* Air pilots
Testimony *See* Witnesses
Testing equipment
See also
Oscilloscopes

Activity A

Use information from the sample *Readers' Guide* page to answer the questions.

1. Give a cross reference for "Temperature."
2. When did *Time* publish an article entitled "The Cosby Show"?
3. Who wrote this article?
4. On what page is it located?
5. In what volume of *Newsweek* will you find an article entitled "Star Search"?
6. Are there any illustrations with this article?
7. What abbreviation indicates this?
8. Name an article written by R.J. La Marche on tennis rackets.
9. In what magazine was it published?
10. If you were interested in articles on test pilots, to what other topic would you refer?

Activity B

Use the *Readers' Guide* to locate a recent article on ten of the following topics. Write down the author of the article (if given), the title, the name of the magazine, the volume number, the date, and the pages.

Motion picture industry	Farmers
Aerobics	Nutrition
Radio broadcasting	Rock music
Basketball, professional	Short stories
Fashion	Medical care
Photography	Transportation
Marriage	Music festivals
Video games	Day care
Women—employment	Journalism
High schools	United Nations

More to Explore

Number your paper from 1 to 12. Name the reference book to which you would refer if you wanted to obtain the following information:

1. the six major divisions/counties of Australia
2. information on bread as the "staff of life"
3. most current information on the president's economic policy
4. background information on John Glenn
5. the names of the governors of each state and the political parties to which they belong
6. a diagram of the human skeleton
7. the cities and geographical features of Nicaragua
8. information on future solar and lunar eclipses
9. information on Dr. Thomas Dooley
10. the airplane and how it flies
11. list of current articles on space flights
12. best route to take from Chicago, Illinois, to Omaha, Nebraska

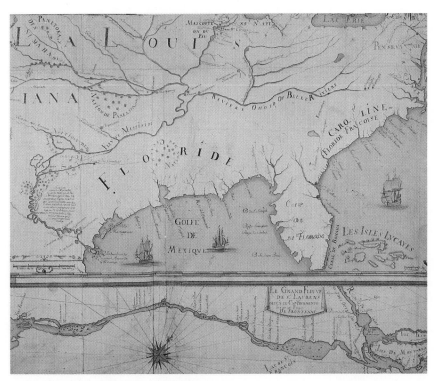

Eighteenth-century map of Louisiana and Florida

Exploring Our Language

Part II

Grammar, Correct Usage, Mechanics

Chapter 1
Nouns

Going Home

by N. Scott Momaday

from *The Way to Rainy Mountain*

I returned to Rainy Mountain in July. My grandmother had died in the spring, and I wanted to be at her grave. She had lived to be very old and at last **infirm.** Her only living daughter was with her when she died, and I was told that in death her face was that of a child.

I like to think of her as a child. When she was born, the Kiowas were living the last great moment of their history. For more than a hundred years they had controlled the open range from the Smoky Hill River to the Red, from the headwaters of the Canadian to the fork of the Arkansas and Cimarron. In **alliance** with the Comanches, they had ruled the whole of the southern Plains. War was their sacred business, and they were among the finest horsemen the world has ever known. But warfare for the Kiowas was preeminently a matter of disposition rather than of survival, and they never understood the grim, unrelenting advance of the U.S. Cavalry. When at last, divided and ill-provisioned, they were driven onto the Staked Plains in the cold rains of autumn, they fell into panic. In Palo Duro Canyon they abandoned their crucial stores to pillage and had nothing then but their lives. In order to save themselves, they surrendered to the soldiers at Fort Sill and were imprisoned in the old stone corral that now stands as a military museum. My grandmother was spared the humiliation of those high gray walls by eight or ten years, but she must have known from birth the affliction of defeat, the dark brooding of old warriors.

Her name was Aho, and she belonged to the last culture to evolve in North America. Her forebears came down from the high country in western Montana nearly three centuries ago. They were a mountain people, a mysterious tribe of hunters whose language

Detail from Crow pictograph, 1880, by White Swan

has never been positively classified in any major group. In the late seventeenth century they began a long migration to the south and east. It was a journey toward the dawn, and it led to a golden age. Along the way the Kiowas were befriended by the Crows, who gave them the culture and religion of the Plains. They acquired horses, and their ancient nomadic spirit was suddenly free of the ground. They acquired Tai-me, the sacred Sun Dance doll, from that moment the object and symbol of their worship, and so shared in the divinity of the sun. Not least, they acquired the sense of destiny, therefore courage and pride. When they entered upon the southern Plains they had been transformed. No longer were they slaves to the simple necessity of survival; they were a lordly and dangerous society of fighters and thieves, hunters and priests of the sun. According to their origin myth, they entered the world through a hollow log. From one point of view, their migration was the fruit of an old prophecy, for indeed they emerged from a sunless world.

Although my grandmother lived out her long life in the shadow of Rainy Mountain, the immense landscape of the continental interior lay like memory in her blood. She could tell of the Crows, whom she had never seen, and of the Black Hills, where she had never been. I wanted to see in reality what she had seen more perfectly in the mind's eye, and traveled fifteen hundred miles to begin my pilgrimage.

The Writer's Craft

1. Momaday returned to Rainy Mountain to be at the grave of his grandmother. Why was his presence there important to him?
2. What was the Kiowas' attitude toward war? Was it different from ours? In what ways? What might account for the differences?
3. Compare the effect of the U.S. Cavalry on the Kiowas with that of internment on Japanese-Americans during World War II.
4. How does the author's use of nouns help convince you that his writing is autobiography and not fiction?

Recalling What You Know

1. What qualities help you recognize a noun?
2. In sentence 1 of the selection "Going Home," change the proper nouns to common nouns.
3. In paragraph 3 find two collective nouns. Then identify the number (singular or plural) and case (nominative, objective, or possessive) of *Aho, forebears,* and *Tai-me.*
4. In paragraph 4 list first the concrete and then the abstract nouns.

Lesson 1 Kinds of Nouns

A noun is a name word.

Proper Nouns and Common Nouns

There are two main classes of nouns, *proper nouns* and *common nouns.*

> A proper noun names a particular person, place, or thing.
>
> A common noun names any one of a class of persons, places, or things.

N. *Scott Momaday* gives *readers* a *view* of Native American *life.*
(proper)   (common) (common)   (common)

Exercise 1

First make a list of all the proper nouns in the following sentences. Then make a list of the common nouns.

1. N. Scott Momaday is a Native American writer.
2. The ancestors of this highly regarded author were Kiowas.
3. His nonfiction stories are about American history and culture.
4. One Kiowa legend he tells is set at the base of the Devil's Tower.
5. It concerns seven sisters—and a brother, who became a bear.
6. In this form the brother chased his sisters to a tree.
7. As the tree spoke to the girls, its branches reached down.
8. Frightened, the sisters climbed the tree to escape the bear.
9. The branches raised the girls into the night sky.
10. That is why Kiowas claim the stars of the Big Dipper as kin.

Collective Nouns

> **A collective noun denotes a group of persons, animals, or things considered as one.**

The *tribe* considers responsibility to the *group* important.

Exercise 2

Make a list of all the collective nouns in the sentences.
1. The 4-H club is going to take a field trip.
2. On the Oklahoma plain a flock of sheep grazes.
3. Every morning the track team practices from seven to eight.
4. The student council is an elected group of students.
5. A bunch of grapes was the dessert of the day.
6. In history class we read about the defeat of the Spanish Armada in 1588.
7. The audience applauded enthusiastically at our play.
8. The tribe has a new president.
9. The school of rare fish was spotted in the lake.
10. Did you know that a herd of goats stopped traffic?

The Spanish Armada

Concrete Nouns

> **Most nouns are concrete nouns. A concrete noun names a person, a place, or a thing that can be seen or touched.**

The following are examples of concrete nouns: *lily, flame, tower, snow, crystal.*

Exercise 3

Make a list of all the concrete nouns in the sentences.
1. The cat purred softly.
2. The roaring train woke everyone in the house.
3. They drilled a well behind the barn.
4. The hawk soars above the field.
5. Subways can be dangerous.
6. His brother plays the saxophone.
7. Our librarian is an excellent storyteller.
8. The stapler is on the desk.
9. The man's strange behavior frightened the children.
10. Enough sleep helps people stay healthy.

A marsh hawk

Abstract Nouns

> **An abstract noun expresses a quality, a condition, or an action apart from any object or thing.**

Justice should be tempered with *mercy*.
Toby's *leadership* was invaluable.

Exercise 4

List all the abstract nouns in the sentences.
1. Ramona showed courage in defending her brother.
2. Tenderness spilled from every line of Herschel's letter.
3. Trust is an important aspect of friendship.
4. Carol's health failed in the spring.
5. The man retained his cheerfulness even after he lost his job.
6. That young woman has a flawless reputation.
7. People kept in slavery respond in different ways.
8. Some people see beauty everywhere.
9. Violence does not solve problems.
10. Jonathan won our confidence.

Words Used as Nouns and Verbs

A noun is a name word. A verb generally expresses action or being.

The play has three *acts*. (*Noun*)
Henry *acts* like a gentleman. (*Verb*)

Exercise 5

Tell whether each word in italics is a verb or a noun.
1. *Drink* the milkshake slowly.
2. Milk is a nourishing *drink*.
3. *Stand* quietly in the corner.
4. Kate left her music on the *stand*.
5. Dr. Wilson will *sign* your note.
6. That *sign* must be removed.
7. Thunder *alarms* some animals.
8. We were awakened by the sound of the *alarms*.
9. Mary Jo took a *walk* through the garden.
10. *Walk* when the light turns green.

Sharpening Your Skills

1. Write ten original sentences using as many *kinds* of nouns as you can.
2. For each of the following words, write two sentences, one using the word as a noun, the other, as a verb: *laugh, crown, rest, watch, catalog*.

Lesson 2 Person, Number, and Gender

Person

Person is that quality of a noun through which the speaker, the one spoken to, or the one spoken about is indicated.

The first person denotes the speaker.
   We, the *citizens*, petitioned the mayor.

The second person denotes the one spoken to.
   Peter, please bring me the tools.

The third person denotes the one spoken about.
   The *Apennine Mountains* run the entire length of Italy.

Exercise 6

Give the person of each noun printed in italics.
   1. You are late, my *friend.*
   2. I, the *president*, do not really care what you choose.
   3. The *teacher* saw a man running away with a blackboard eraser.
   4. "Stop, *sir*," she called.
   5. We, the *students*, wondered why the man wanted an eraser.
   6. *Stephano* saw a store nearby with a new chalkboard sign.
   7. Someone, perhaps that same *man*, had erased the sign.
   8. *Neighbors*, it is your duty to vote.
   9. We, the *pedestrians*, demand proper crosswalks.
   10. *Bicyclists*, too, need more protection.

Number

Number is the quality of a noun that denotes whether it refers to one person or thing (singular number) or more than one (plural number).

One of the three *branches* of the government is the executive *branch*. (*branches*, plural; *branch*, singular)

Methods of Forming the Plural

There are seventeen well-known rules for forming the plurals of various types of nouns. If you wish to use the plural of some noun that does not seem to be included in the rules, consult the dictionary. A choice of plural forms is given for some words; for example, the plural of *scarf* may be *scarfs* or *scarves*.

1. Most nouns form the plural by adding *s* to the singular.

   SINGULAR: *miracle*   PLURAL: *miracles*

2. For the sake of a pleasing sound (euphony), nouns ending in *s, x, z, ch,* and *sh* form the plural by adding *es* to the singular.

   SINGULAR: *tax*   PLURAL: *taxes*

3. Nouns ending in *y* preceded by a consonant form the plural by changing the *y* to *i* and adding *es*.

   SINGULAR: *victory*   PLURAL: *victories*

   NOTE: Nouns ending in *y* preceded by a vowel form the plural by adding *s* to the singular.

   SINGULAR: *valley*   PLURAL: *valleys*

4. The following nouns form the plural by changing the *f* or *fe* to *ves*: calf, elf, half, knife, leaf, life, loaf, self, shelf, thief, wife, wolf.

   SINGULAR: *leaf*   PLURAL: *leaves*

5. Nouns ending in *o*:

   a. All nouns ending in *o* preceded by a vowel form the plural by adding *s* to the singular.

   SINGULAR: *igloo*   PLURAL: *igloos*

   b. Nouns ending in *o* preceded by a consonant generally form the plural by adding *es* to the singular.

   SINGULAR: *potato*   PLURAL: *potatoes*

   c. Some nouns ending in *o* preceded by a consonant form the plural by adding *s* to the singular.

   SINGULAR: *silo*   PLURAL: *silos*

   d. Some nouns ending in *o* preceded by a consonant form the plural by adding *s* or *es* to the singular.

   SINGULAR: *buffalo*   PLURAL: *buffaloes* or *buffalos*.

6. A few nouns form the plural by a change within the singular.

   SINGULAR: *man*   PLURAL: *men*

7. A few nouns form the plural by the addition of the Old English ending *en*.

   SINGULAR: *ox*   PLURAL: *oxen*

8. A few nouns retain the same form in the plural as in the singular.

SINGULAR	PLURAL	SINGULAR	PLURAL
series	series	corps	corps
species	species	salmon	salmon
sheep	sheep	cod	cod
deer	deer	trout	trout
swine	swine	Portuguese	Portuguese

9. When a name is preceded by a title, either the name or the title may be pluralized.

SINGULAR	PLURAL
Miss Lee	The Misses Lee, The Miss Lees, or The Ms. Lees
Mr. Snyder	The Messrs. Snyder or the Mr. Snyders
Dr. Heard	The Doctors Heard or The Dr. Heards

NOTE: The title *Mrs.* is an exception to this rule, as it cannot be pluralized.

SINGULAR: *Mrs. Fisher* PLURAL: *The Mrs. Fishers*

10. Some nouns taken from foreign languages retain their foreign plurals.

SINGULAR	PLURAL	SINGULAR	PLURAL
radius	radii	crisis	crises
alumna	alumnae	oasis	oases
alumnus	alumni	larva	larvae
basis	bases	thesis	theses
analysis	analyses	stratum	strata
synopsis	synopses	vertebra	vertebrae
datum	data	bacterium	bacteria

11. Some nouns taken from foreign languages have both a foreign and an English plural. The English form is preferred.

SINGULAR	ENGLISH PLURAL	FOREIGN PLURAL
formula	formulas	formulae
memorandum	memorandums	memoranda
curriculum	curriculums	curricula
appendix	appendixes	appendices
index	indexes	indices
tableau	tableaus	tableaux

12. Some nouns are used only in the plural.

clothes	pliers	trousers
goods	scissors	tweezers

13. Some nouns are plural in form, but singular in meaning and use.

> civics physics aeronautics
> mathematics measles news

14. Compound nouns usually form the plural by adding *s* to the most important word or words.

SINGULAR	PLURAL
governor general	governors general
sergeant-at-arms	sergeants-at-arms
drive-in	drive-ins

15. Compound nouns ending in *ful* form the plural by adding *s* to the last syllable.

> SINGULAR: *handful* PLURAL: *handfuls*

NOTE: If more than one hand, pail, or glass is filled, two words are used; as in *two hands full, three glasses full.*

16. Letters form the plural by adding *s* or *'s*. Lowercase letters and capital letters that would be confusing if *s* alone were added form the plural by adding *'s*.

SINGULAR	PLURAL
TV	TVs
i	i's
A	A's

17. The plural of numbers is formed by adding *s* with no apostrophe.

SINGULAR	PLURAL
1980	1980s
87	87s

Exercise 7

Write the plural of each noun.

lady	kimono	floor
suffix	mumps	pulley
trespass	shelf	tiff
sash	alumnus	infant
dispatch	appendix	politics
heresy	8	Mrs. Teng
jockey	sketch	child
John	salmon	radio
chimney	dishful	Chinese

Exercise 8

Arrange the following nouns in two columns. In the first column, put the singular nouns; in the second, the plural nouns.

beef	spoonfuls	allies	piano
alley	gentlemen	wives	sheriffs
trolleys	queries	fox	iris
switch	porches	galoshes	sandwich
alms	memento	tomatoes	cameos
valleys	jellies	Eleanors	trios
buoy	The Misses Butler	industries	oasis
mice	trout	pocketful	4
d	mother-in-law	pliers	Donalds
peach	salesperson	altos	briefcase

Gender

> **Gender is that quality of a noun by which sex is distinguished. There are three genders: masculine, feminine, and neuter.**

The masculine gender denotes the male sex.
man, boy, uncle, brother

The feminine gender denotes the female sex.
woman, girl, grandmother, niece

The neuter gender denotes objects that have no sex.
house, football, telephone, tree

Some nouns may be taken as either masculine or feminine.
teacher, senator, writer, supervisor

NOTE: Several nouns that traditionally denoted the masculine gender in certain occupations are no longer used. One form is now used for both genders.

Traditional	Current
fireman	firefighter
councilman	councillor
repairman	repairer
mailman	mail carrier
policeman	police officer

The gender of a pronoun should agree with that of its antecedent. When the antecedent of a singular possessive pronoun may be either masculine or feminine, the form *his or her* is now considered acceptable.

Exercise 9

Give the gender of each noun.

widower	lamp	alumnus	invalid	kitchen
boy	relative	scout	Marie	friend
doctor	juror	ladder	lad	bridesmaid
stepbrother	costume	prophet	book	library
house	ewe	ship	goddess	cousin

Sharpening Your Skills

Write one sentence that contains
1. a third person, plural, neuter noun
2. two third person, singular, masculine nouns
3. a second person, plural, feminine noun
4. a first person, plural, masculine noun
5. a third person, singular, feminine noun
6. a third person, plural, feminine noun
7. a second person, singular, masculine noun
8. a second person, singular, feminine noun
9. two third person, plural, masculine or feminine nouns
10. a first person, singular, masculine or feminine noun

Lesson 3 Nominative Case

Case is that quality of a noun that shows its relation to some other word or words in the sentence. There are three cases: nominative, possessive, and objective.

Before a noun can be classified according to case, its use or syntax must be determined. The uses of the *nominative case* that have been studied in previous years are as follows:

Subject. A noun used as the subject of a finite verb is in the nominative case.

Cairo is the capital of Egypt.
Through the Panama Canal sail *ships* of many nations.
An important *crop* of France is the grape.

Subjective Complement. A noun used as a subjective complement is in the nominative case.

A noun that follows a copulative or linking verb is in the nominative case if it refers to the same person or thing as its subject.

Winston Churchill became *prime minister* of England during World War II.
Sherlock Holmes is a famous *detective* of English fiction.
The child was named *John*.

Apposition. A noun in apposition is in the same case as the noun it explains.

A noun that explains a subject or a subjective complement is in the nominative case.

Rome, the *capital* of Italy, is called the "Eternal City."
Margaret Chase, the *mayor*, was reelected to a third term.
Wanda's favorite food is pizza, a tomato–cheese *pie*.

Address. A noun used in direct address is in the nominative case.

Tony, will you go with me to the game?
Senators, let us vote on the resolution.
Obey the traffic signals, *drivers.*

Exclamation. A noun used independently to express a strong emotion is in the nominative case.

Action! The play needs action.
Theresa! She has won the award.
The poor *man!* We feel so sorry for him.

Nominative Absolute. A noun before a participle in an independent phrase is in the nominative case absolute.

A participle, a word that does the twofold work of a verb and an adjective, is sometimes used with a noun or a pronoun in an independent adverbial phrase to express the time, the condition, the cause, or the circumstances of the action expressed by the main verb in the sentence. The noun or the pronoun used in this absolute construction is in the nominative case.

The *salute* having been given, the soldier marched on.
Winter coming on, the geese flew south.
The *work* having been completed, we went to the zoo.

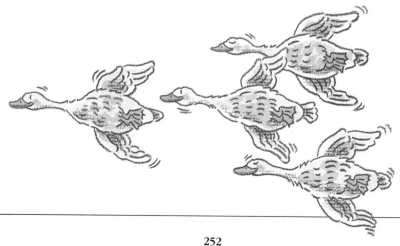

Exercise 10

Select the nouns in the nominative case and give the syntax (use) of each.

1. Water power is sometimes called white coal.
2. Lincoln having been assassinated, Johnson succeeded him.
3. Brussels is the capital of Belgium.
4. Sven, the new librarian, works evenings and Saturdays.
5. The river! It is flooding the town.
6. Jerome remained captain of the team.
7. My aunt, Barbara, works as a nurse.
8. The play being delayed slightly, the director addressed the audience.
9. Ricardo won ten dollars in the raffle. Lucky boy!
10. Ms. Tobias, may we race to the corner?
11. Oxygen and nitrogen are the chief gases in the air.
12. Erin, the smallest girl in the class, has beautiful red hair.
13. William is a prince in England.
14. The small animal scurried away before we could tell what it was.
15. Jacob, please be home for dinner.

Exercise 11

Complete each sentence with a noun in the nominative case, and tell how the noun is used in the sentence.

1. _____ has been a good friend of mine for many years.
2. Into the fort stumbled the exhausted _____ .
3. _____ encouraged the team.
4. Our lifeguard, _____ , is very concerned about water safety.
5. Fritz is a talented _____ .
6. It was _____ who set off the fire alarm by mistake.
7. Keep your hands inside the windows, _____ .
8. My cousin, _____ , visited China.
9. Her computer _____ would not work properly.
10. _____ used a power saw to remove the dead branches.

Sharpening Your Skills

Compose a total of six sentences illustrating each type of noun in the nominative case.

Lesson 4 Possessive Case

> **A noun that expresses possession, ownership, or connection is in the possessive case.**

The sign of the possessive case is the apostrophe and *s*.
Beethoven's "Eroica" is a popular symphony.

Methods of Forming the Possessive Case of Nouns

1. To form the singular possessive, add *'s* to the singular form of the noun.

    Joseph, Joseph's; captain, captain's

    The apostrophe and *s* is *not* used with nouns relating to inanimate things.

    steeple of the church (*not* church's steeple)

    The apostrophe and *s is* used with the names of certain inanimate objects which have become idiomatic from common usage.

    earth's surface; sun's rays

2. To form the plural possessive of nouns ending in *s*, add the apostrophe only.

    boys, boys'; baby, babies'

    If the plural form of the noun does not end in *s*, add *'s*.

    children, children's; oxen, oxen's

3. Proper names ending in *s* usually form the possessive case by adding *'s*.

    Mr. Burns, Mr. Burns's; Dickens, Dickens's

4. In compound nouns the *'s* is added to the end of the word.

NOUN	SINGULAR POSSESSIVE	PLURAL POSSESSIVE
father-in-law	father-in-law's	fathers-in-law's

Exercise 12

Write the singular possessive form and the plural possessive form
of each noun.

brother-in-law	student	professor	mouse
woman	man	gentleman	horse
sergeant-at-arm	lady	sister	ox
sheep	child	Thomas	deer
attorney general	Jane	king	goose
stepsister	boy	princess	bird
Mr. Swenson	scout	pupil	animal
maid of honor	girl	father	lion

Exercise 13

Write the possessive form of the word in parentheses that will
correctly complete each sentence. In some sentences, you will use the
singular number, and in other sentences, the plural.

1. The early (settler) homes were very crude.
2. The blind (child) classmates study with her, reading their
   textbooks aloud and discussing the subjects.
3. You may enjoy reading (Shakespeare) *Romeo and Juliet*.
4. The (deer) horns are shed and renewed annually.
5. The (boy) team finished third.
6. In February, we celebrate (Washington) birthday.
7. Jean works in her (sister) store.
8. The general tried to discover the (enemy) strategy.
9. Three thousand people heard (Stephanie) speech.
10. We saw a dramatization of one of (Dickens) novels on television.
11. The (astronaut) spacesuit failed to function properly.
12. Bernardo found a (bird) nest.
13. Beth put some food in the (dog) dish.
14. (Men) clothing is sold on the third floor.

Separate and Joint Possession or Ownership

If two or more nouns are used together to indicate separate ownership—that is, to show that each person possesses something independently of the other—the 's is used after each noun.

> *Irving's and Scott's* literary works are well worth reading.
> *Webster's and Hayne's* speeches have been studied by many orators.

If two or more nouns are used together to indicate joint ownership—that is, to show that one thing is possessed by the group jointly—the 's is used after the last noun only.

> *The secretary and the treasurer's* office is on the third floor.
> *Garcia and King's* store has been remodeled.

Exercise 14

Number a sheet of paper from 1 to 15 and write the correct possessive forms of the nouns.

1. Janice and Maria compositions describe the animal life in caves.
2. Campbell and Luciano market sells imported cheese.
3. Pattie and Richard father's blood pressure is too high.
4. We received the doctor and the nurse reports.
5. Keats and Tennyson poems are among my favorites.
6. Da Vinci and Picasso paintings hang in important museums.
7. Laura and Katie mother seems very young.
8. Did you see Pedro and Dianne new town houses?
9. Neiman-Marcus and Saks Fifth Avenue Christmas window displays attract many shoppers.
10. David and Susan parents live in a small town in Mississippi.
11. Emerson and Thoreau writings are important contributions to American literature.
12. Radio and television effects on viewers are only beginning to be studied.
13. Laurel and Hardy film career was long and revered.
14. Last week was Lois and George twenty-fifth wedding anniversary.
15. Pam and Jim car has a dead battery.

Sharpening Your Skills

Compose six sentences using the nouns from Exercise 12. Be sure to use both singular and plural possessives. Write four sentences using separate and joint ownership correctly.

Lesson 5 Objective Case

The uses of the objective case are as follows:

> *Direct Object.* **A noun used as the direct object of a verb is in the objective case.**

Thaddeus Kosciuszko drew the *plans* for West Point.
Dylan Thomas wrote beautiful *poems.*
The villagers planned a *celebration.*

> *Indirect Object.* **A noun used as the indirect object of a verb is in the objective case.**

Terri sent *Benjamin* the directions.
Buy your *brother* some candy.
They gave the *bride* beautiful flowers.

NOTE: The preposition *to* or *for* can usually be inserted before the indirect object without changing the meaning of the sentence.

> *Object of a Preposition.* **A noun used as the object of a preposition is in the objective case.**

Water evaporates in *sunlight.*
The lawyer performed his duties with great *courage.*
The farmers objected to a protective *tariff.*

> **Apposition.** A noun in apposition is in the same case as the noun it explains. A noun that explains a direct object, an indirect object, or an object of a preposition is in the objective case.

Kent Jackson won the first prize, an *automobile*.

We gave Rose, our *captain*, the trophy.

John gave the message to the coach, his *uncle*.

> **Adverbial Objective.** A noun used as an adverbial objective is in the objective case.

The athlete exercises every *day*.
Linda can jump five *feet*.
This *morning* the ground was covered with frost.

NOTE: An adverbial objective is a noun used as an adverb. Adverbial objectives may tell when, where, how long, or how far.

> **Objective Complement.** A noun used as an objective complement is in the objective case.

The parents named the baby *Paul*.
The owner appointed Julia *treasurer*.
The team chose Saul *captain*.

NOTE: In the first sentence, the noun *Paul* completes the meaning of the verb *named* and refers to the direct object, *baby*.

Some common verbs that may take objective complements are *appoint, call, choose, elect, make, name.*

> **Cognate Object.** A noun used as a cognate object is in the objective case.

He dreamed a *dream* of future greatness.
The boxer fought a good *fight*.
Anne sang a *song* of joy.

NOTE: A cognate object is a noun that repeats the meaning of and closely resembles the verb of which it is the object.

Exercise 15

Each italicized noun is in the objective case. Give the syntax (use) of each.

1. Many people take the *train* to *work*.
2. Bette Midler sang a very unusual *song*.
3. The team selected *Albert* team *captain*.
4. Going into the New York *subway* is an artistic experience.
5. The author told the *class* a *story*.
6. We must wait two *hours*.
7. Ross Brown, our group leader, gave *Scott* a new *program*.
8. The commissioner gave *Reggie Jackson* a batting *award*.
9. The actors danced the *dance* of the sea *creatures*.
10. Pepe waited twenty *minutes* at the *station*.
11. Sarah consulted *Jennie*, her *doctor*.
12. Ollie named his *dog Dynamite*.
13. He gave *George*, my *brother*, his old *watch*.
14. The class called *Eddie "Whiz Kid."*
15. The President can veto *acts* of *Congress*.

Exercise 16

Choose a noun in the objective case to complete each sentence, and then tell how the noun is used in the sentence. Be sure to use each possible objective case syntax at least once.

1. Jerre gets up every morning three ____ before she has to leave for school.
2. Florence, the _____, read the minutes of the last meeting.
3. José prayed a ____ of thanksgiving.
4. Judy painted a small ___.
5. The students chose _____ captain.
6. Ben enjoyed the book _____.
7. Lisa gave _____ some flowers.
8. They elected Robert _____.
9. The coach taught _____ a new ___.
10. Orbiting satellites travel around _____.

You Are the Author

Momaday describes his grandmother and her background. Write a description of one of your grandparents and either his or her background or your grandparent's influence on you.

Chapter Challenge

Read this selection very carefully and then answer the questions that follow.

[1]In the Louvre in Paris hangs a painting by the celebrated American artist James McNeill Whistler. [2]*An Arrangement in Gray and Black* is the imposing title of this portrait, but to the millions who know and love it, the likeness is known as "The Artist's Mother." [3]The picture, when it first appeared, was given very little attention, and it brought the artist scant recognition. [4]Many years later, however, it was the opinion of more than one committee of critics that this picture alone would have made Whistler a leader among painters. [5]For connoisseurs of art, the beauty of this painting lies in the harmony achieved by perfect spacing and the many tones of gray produced by skillful blending. [6]Its appeal to the heart of the ordinary person rests in the noble traits of motherhood that Whistler has captured and enshrined forever on canvas.

1. Name the proper nouns in the first sentence.
2. What is the subject in the first sentence? What is its case?
3. Find an appositive in the first sentence. What is its case?
4. What is the case of the noun *Artist's* in the second sentence?
5. In what case is the noun *title* in the second sentence? Why?
6. Find the direct and the indirect objects in the third sentence.
7. Find a masculine noun and a neuter noun in the third sentence.
8. Find an adverbial objective in the fourth sentence.
9. Select a collective noun in the fourth sentence.
10. Name an objective complement in the fourth sentence.
11. Write the singular form of *connoisseurs* in the fifth sentence.
12. Which nouns in the fifth sentence are objects of prepositions?
13. What kind of noun is *motherhood* in the sixth sentence?
14. Find an abstract and a concrete noun in the sixth sentence.
15. In what person is this selection written?

The Artist's Mother by
James McNeill Whistler

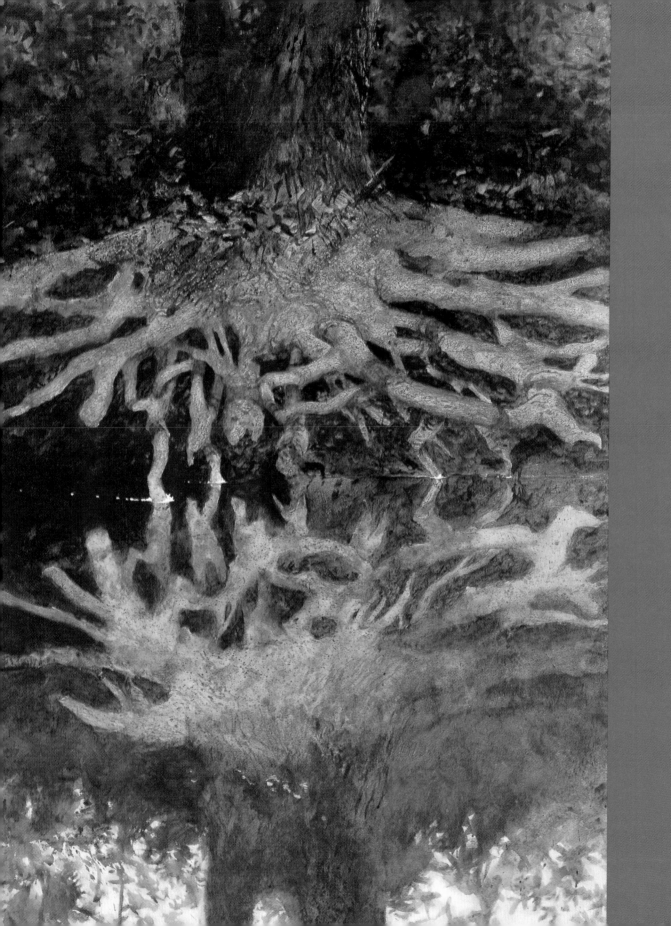

Chapter 2

Pronouns

The Devil and Tom Walker

by Washington Irving

from *Rip Van Winkle and Other Stories*

A few miles from Boston in Massachusetts, there is a deep inlet, winding several miles into the interior of the country from Charles Bay, and terminating in a thickly wooded swamp or morass. On one side of this inlet is a beautiful dark grove; on the opposite side the land rises abruptly from the water's edge into a high ridge, on which grow a few scattered oaks of great age and immense size.

About the year 1727, just at the time that earthquakes were prevalent in New England and shook many tall sinners down upon their knees, there lived near this place a meager, miserly fellow, of the name of Tom Walker. He had a wife as miserly as himself: they were so miserly that they even conspired to cheat each other.

One day that Tom Walker had been to a distant part of the neighborhood, he took what he considered a shortcut homeward, through the swamp. Like most shortcuts, it was an ill-chosen route. The swamp was thickly grown with great gloomy pines and hemlocks, some of them ninety feet high, which made it dark at noonday, and a retreat for all the owls of the neighborhood. It was full of pits and quagmires, partly covered with weeds and mosses, where the green surface often betrayed the traveller into a gulf of black, smothering mud: there were also dark and stagnant pools, the abodes of the tadpole, the bullfrog, and the water snake; where the trunks of pines and hemlocks lay half drowned, half rotting, looking like alligators sleeping in the mire.

It was late in the dusk of evening when Tom Walker reached an old fort, and he paused there awhile to rest himself. Tom lifted up his eyes, and beheld a great dark man seated directly opposite him, on the stump of a tree. He was exceedingly surprised, having neither heard nor seen any one approach; and he was still more

Where W. Rat Lives by Jamie Wyeth

perplexed on observing, as well as the gathering gloom would permit, that the stranger was neither Negro nor Indian. It is true he was dressed in a rude half-Indian garb, and had a red belt or sash swathed round his body! But his face was neither black nor copper-color, but swarthy and dingy, and begrimed with soot, as if he had been accustomed to toil among fires and forges. He had a shock of coarse black hair, that stood out from his head in all directions, and bore an axe on his shoulder.

He scowled for a moment at Tom with a pair of great red eyes.

"What are you doing on my grounds?" said the man, with a hoarse, growling voice.

"Your grounds!" said Tom, with a sneer, "no more your grounds than mine; they belong to Deacon Peabody."

"Deacon Peabody be d——d," said the stranger, "as I flatter myself he will be, if he does not look more to his own sins and less to those of his neighbors. Look yonder, and see how Deacon Peabody is faring."

Tom looked in the direction that the stranger pointed, and beheld one of the great trees, fair and flourishing without, but rotten at the core, and saw that it had been nearly hewn through, so that the first high wind was likely to blow it down. On the bark of the tree was scored the name of Deacon Peabody, an eminent man, who had waxed wealthy by driving shrewd bargains with the Indians. He now looked around, and found most of the tall trees marked with the name of some great man of the colony, and all more or less scored by the axe. The one on which he had been seated, and which had evidently just been hewn down, bore the name of Crowninshield; and he recollected a mighty rich man of that name, who made a vulgar display of wealth, which it was whispered he had acquired by **buccaneering.**

"He's just ready for burning!" said the stranger, with a growl of triumph. "You see I am likely to have a good stock of firewood for winter."

"But what right have you," said Tom, "to cut down Deacon Peabody's timber?"

"The right of a prior claim," said the other. "This woodland belonged to me long before one of your white-faced race put foot upon the soil."

"And pray, who are you, if I may be so bold?" said Tom.

"Oh, I go by various names. I am the wild huntsman in some countries; the black miner in others. I am the great patron and prompter of slave-dealers, and the grand-master of the Salem witches."

"The upshot of all which is that, if I mistake not," said Tom, sturdily, "you are he commonly called Old Scratch."

"The same, at your service!" replied the other man, with a half-civil nod.

It is said that after this commencement they had a long and earnest conversation together, as Tom returned homeward. Old Scratch told him of great sums of money buried by Kidd the pirate, under the oak trees on the high ridge, not far from the morass. All these were under his command, and protected by his power, so that none could find them but such as **propitiated** his favor. These he offered to place within Tom Walker's reach, having conceived an especial kindness for him; but they were to be had only on certain conditions.

There was one condition which need not be mentioned, being generally understood in all cases where the devil grants favors; but there were others about which, though of less importance, he was inflexibly **obstinate.** He insisted that the money found through his means should be employed in his service.

Foot by Jamie Wyeth

He proposed that Tom should turn **usurer;** the devil being extremely anxious for the increase of usurers, looking upon them as his peculiar people.

To this no objections were made, for it was just to Tom's taste.

"You shall open a broker's shop in Boston next month," said Old Scratch.

"I'll do it tomorrow, if you wish," said Tom Walker.

"You shall lend money at two per cent a month."

"Egad, I'll charge four!" replied Tom Walker.

"You shall extort bonds, foreclose mortgages, drive the merchants to bankruptcy—"

"I'll drive them to the d——l," cried Tom Walker.

"You are the usurer for my money!" said sooty legs with delight. "When will you want the **rhino**?"

"This very night."

"Done!" said the devil.

"Done!" said Tom Walker. So they shook hands and struck a bargain.

A few days' time saw Tom Walker seated behind his desk in a counting-house in Boston.

The Writer's Craft

1. Did you enjoy the excerpt? Why or why not? How do you think the story might turn out?
2. Do you agree that Tom's shortcut "was an ill-chosen route"? Discuss.
3. What do you think was "the condition which need not be mentioned" in the agreement between Tom and the devil?
4. The pronoun that the author uses most frequently in this excerpt is *he*. To whom does it usually refer? Why do you think the reader rarely confuses references to the devil with those to Tom—even though *he* could apply to both?

Recalling What You Know

1. What nouns does the pronoun replace? *Tom and Old Scratch meet, and they strike a bargain.*
2. What are the qualities (person, number, gender, and case) of the personal pronouns *I* and *her?*
3. A possessive pronoun shows ownership. What possessive pronouns might fit in the blanks? *A pirate buried ____ money under an oak tree. ____ leaves turn brown in autumn.*

Lesson 1 Personal Pronouns: Review, Nominative Case

A pronoun is a word used in place of a noun.

When Tom reached the old fort, he paused to rest.

The word to which a pronoun refers is its *antecedent.* In the sentence the antecedent of the pronoun *he* is *Tom.*

Personal Pronouns, A Review

> **A personal pronoun is a pronoun that denotes by its form the speaker, the person spoken to, or the person or the thing spoken of.**

I enjoyed this story as much as *you* did.
They would like *you* to lend *them* the book.

The pronouns of the first person (the speaker) are *I, mine, me, we, ours, us.* The pronouns of the second person (the person spoken to) are *you* and *yours.* The pronouns of the third person (the person, the place, or the thing spoken of) are *he, she, it, his, hers, its, him, her, they, theirs, them.*

Pronouns change form to denote case and number. Use the *nominative case* when the pronoun is the subject of a sentence, a subjective complement, or in the nominative absolute. Use the *possessive case* to denote possession. Use the *objective case* for a direct object, an indirect object, or the object of a preposition.

The personal pronouns are declined in the following way. In the third person singular there are distinct forms for masculine, feminine, and neuter genders.

Declension of the Personal Pronouns

First Person

Case	Singular	Plural
NOMINATIVE	I	we
POSSESSIVE	my,* mine	our,* ours
OBJECTIVE	me	us

Second Person

	Singular	Plural
NOMINATIVE	you	you
POSSESSIVE	your,* yours	your,* yours
OBJECTIVE	you	you

Third Person

	Singular	Plural
NOMINATIVE	he, she, it	they
POSSESSIVE	his, her,* hers, its	their,* theirs
OBJECTIVE	him, her, it	them

Exercise 17

Name the personal pronouns and give the person, number, gender, and case of each.

1. After Irving had spent several years in England, he took a trip to Germany.
2. He gave American settings to some German tales.
3. Among them were "Rip Van Winkle" and "The Legend of Sleepy Hollow."
4. They are both set in New York.
5. Which story do you like better?
6. She likes "The Legend of Sleepy Hollow" because it is spooky.
7. In 1832 Americans honored him as a great man of letters.
8. He mixed realistic and supernatural elements in his stories.
9. I think Irving had a large vocabulary.
10. Some stories teach us about human values.

*The possessive adjectives *my, our,* and so forth, are included in this table for the sake of completeness.

Correct Use of the Nominative Case
Subject of a Verb

> A pronoun used as the subject of a verb is in the nominative case.

Grace and (I, me) swim together.

The correct form is Grace and *I* swim together.

Exercise 18

Select the correct form of the personal pronoun and give the reason for your choice.

1. (He, Him) and (her, she) drove here together.
2. Ira and (me, I) will pack the lunch.
3. The group leader and (he, him) wrote the program in BASIC.
4. (Her, She) and Adrienne wrote a program in Logo.
5. (They, Them) and (us, we) only speak English.
6. Eddie and (I, me) studied atomic fission.
7. Wilma and (her, she) opened the mystery package.
8. (He, Him) and (I, me) discovered a gold coin near the wall.
9. (They, Them) and (we, us) live on the same street.
10. Ruth and (me, I) were invited to a party.

Subjective Complement

> A pronoun that follows a linking verb is used as a subjective complement and is in the nominative case.

It is (he, him).

It is *he* is the correct form. *He* follows the linking verb *is* and refers to the word *it*.

Exercise 19

Select the correct form of the personal pronoun and give the reason for your choice.

1. The winner of the prize was (she, her).
2. This is (him, he).
3. Did you know it was (me, I) who called?
4. The youngest couple could be (they, them).
5. The people called were (we, us).
6. Was it (her, she)?
7. The man carrying the sign was (he, him).
8. The first to arrive were (them, they).
9. It might have been (I, me).
10. It is (I, me) dressed in the costume.

Exercise 20

Of the two words in parentheses in each sentence, select the word that correctly completes the sentence. Then tell whether the word selected is used as a subject or as a subjective complement.

1. Margie and (I, me) saw the snake shed its skin.
2. Tony and (him, he) are brothers.
3. Abraham thought the caller was (her, she).
4. It was (us, we) whom they met at the studio.
5. Doug, Joan, and (me, I) toured NASA in Houston.
6. Paco and (they, them) are skydivers.
7. It was (he, him) who found the extra holes in the parachute.
8. Bernie and (him, he) spoke about the dangers of smoking.
9. Andy and (me, I) are going to the opera.
10. It was (she, her) who played the lead.

Exercise 21

Choose a personal pronoun to complete each sentence. Tell whether the pronoun is used as subject or subjective complement.

1. _____ am eager to see the World Series in person.
2. Is that you? Yes, it is _____ .
3. Corita and _____ met at the library.
4. _____ intends to study Aztec civilization.
5. Jasper and _____ will compete in the race.
6. It is _____ who will win.
7. _____ saw the Super Bowl last year.

8. Was it _____ who made the touchdown in the game this afternoon?
9. Vince and _____ were collecting stamps.
10. It was _____ who found the lost wallet.
11. You know that the guilty person is _____ .
12. Was it _____ who answered the door?
13. Here are Frieda and _____ .
14. Students from technical college who came to the party were Sally, Roth, and _____ .
15. He and _____ were delighted with their new puppy.
16. Will _____ be ready on time?
17. You must admit that the best hula dancer was _____ .
18. My brother and _____ will attend the senior play.
19. It was _____ who wrote the poem.
20. Either Tom or _____ caught the shark.

Lesson 2 Personal Pronouns: Objective Case

Direct Object

A pronoun used as the direct object of a verb is in the objective case.

I met David and (he, him) at the station.

The correct form is: I met David and *him* at the station.

Exercise 22

Copy each sentence, using the correct form of the pronoun. Give the reason for your choice.
1. Carmela took Monica and (I, me) for a ride in her new car.
2. The guard helped (he, him) look for the lost keys.
3. The teacher rewarded Tom and (her, she) for their consistent effort.
4. Mr. Winslow directed Kathleen and (I, me) in the school play.
5. The judge warned Lucinda and (her, she) about riding their bicycles on city streets.

6. They thanked the policeman and (him, he) for helping.
7. The firefighter congratulated (we, us) on our fire prevention activities.
8. Ten people helped Nicholas and (me, I) find the dog.
9. Charles instructed (they, them) in the art of wood carving.
10. Grandfather took Stella and (us, we) out for dinner.

Indirect Object

> **A pronoun used as the indirect object of a verb is in the objective case.**

Give Coretta and (I, me) the papers.

The correct form is: Give Coretta and *me* the papers.

NOTE: The preposition *to* or *for* can usually be inserted before the indirect object without changing the meaning of the sentence.

Give *to* Coretta and me the papers.

Exercise 23

Copy each sentence, using the correct form of the pronoun. Mentally insert the preposition before the indirect object as shown in the example above.

1. Claude wrote Sam and (me, I) a long letter.
2. He told (we, us) facts about life in Thailand.
3. Marita brought Jeff and (her, she) some fresh pineapple from Hawaii.
4. A guide showed Rosemary and (them, they) the Monet exhibit at the art museum.
5. My brother lent Bill and (he, him) the car.
6. The bullfighter gave (me, I) his red cape.
7. Tod threw (her, she) the ball.
8. The vendor offered (he, him) and (I, me) some peanuts.
9. The Smiths owe Mrs. Fernandez and (him, he) three thousand dollars.
10. Olga lends (we, us) her computer on Tuesdays.

Object of a Preposition

> **A pronoun used as the object of a preposition is in the objective case.**

I have not heard from Jean or (she, her).

The correct form is: I have not heard from Jean or *her*.

Exercise 24

Copy each sentence, using the correct form of the pronoun. Give the reason for your choice.

1. This puzzle is too difficult for (I, me).
2. We went sledding with him and (her, she).
3. Lloyd gave the keys to (him, he).
4. Maria voted for (they, them).
5. John showed mother a painting by (her, she).
6. Casimir, sit between (he, him) and (I, me).
7. Alfred walked beside (us, we) toward the fire.
8. We went to the computer store with (her, she).
9. The man did not want to talk with (we, us).
10. Lenny may stand between Kermit and (she, her).

Exercise 25

Write the correct form of the personal pronoun in the objective case.

1. The crowd separated Greg from (*1st person, plural*).
2. Is this mail for (*3rd person, sing., masc.*) or (*1st person, sing.*)?
3. Regina is singing with (*2nd person, sing.*).
4. The artist painted a picture of (*3rd person, sing., fem.*).
5. His brother brought (*3rd person, sing., masc.*) a spotted puppy.
6. The salesperson did not want to help (*3rd person, plural*).
7. Andrew told (*1st person, sing.*) an exciting story.
8. These things are important to you and (*3rd person, sing., masc.*).
9. Shelly asked Dave and (*3rd person, sing., fem.*) for a ticket.
10. Take (*3rd person, plural*) with you.
11. Stan did not ride with (*1st person, plural*).
12. Between you and (*3rd person, sing., masc.*) there should be no quarrels.

13. Give Julio and (*1st person, sing.*) the directions.
14. The mouse was behind Helen and (*2nd person, sing.*).
15. Alice called (*3rd person, sing., fem.*) to the door.
16. That phone call was for (*2nd person, sing.*).
17. Lucinda gave (*3rd person, sing., fem.*) a massage.
18. The librarian saved (*3rd person, sing., neut.*) for us.
19. These tests are very difficult for (*3rd person, sing., masc.*).
20. We watched (*3rd person, plural*) play the tubas.

Exercise 26

Copy these sentences, filling in each blank with the proper form of a personal pronoun. Tell how the pronoun is used: direct object, indirect object, object of a preposition.

1. We went with _____ to see the game.
2. The English prizes were won by Mary and _____ .
3. Wanda gave _____ her fishing pole.
4. His father promised _____ a trip to the lake.
5. They visited _____ over the weekend.
6. He saw _____ at the theater.
7. Jim offered _____ some popcorn.
8. The noise startled _____ .
9. Will you take _____ to the basketball game?
10. Did you call _____ before school?
11. The storm carried _____ out to sea.
12. They want to take us with _____ .
13. The magician divided the cards between _____ and _____ .
14. Tod showed _____ the secret formula.
15. Theresa gave Chris and _____ this intricate teapot.

The Case Used after *Than* and *As*

After the conjunctions *than* and *as* there is an omission of words. The pronoun following these conjunctions must be in the same case as the word with which it is compared.

Marcia reads better than (she, her).

The correct form is: Marcia reads better than *she* (reads).

We saw him before (she, her).

The correct form is: We saw him before (we saw) *her*.
or We saw him before *she* (saw him).

Exercise 27

Select the correct form of the pronoun. Then give the words that are omitted but understood.
1. Evelyn walks more quickly than (she, her).
2. Fred sings better than (I, me).
3. Anne swims as fast as (he, him).
4. That band is as good as (we, us).
5. Bernardo is older than (I, me).
6. I hope to be as proficient as (she, her).
7. Francine studies more diligently than (they, them).
8. She prepares her work better than (I, me).
9. Dave is not so witty as (he, him).
10. Antonio climbs as well as (she, her).
11. He drove no faster than (we, us).
12. Maria skied down a steeper trail than (he, him).
13. I wish I were as successful as (she, her).
14. Ed recognized the star sooner than (she, her).
15. Our sprinters are faster than (they, them).
16. Amy is more efficient than (we, us).
17. Jan and Tom are shorter than (I, me).
18. Is that computer as organized as (she, her)?
19. Mick is more patient than (I, me).
20. They nominated him as well as (she, her).

Exercise 28

Choose the correct pronoun in each of the following sentences.
Give the reason for your choice.

1. We thought that it was (she, her).
2. May (we, us) three leave early?
3. The cat followed (he, him) and (I, me).
4. Did the nurse ask Ted and (she, her) a question?
5. That tall boy is (he, him).
6. All were excused except Ann and (she, her).
7. (He, Him) and (I, me) were invited to the costume party.
8. It was (I, me) who called.
9. The woman saw (they, them) from her kitchen window.
10. Is it (she, her) you want?
11. All of (we, us) play soccer.
12. Everyone but you and (he, him) went to the movie.
13. The argument was between (they, them) and (we, us).
14. Did you think it was (she, her) who found it?
15. Would you go if you were (I, me)?

Exercise 29

Substitute a pronoun for the italicized words in each sentence.
Tell the case of the pronoun and how it is used in the sentence.

1. The best musician in the class is *Francine*.
2. The tour continued without *the three children*.
3. *The group* sat in a circle around the campfire.
4. My mother told Carmen and *Jeff* a bedtime story.
5. The firemen saw *the cat* hanging from the roof.
6. I knew it was *Gabrielle* as soon as I turned the corner.
7. *Jason and I* signed up for the field trip.
8. *The field trip* was a tour through the Air Force Academy.
9. Jason and I were grateful to *the tour guides* for their time.
10. I had seen *the academy* from the outside, but never the inside.

Sharpening Your Skills

Your mom is not at home. Write a note to her explaining what you
and a friend are planning for the day. Underline the pronouns
you use.

Lesson 3 Possessive and Compound Personal Pronouns

Possessive Pronouns

> A possessive pronoun is a pronoun used to denote possession or ownership by the speaker, the person spoken to, or the person, place, or thing spoken of.

The possessive pronouns *mine, ours, yours, his, hers, its*, and *theirs* are sometimes called independent possessives because they may be used alone to take the place of nouns. *My, our, your, his, her, its*, and *their* modify nouns. The possessives that modify nouns are called possessive adjectives.

Possessive Pronouns	Possessive Adjectives
Mine is blue.	*My* uniform is blue.
This is *yours*.	This is *your* pen.
Mr. Cook sold *his*.	Mr. Cook sold *his* car.
They have examined *theirs*.	They have examined *their* posters.

When a possessive pronoun or a possessive noun is used independently, its case is determined by its use in the sentence.

Leo's is here.	*His* is here.	(*Subject*)
She saw *Helen's*.	She saw *yours*.	(*Direct object*)
This is *Blanche's*.	This is *mine*.	(*Subjective complement*)

Exercise 30

Complete each sentence with an appropriate possessive pronoun.
1. That blue sweater is not _____.
2. Take _____, but leave _____.
3. _____ is not as warm as _____.
4. This book is _____ but that is _____.
5. Mrs. Rodriguez sold _____.
6. _____ ran away.
7. The umbrella with purple stripes is _____.
8. Someone stole _____.
9. _____ was left on their beach.
10. _____ were in a box on my desk.

Compound Personal Pronouns

> Compound personal pronouns are pronouns made by
> adding *self* or *selves* to certain forms of the
> personal pronouns.

Forms of the Compound Personal Pronouns

	Singular	*Plural*
FIRST PERSON	myself	ourselves
SECOND PERSON	yourself	yourselves
THIRD PERSON	himself, herself, itself	themselves

A compound personal pronoun may be used to give emphasis to a
noun, or as an object referring to the subject.

> An intensive pronoun is used to emphasize a preceding
> noun or pronoun.

The land *itself* was very fertile.

> A reflexive pronoun is used as an object referring to and denoting the same person or thing as the subject.

We must prepare *ourselves* for the examination.

Exercise 31

List the compound personal pronouns and tell whether they are intensive or reflexive.

1. The robbers saw a reflection of themselves in the bank's spotless windows.
2. The gunman frightened himself.
3. A customer herself kicked the pistol from his hand.
4. The bank guard himself was stunned by her act.
5. The police officers put themselves between the robbers and everyone else.
6. I myself could not explain my behavior.
7. Rome took its name from Romulus himself.
8. Napoleon crowned himself emperor.
9. The people support themselves by begging.
10. Pat yourself on the back, Jillian.

Agreement of Compound Personal Pronouns

> A compound personal pronoun must agree with its antecedent in person, number, and gender.

Compound personal pronouns have two distinct uses, as intensive and as reflexive pronouns.

King Ethelbert *himself* received the explorers. (*Intensive*)
We seldom see *ourselves* as others see us. (*Reflexive*)

The antecedent of *himself* is *King Ethelbert*. *King Ethelbert* is third person, singular, masculine; so, too, is *himself*. The antecedent of *ourselves* is *we*. *We* is first person, plural, masculine or feminine; so, too, is *ourselves*.

Exercise 32

Select the correct compound personal pronoun for each of the following sentences. Then tell whether the selected pronoun is intensive or reflexive, and give its antecedent.

1. Roger blamed _____ for the misunderstanding.
2. Margie cut _____ on the pieces of the broken catsup bottle.
3. Every woman must answer for _____.
4. The fire fighters _____ could not find the source of the smoke.
5. David _____ had been smoking in the forest that afternoon.
6. You _____ heard the verdict.
7. The fugitives hid _____ from the sheriff.
8. We _____ were responsible for the broken window.
9. Kim's turtle hid _____ behind a pile of stuffed animals.
10. The voters disagreed among _____.
11. She did the job _____.
12. The couple _____ had not seen the videotape of the wedding.
13. Louis XIV called _____ the Sun King.
14. Ben changed the tire _____.
15. Ellen _____ composed the song for the school play.

Sharpening Your Skills

You took your brother's (sister's) books to school. He (she) took yours. In five or six sentences, explain how this happened. Use possessive and compound personal pronouns.

Lesson 4 Interrogative Pronouns

An interrogative pronoun is a pronoun used in asking a question.

The interrogative pronouns are *who, whose, whom, which,* and *what.* They are used in both direct and indirect questions.

Direct questions: By *whom* was it written? *Who* is Tom?
Indirect questions: She asked *whom* we wanted. He wondered *whose* book it was.

Use *who, whose,* and *whom* in speaking of persons. Use *which* in speaking of places and things or to denote one of a definite class. Use *what* in speaking of places and things and in seeking information.

Declension of *Who*

	Singular	*Plural*
NOMINATIVE	who	who
POSSESSIVE	whose	whose
OBJECTIVE	whom	whom

Exercise 33

List the interrogative pronoun in each of the following sentences and tell what it refers to by writing *person(s), thing(s),* or *information.*
Give the case of each interrogative pronoun in the sentence.

1. What were the direct causes of the First World War?
2. To whom did you give your job application?
3. Whom did you meet at the White House?
4. From what is rayon made?
5. Which of those movies would you like to see?
6. Whom will you escort to the dance?
7. Rose asked who lived in that house.
8. Of whom did you ask the question?
9. Who wrote *The Mill on the Floss*?
10. What was the result of the recycling project?

Exercise 34

For each blank, provide an appropriate interrogative pronoun.
1. By _____ of the political parties was she nominated?
2. _____ was the result of the election?
3. By _____ were the votes tallied?
4. _____ was charging vote fraud?
5. For _____ did you cast your ballot?
6. _____ led the fight for Haitian independence?
7. They asked _____ was the fastest means of transportation.
8. _____ is the function of the motor nerves?
9. _____ would be your choice if you could never change your mind?
10. Leslie asked _____ had been to see the dolphins.

Correct Use of Interrogative Pronouns *Who* and *Whom*

> The interrogative pronoun *who* is used when the sentence requires a pronoun in the nominative case.
>
> The interrogative pronoun *whom* is used when the sentence requires a pronoun in the objective case.

To help determine the correct use of *who* and *whom*, answer the question by filling in a name.

Subject
Who picked the winning number?
Chris picked the winning number.

Object of a Preposition
With whom does Anita plan to work?
Anita plans to work *with Sally*.

Direct Object
Whom did you invite to your party?
I invited *the entire class* to my party.

Folk painting depicting
Haitian independence

Exercise 35

Complete each sentence with the correct form of *who* or *whom*.

1. _____ is the first person in line?
2. By _____ were you told?
3. _____ do you think is at the door, wearing pink tennis shoes?
4. With _____ did you come to the party?
5. _____ went with you to see the blue whale?
6. To _____ do we owe thanks for these season theater tickets?
7. _____ brought the pizza?
8. _____ was chosen to be captain of the soccer team?
9. To _____ did you explain your absence?
10. By _____ was this video game created?
11. _____ usually picks the flowers in the morning?
12. For _____ are these remarks intended?
13. _____ left the test tube where that child could get near it?
14. _____ will they choose to explain the problem?
15. _____ do you think will have the graduation party?
16. _____ are your friends?
17. _____ shall we invite this time?
18. To _____ have you already mailed cards?
19. By _____ was that moving documentary on nuclear power prepared?
20. _____ can solve this riddle?

Sharpening Your Skills

Compose six sentences showing the correct use of interrogative pronouns. Answer your own questions.

Lesson 5 Relative Pronouns

A relative pronoun is a pronoun that does the work of a conjunction. A relative pronoun joins the subordinate clause to the antecedent in the principal clause.

Examine these two sentences:

Dominic went to the house of his friend *who* was ill.
The bear *that* roamed the countryside was finally caught.

In the first sentence, *who* joins the subordinate clause *who was ill* to the antecedent *friend* in the principal clause. In the second sentence, *that* joins the subordinate clause *that roamed the countryside* to the antecedent *bear* in the principal clause.

The relative pronouns *who, whose,* and *whom* refer to persons; *which* refers to animals and things; *that* refers to persons, places, or things; and *what* refers to things.

Exercise 36

Name the relative pronouns and their antecedents.
1. The Andes Mountains, which run the length of South America, are rugged and beautiful.
2. There is no person here who can solve the math problem.
3. The letter that you wrote to the president may have some effect.
4. Ms. Sysmanski was the lawyer who handled Ronald's case.
5. The rug that I wove has been entered in the art show.
6. He who debates the issue is a fool.
7. Thomas Jefferson, who wrote the Declaration of Independence, also owned slaves.
8. None who do battle want to die in the process.
9. They redesigned the museum that overlooks the river.
10. The Goldbergs, who moved into the house next door, have three cats and two dogs.
11. The storm, which kept us from getting to the store, left twelve inches of snow on the ground.
12. Dublin is located on the Liffey, which is a principal river of Ireland.

13. The river that divides the United States is the Mississippi.
14. People who race in marathons must run many miles in practice.
15. Only those who are prepared finish the race.

Correct Use of Relative Pronouns *Who* and *Whom*

> The relative pronoun *who* is used when the pronoun is the subject of a verb.
>
> The relative pronoun *whom* is used when the pronoun is the object of a verb or of a preposition.

Christina Rossetti is the person *who* wrote that poem.
(*Subject of* wrote)
Louisa is the one *whom* they selected for the play.
(*Object of* selected)

Since the relative pronoun relates to a word (antecedent) in the principal clause, you can discover whether you are using the correct pronoun by

1. writing the sentence as two sentences, substituting the antecedent for the relative pronoun.

> Christina Rossetti is the person. Christina Rossetti wrote that poem.

> Louisa is the one. They selected Louisa for the play.

2. determining whether the antecedent in the second sentence is in the nominative case or the objective case.

> Christina Rossetti is the person. *Christina Rossetti* wrote that poem. (*Nominative case*)

> Louisa is the one. They selected *Louisa* for the play. (*Objective case*)

Exercise 37

Choose the correct pronoun to complete each sentence.
1. The mayor is a woman in (who, whom) I have great confidence.
2. I will send a messenger (who, whom) you can trust.
3. Paul is a nurse (who, whom) will give good service.
4. Lincoln Hopkins, from (who, whom) we bought the car, is an honest person.
5. We have a friend (who, whom) will entertain you.
6. We have a friend (who, whom) you will like.
7. Was it Juanita to (who, whom) you spoke?
8. Thom is the person for (who, whom) you have been waiting.
9. Do you know the person with (who, whom) he is sitting?
10. Are they the cousins (who, whom) are visiting you?
11. We watched the workers (who, whom) were building the bridge.
12. The boy (who, whom) owns that blue convertible is my neighbor.
13. Theresa, (who, whom) has a very clear voice, will introduce the speaker.
14. Sally was the only player (who, whom) scored a point.
15. Someone (who, whom) she respects will have to tell her.

Agreement of Relative Pronouns

> A relative pronoun agrees with its antecedent in person, number, and gender, but its case depends upon its use in the subordinate clause.

Jake Hamlin, to *whom* we gave this award, was very happy.

In this sentence, the relative pronoun is in the third person, singular number, masculine gender to agree with its antecedent, *Jake Hamlin*. It is in the objective case because it is the object of the preposition *to*.

Exercise 38

For each of the following sentences, name the relative pronoun and its antecedent. Give the person, number, gender, and case of each relative pronoun.

1. The skiers who swooped down the snowy hill seemed to enjoy the cold.
2. The workers voted for the person whom they knew best.
3. The jockey who rode the winning horse was very happy.
4. Scott's shirt is made of cotton, which is a soft, natural fabric.
5. Benjamin Disraeli, who served as the English prime minister, was also a writer.
6. The nerves that carry messages to the brain are called sensory nerves.
7. The umpire handed the catcher the ball that was to be used in the game.
8. She did not know the man who had taken the car.
9. The videotape that he made for a class project won first prize.
10. Robin, for whom the present was intended, did not come.

Compound Relative Pronouns

> Compound relative pronouns are pronouns formed by
> adding *ever* or *soever* to *who*, *whom*, *which*, and *what*.

The compound relatives usually contain their own antecedents.

> Give the letter to *whoever* answers the door. (*Subject of* answers)
> He needs *whatever* is on the desk. (*Subject of* is)

REMEMBER: The case of a relative pronoun depends upon its use
in the subordinate clause.

Exercise 39

Give the syntax of the compound relative pronouns in the following
sentences. The subordinate clauses are italicized.
1. The prize goes to *whoever achieves the highest total score.*
2. The campers took *whatever was necessary for the trip.*
3. You may keep *whatever you desire.*
4. We rewarded *whoever was most diligent.*
5. *Whoever wants this map* may have it.
6. Write about *whatever interests you.*
7. *Whoever is easily moved* cries often.
8. Mr. Pisani gives pie to *whoever wants some.*
9. Do *whatever you can for your friend.*
10. Jack spoke to *whomever he met.*

Sharpening Your Skills

Practice expanding each sentence with a relative pronoun and a
subordinate clause in the place indicated (ʌ).
1. The campgroundʌwas open all year round.
2. My friend and I were lucky to have a large camperʌ.
3. My friendʌloved to see as many interesting places as possible.
4. Most of our vacation daysʌwere sunny and warm.
5. On the morning we left, we vowed to take another tripʌ.

Lesson 6 Pronominals

A pronominal is a pronoun that can also be used as an adjective.

In this lesson all pronominals will be used as pronouns. The common pronominals are possessive, interrogative, demonstrative, indefinite, and distributive pronouns.

Demonstrative Pronouns

A demonstrative pronoun is a pronoun that points out a definite person, place, or thing.

The demonstrative pronouns are *this, that, these,* and *those. This* and *these* denote objects that are near. *That* and *those* denote distant objects.

Exercise 40

Choose an appropriate demonstrative pronoun to complete each of the following sentences. Then tell whether the pronoun you have selected refers to things near or to things far.

1. _____ were grown in Israel.
2. _____ is from the South.
3. Do you prefer _____?
4. _____ is not balanced.
5. _____ is the best food you can eat.
6. I have never seen a river as polluted as _____ is.
7. _____ are located on the Fall Line.
8. Is _____ a model of *Apollo 11*?
9. _____ did not end the debate.
10. _____ is the only white tiger in captivity.

Indefinite Pronouns

> **An indefinite pronoun is a pronoun that points out no particular person, place, or thing.**

Many of the Conquistadores suffered hardships.
Some returned to Europe, but *some* remained.

In all, there are about thirty indefinite pronouns. The most commonly used are:

all	anyone	everyone	much	one	somebody
another	anything	everything	nobody	same	someone
any	both	few	none	several	something
anybody	everybody	many	no one	some	such

Exercise 41

Find the indefinite pronouns in the sentences and tell how they are used: subject, direct object, object of preposition.

1. No one saw the comet.
2. Everybody on the team ran his or her best.
3. Anyone who works hard enough can achieve his or her goal.
4. Much of this is news to me.
5. Few of us manage to do everything we want to do.
6. You may have both.
7. Someone saw the gorilla eat the hat.
8. Many of the South American rivers are infested with piranhas.
9. Have they questioned everyone about the accident?
10. Several should be able to complete the project.
11. Before the Industrial Revolution, much of the work was done in the home.
12. The tornado lifted everything in its path.
13. Some work at night.
14. All of the cows rested in the shade of the huge oaks.
15. Is Cheryl waiting for somebody?

Distributive Pronouns

A distributive pronoun is a pronoun that refers to each person, place, or thing separately.

Each of the soldiers reported promptly.

The distributive pronouns are *each, either,* and *neither*.

Exercise 42

Identify the distributive pronouns in the sentences.
1. Each of the burglars revealed the guilt of the others.
2. Hank will be pleased with either.
3. Neither of the countries turned away the refugees.
4. Each was told to take care of his or her own things.
5. Do you prefer either of these clocks?
6. Each expected the other to make the decision.
7. Neither wanted to take the risk.
8. Either of the men could have spoken first.
9. Sheila may be living in either of the provinces.
10. Each of the objects is crafted by hand.

Agreement with Distributive and Indefinite Pronouns

> **Personal pronouns and possessive adjectives must agree with their antecedents in person, number, and gender.**

The distributive pronouns *each, either, neither,* and the indefinite pronouns *one, anyone, no one, anybody, nobody, everyone, everybody, someone, somebody* are always singular. Pronouns and possessive adjectives referring to these pronouns as antecedents must be singular in number.

Group of People in a Woody Place a Long Time Ago **by Carroll Cloar**

Such indefinite pronouns as *all, both, few, many, several,* and *some* are generally plural. Pronouns and possessive adjectives referring to these pronouns as antecedents must be plural.

Each did *her* best.
Both did *their* best.

Exercise 43

Identify the indefinite or distributive pronoun in each sentence. Then select the pronoun or adjective that agrees with the indefinite or distributive pronoun.

1. Everyone in the class agreed to give some of (his or her, their) money to the Save the Whales fund.
2. Each of the students thought that (his or her, their) own social studies project should win first prize.
3. Neither of the runners thought that (she, they) had tripped the other in the race.
4. Everyone must wait (his or her, their) turn to work on the computer.
5. Many of the employees ate (his or her, their) lunch at Ernie's Diner.
6. Everybody who has red hair was asked if (he or she, they) would try the new shampoo.
7. All of the candidates did (his or her, their) best to win.
8. A few of the students complained that (his or her, their) names were misspelled in the yearbook.
9. If everyone does (his or her, their) best, it doesn't matter if we lose the game.
10. Both of the boys forgot to bring (his, their) skates.

Exercise 44

Choose a pronoun or adjective to complete each sentence correctly.

1. If anyone wishes to start the program with a song, _____ may do so now.
2. Both of the scouts spent an hour loading _____ camping equipment into the old blue truck.
3. Each of the newspaper carriers was given a bonus at the end of the year based on _____ service to old customers and sales to new customers.
4. No one could take any of the tiny kittens into _____ home until we had taken them to the veterinarian.
5. Anyone who has finished _____ dinner may help clear the table now.

You Are the Author

Choose one.

1. Imagine that you are a reporter for *The Boston Scoop*. Write a front-page story on "The Devil and Tom Walker." If you wish, interview partners (to act as townspeople) for the article. Be sure to use a variety of pronouns correctly.
2. Think of a value you believe to be unyielding. Write a paragraph that promotes this value. Use at least four or five sentences to support your point of view.

Chapter Challenge

Read this section carefully and then answer orally the questions that follow.

> ¹Each of you, boys and girls, belongs to two important societies: the family and the state. ²"What," you may ask, "is the obligation that is imposed by membership in these societies?" ³The answer is this. ⁴You must give a respectful obedience to those in authority, perform your duties conscientiously, and strive to live in harmony with other persons. ⁵In other words, you must develop in yourself whatever will make you a valued member of each group. ⁶Such is the attitude of every worthwhile person. ⁷It should also be yours.

1. Name a personal pronoun found in the first sentence.
2. In what person is the pronoun *you* in the second sentence?
3. Name the demonstrative pronoun in the third sentence.
4. In the fourth sentence, select a personal pronoun that is used as the subject.
5. Find a compound personal pronoun in the fifth sentence.
6. Is the compound personal pronoun in the fifth sentence used intensively or reflexively?
7. Find an interrogative pronoun in the second sentence.
8. In what case is the interrogative pronoun?
9. Name a personal pronoun in the seventh sentence that is neuter gender.
10. Find a relative pronoun in the second sentence. What is the antecedent of that relative pronoun?
11. What kind of pronoun is the first word in the paragraph?
12. What kind of pronoun does the sixth sentence contain?
13. Name the possessive pronoun in the seventh sentence.

Chapter 3

Adjectives

The Scholarship Jacket
by Marta Salinas

The small Texas school that I attended carried out a tradition every year during the eighth-grade graduation; a beautiful gold and green jacket, the school colors, was awarded to the class **valedictorian,** the student who had maintained the highest grades for eight years. The scholarship jacket had a big gold *S* on the left front side and the winner's name was written in gold letters on the pocket.

My oldest sister Rosie had won the jacket a few years back, and I fully expected to win also. I was fourteen and in the eighth grade. I had been a straight A student since the first grade, and last year I had looked forward to owning that jacket. My father was a farm laborer who couldn't earn enough money to feed eight children, so when I was six I was given to my grandparents to raise. We couldn't participate in sports at school because there were registration fees, uniform costs, and trips out of town; so even though we were quite agile and athletic, there would never be a sports school jacket for us. This one, the scholarship jacket, was our only chance.

In May, close to graduation, spring fever struck, and no one paid any attention in class; instead we stared out the windows and at each other, wanting to speed up the last few weeks of school. I despaired every time I looked in the mirror. Pencil thin, not a curve anywhere, I was called "Beanpole" and "String Bean," and I knew that's what I looked like. A flat chest, no hips, and a brain, that's what I had. That really isn't much for a fourteen-year-old to work with, I thought, as I absentmindedly wandered from my history class to the gym. Another hour of sweating in basketball and displaying my toothpick legs was coming up. Then I remembered my P.E. shorts were still in a bag under my desk where I'd forgotten them. I had to walk all the way back and get them. Coach Thompson was a real bear if anyone wasn't dressed for P.E. She had said

Detail from *Road to Lamy* by Andrew Michael Dasburg

I was a good forward and once she even tried to talk Grandma into letting me join the team. Grandma, of course, said no.

I was almost back at my classroom's door when I heard angry voices and arguing. I stopped. I didn't mean to eavesdrop; I just hesitated, not knowing what to do. I needed those shorts and I was going to be late, but I didn't want to interrupt an argument between my teachers. I recognized the voices: Mr. Schmidt, my history teacher, and Mr. Boone, my math teacher. They seemed to be arguing about me. I couldn't believe it. I still remember the shock that rooted me flat against the wall as if I were trying to blend in with the graffiti written there.

"I refuse to do it! I don't care who her father is, her grades don't even begin to compare to Martha's. I won't lie or **falsify** records. Martha has a straight A plus average, and you know it." That was Mr. Schmidt and he sounded very angry. Mr. Boone's voice sounded calm and quiet.

"Look, Joann's father is not only on the Board, he owns the only store in town; we could say it was a close tie and—"

The pounding in my ears drowned out the rest of the words, only a word here and there filtered through. ". . . Martha is Mexican . . . resign . . . won't do it . . ." Mr. Schmidt came rushing out, and luckily for me went down the opposite way toward the auditorium, so he didn't see me. Shaking, I waited a few minutes and then went in and grabbed my bag and fled from the room. Mr. Boone looked up when I came in but didn't say anything. To this day I don't remember if I got in trouble in P.E. for being late or how I made it through the rest of the afternoon. I went home very sad and cried into my pillow that night so grandmother wouldn't hear me. It seemed a cruel coincidence that I had overheard that conversation.

The next day when the principal called me into his office, I knew what it would be about. He looked uncomfortable and unhappy. I decided I wasn't going to make it any easier for him so I looked him straight in the eye. He looked away and fidgeted with the papers on his desk.

"Martha," he said, "there's been a change in policy this year regarding the scholarship jacket. As you know, it has always been free." He cleared his throat and continued. "This year the Board decided to charge fifteen dollars—which still won't cover the complete cost of the jacket."

I stared at him in shock and a small sound of dismay escaped my throat. I hadn't expected this. He still avoided looking in my eyes.

"So if you are unable to pay the fifteen dollars for the jacket, it will be given to the next one in line."

Standing with all the dignity I could muster, I said, "I'll speak to my grandfather about it, sir, and let you know tomorrow." I cried on the walk home from the bus stop. The dirt road was a quarter of a mile from the highway, so by the time I got home, my eyes were red and puffy.

"Where's Grandpa?" I asked Grandma, looking down at the floor so she wouldn't ask me why I'd been crying. She was sewing on a quilt and didn't look up.

"I think he's out working in the bean field."

I went outside and looked out at the fields. There he was. I could see him walking between the rows, his body bent over the little plants, hoe in hand. I walked slowly out to him, trying to think how

Landscape, New Mexico, 1923, by Marsden Hartley

I could best ask him for the money. There was a cool breeze blowing and a sweet smell of **mesquite** in the air, but I didn't appreciate it. I kicked at a dirt clod. I wanted that jacket so much. It was more than just being a valedictorian and giving a little thank-you speech for the jacket on graduation night. It represented eight years of hard work and expectation. I knew I had to be honest with Grandpa; it was my only chance. He saw me and looked up.

He waited for me to speak. I cleared my throat nervously and clasped my hands behind my back so he wouldn't see them shaking. "Grandpa, I have a big favor to ask you," I said in Spanish, the only language he knew. He still waited silently. I tried again. "Grandpa, this year the principal said the scholarship jacket is not going to be free. It's going to cost fifteen dollars, and I have to take the money in tomorrow, otherwise it'll be given to someone else." The last words came out in an eager rush. Grandpa straightened up tiredly and leaned his chin on the hoe handle. He looked out over the field that was filled with the tiny green bean plants. I waited, desperately hoping he'd say I could have the money.

He turned to me and asked quietly, "What does a scholarship jacket mean?"

I answered quickly; maybe there was a chance. "It means you've earned it by having the highest grades for eight years and that's why they're giving it to you." Too late I realized the significance of my words. Grandpa knew that I understood it was not a matter of money. It wasn't that. He went back to hoeing the weeds that sprang up between the delicate little bean plants. It was a time-consuming job; sometimes the small shoots were right next to each other. Finally he spoke again.

"Then if you pay for it, Marta, it's not a scholarship jacket, is it? Tell your principal I will not pay the fifteen dollars."

I walked back to the house and locked myself in the bathroom for a long time. I was angry with grandfather even though I knew he was right, and I was angry with the Board, whoever they were. Why did they have to change the rules just when it was my turn to win the jacket?

It was a very sad and withdrawn girl who dragged into the principal's office the next day. This time he did look me in the eyes.

"What did your grandfather say?"

I sat very straight in my chair.

"He said to tell you he won't pay the fifteen dollars."

The principal muttered something I couldn't understand under his breath, and walked over to the window. He stood looking out at something outside. He looked bigger than usual when he stood

up; he was a tall, gaunt man with gray hair, and I watched the back of his head while I waited for him to speak.

"Why?" he finally asked. "Your grandfather has the money. Doesn't he own a small bean farm?"

I looked at him, forcing my eyes to stay dry. "He said if I had to pay for it, then it wouldn't be a scholarship jacket," I said and stood up to leave. "I guess you'll just have to give it to Joann." I hadn't meant to say that; it had just slipped out. I was almost to the door when he stopped me.

"Martha—wait."

I turned and looked at him, waiting. What did he want now? I could feel my heart pounding. Something bitter and vile tasting was coming up in my mouth; I was afraid I was going to be sick. I didn't need any sympathy speeches. He sighed loudly and went back to his big desk. He looked at me, biting his lip, as if thinking.

"Okay, damn it. We'll make an exception in your case. I'll tell the Board, you'll get your jacket."

I could hardly believe it. I spoke in a trembling rush. "Oh, thank you sir!" Suddenly I felt great. I didn't know about **adrenaline** in those days, but I knew something was pumping through me, making me feel as tall as the sky. I wanted to yell, jump, run the mile, do something. I ran out so I could cry in the hall where there was no one to see me. At the end of the day, Mr. Schmidt winked at me and said, "I hear you're getting a scholarship jacket this year."

His face looked as happy and innocent as a baby's, but I knew better. Without answering I gave him a quick hug and ran to the bus. I cried on the walk home again, but this time because I was so happy. I couldn't wait to tell Grandpa and ran straight to the field. I joined him in the row where he was working and without saying anything I crouched down and started pulling up the weeds with my hands. Grandpa worked alongside me for a few minutes, but he didn't ask what had happened. After I had a little pile of weeds between the rows, I stood up and faced him.

"The principal said he's making an exception for me, Grandpa, and I'm getting the jacket after all. That's after I told him what you said."

Grandpa didn't say anything; he just gave me a pat on the shoulder and a smile. He pulled out the crumpled red handkerchief that he always carried in his back pocket and wiped the sweat off his forehead.

"Better go see if your grandmother needs any help with supper."

I gave him a big grin. He didn't fool me. I skipped and ran back to the house whistling some silly tune.

The Writer's Craft

1. What is the injustice described in this story? How does the author lead you to expect it?
2. What does Martha's grandfather mean when he says, "Then if you pay for it, Marta, it's not a scholarship jacket, is it?" Discuss.
3. Do you think the author made a good choice when she wrote "The Scholarship Jacket" as a short story rather than in a longer form? Why or why not?
4. Why do you think the author uses such different adjectives to describe Martha's principal on two occasions in the selection?
5. Mr. Schmidt and Mr. Boone disagree over who should be awarded the scholarship jacket. How do their opinions differ? Use an adjective to describe each teacher's character.

Road to Lamy by Andrew Michael Dasburg

Recalling What You Know

1. You will recall that adjectives can modify nouns and pronouns in different ways. What are the main kinds of adjectives?
2. Locate the descriptive adjectives in the first paragraph.
3. Find the numeral adjectives used in the second paragraph and state the word that each one modifies.
4. List the indefinite adjectives in the third paragraph.
5. Name the demonstrative adjectives in the fourth paragraph.

Lesson 1   Descriptive Adjectives

An adjective is a word that describes or limits a noun or a pronoun.

Adjectives may be divided into two general classes, *descriptive adjectives* and *limiting adjectives*. Limiting adjectives will be studied in lesson 2.

> **A descriptive adjective is an adjective that describes a noun or a pronoun.**

He pulled out the *crumpled red* handkerchief.

There are two types of descriptive adjectives, *proper adjectives* and *common adjectives*.

> **A proper adjective is an adjective that is formed from a proper noun.**
>
> **A common adjective is an adjective that expresses the ordinary qualities of a noun or a pronoun.**

Marta Salinas is a writer of *Chicano* stories. (*Proper adjective*)
The author was an *intelligent* girl. (*Common adjective*)

NOTE: Many participles may be used as descriptive adjectives.
   A *despairing* young girl looked at herself in the mirror.
   (*Despairing* comes from the verb *to despair*.)
   A sad, *withdrawn* girl went to the principal's office.
   (*Withdrawn* comes from the verb *to withdraw*.)

Exercise 45

Find all of the descriptive adjectives. Tell whether they are common or proper.

1. Marta Salinas wrote about Mexican agricultural workers.
2. She gave her stories American settings.
3. The tales are about poor children, but they touch others too.
4. Rodolfo Gonzales, the son of a migrant worker, is active in the Mexican-American civil-rights movement.
5. Author Ernesto Galarza was born in western Mexico.
6. Did you know that his *Barrio Boy* is the true account of his family's migration to sunny California?
7. A *barrio* is the Spanish-speaking district in a town.
8. The inhabitants definitely consider it their exclusive territory!
9. Americo Parades has edited interesting anthologies of writings.
10. They contain Mexican folklore and ancient legends.

Exercise 46

Complete each of the following sentences with adjectives. Remember to use both common and proper adjectives.

1. The _____ guard has _____ eyes.
2. In the _____ museum, we saw paintings of _____ artists.
3. Remember that _____ objects break easily.
4. Dan's _____ bicycle has _____ handlebars.
5. _____ citizens vote in _____ elections.
6. Many nations import _____ oil.
7. The _____ mountains tower above the _____ ravine.
8. People from _____ climates have trouble adjusting to weather.
9. Ms. Keller, the _____ coach, gave us some _____ cake.
10. Sometimes _____ diplomats work in _____ places.

Position of Descriptive Adjectives

The usual position of a descriptive adjective is before a noun, but sometimes it comes after the noun.

> Eric has *bright blue* eyes.
> The colors, *sharp* and *vivid*, helped make the picture come alive.

A descriptive adjective used as a subjective complement follows and completes a linking verb.

> The room is *large* and *comfortable*. (This is a *large* and *comfortable* room.)

A descriptive adjective that follows the direct object and at the same time completes the thought expressed by a transitive verb is called an objective complement.

> The announcement made him *angry*.

Exercise 47

Identify the adjectives and tell how each is used.
1. Sam keeps his motorcycle clean.
2. The gray cat is blind.
3. Philadelphia pretzels are famous around the world.
4. The new car, small and sporty, drives like a dream.
5. Jane appears indifferent.
6. Workers paved the road smooth.
7. The pizza, hot and bubbly, arrived exactly at noon.
8. The baby's high fever caused alarm.
9. Steven looks ill.
10. She painted the house red.

Words Used as Nouns and Adjectives

The use of a word in the sentence determines the part of speech. Very frequently the same word may be used both as a noun and as an adjective.

A noun is a name word; an adjective describes or limits a noun.

> The *iron* is very hot. (*Noun*)
> An *iron* pot hung over the fireplace. (*Adjective*)

Exercise 48

Identify each word in italics as a noun or an adjective.

1. The white *brick* became the cornerstone of the building.
2. The *brick* wall cracked this morning.
3. The *inside* door to their building opened with a triangular key.
4. Let me see the *inside*.
5. Leroy has a new hat with a *feather* in it.
6. Grandmother has *feather* pillows on her bed.
7. Draw a *square* figure at the top of the page.
8. The town *square* was full of people.
9. The *past* cannot be relived.
10. During the *past* hour, the telephone has rung seven times.

Sharpening Your Skills

Write a paragraph about the picture on the opposite page. Use different kinds of descriptive adjectives, and use them in various positions in the sentences.

Fire Down on the Labrador
by David Blackwood

Lesson 2 Limiting Adjectives

> **A limiting adjective is an adjective that either points out an object or denotes number.**

The limiting adjectives may be subdivided into the following three classes: (1) articles, (2) numeral adjectives, and (3) pronominal adjectives.

> **The articles *the*, *an*, and *a* show whether the noun is used definitely or indefinitely.**

The parade was very colorful. (*Definite:* a *specific* parade)
An artist must use his imagination. (*Indefinite:* *any* artist)

> **A numeral adjective is an adjective that denotes exact number.**

Mat paid *fifty* cents for his *second* ride.

> **A pronominal adjective is an adjective that may also be used as a pronoun.**

Pronominal adjectives are usually divided into the following five classes:

> A **demonstrative adjective** is an adjective that points out a definite person, place, or thing (*this, that, these, those*).
>
> A **possessive adjective** is an adjective that denotes ownership (*my, our, your, his, her, its, their*).
>
> A **distributive adjective** is an adjective that refers to each person, place, or thing separately (*each, every, either, neither*).
>
> An **indefinite adjective** is an adjective that points out no particular person, place, or thing (*any, all, another, both, few, many, much, several, some, such*, and so forth).
>
> An **interrogative adjective** is an adjective that is used in asking a question (*which, what*).

Exercise 49

Find the limiting adjectives in the following sentences. Identify each as an article, a numeral adjective, or a pronominal adjective.

1. Several airplanes flew over the stadium.
2. Do you know the names of the ten animals?
3. Many actors will appear in the play.
4. His boomerang was lost.
5. Which debater gave the longest speech?
6. The United States has five important forest belts.
7. That bag is filled with her candy.
8. A man took Pat's twenty dollars and gave it to two other people.
9. The sailors saved many lives.
10. Each member of the board cast one vote.
11. The truck hit my car.
12. The diameter of that soft rock is twelve centimeters.

Exercise 50

Select the pronominal adjectives and tell to which class each belongs.
1. Some clowns arrived early.
2. We had never seen such outfits before.
3. Each clown had brought an extra arm.
4. The clowns shook hands with a few people in the audience.
5. Several people were shocked when they found themselves holding rubber arms.
6. Those people were fooled.
7. There was much laughter as many clowns tumbled out of a tiny car.
8. Which person in my family laughed the hardest?
9. Even my grandparents enjoyed the antics of those clowns.
10. We had such fun we wanted to see every performance.

Exercise 51

Complete each sentence with an appropriate pronominal adjective.
1. _____ member of the panel gave a short talk on _____ part of the topic.
2. _____ work requires great strength.
3. _____ tree is an elm.
4. _____ politicians talk too much.
5. _____ worker has _____ job to do.
6. Mike wants _____ day to be more fun than the one before.
7. Our vacation was terrible because of _____ rudeness.
8. _____ state has two senators in Congress.
9. You may have _____ chance.
10. _____ statue was given to _____ country by France.

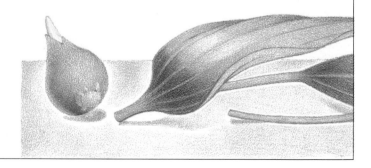

Correct Use of the Demonstrative Adjectives *This* and *That*

> **The demonstrative adjectives *this* and *that* agree in number with the nouns they modify.**

This book   *These* books
That kind of shoe   *Those* kinds of shoes

This and *these* denote objects that are near. *That* and *those* denote more distant objects.

Exercise 52

Choose the correct form of the indicated type of demonstrative adjective.

1. ____ coffee tastes like seaweed. (*near*)
2. My mother has one of ____ pink toasters. (*distant*)
3. ____ computer has enough memory to run any program on the market. (*distant*)
4. ____ hybrid tulip must have come from Holland. (*near*)
5. Why does she refuse to watch ____ kind of television show? (*distant*)
6. ____ shoes may not last until the end of the day. (*distant*)
7. What did ____ men say to you? (*distant*)
8. She has many agates of ____ color in her rock collection. (*distant*)
9. ____ printer uses too many ribbons. (*near*)
10. Leonard finally decided to raise ____ salaries. (*distant*)

The Repetition of the Article

The repetition of the article changes the meaning of a sentence.

> I know *the* director and *the* producer.

Here the article is placed before both nouns to show that they refer to two separate persons.

> I know *the* director and producer.

In this sentence the article is placed *only* before the first noun to show that both positions (director and producer) are held by one individual.

Exercise 53

Determine whether the article in parentheses is needed. Give a reason for your choice.

1. We had a plum and (a) peach for our lunch.
2. The Danube and (the) Rhine are major German rivers.
3. The co-captain and (the) center is wearing number 51.
4. A blue and (a) yellow pencil are in the case.
5. The French bakery and (the) café has moved to a new location.
6. The president and (the) manager have gone to Madrid.
7. The secretary and (the) treasurer has written the report about the angry citizens who came to the meeting.
8. The captain and (the) pilot were asking the ground crew for help.
9. The ranchers and (the) farmers made a treaty.
10. A canoe and (a) rowboat were still on the lake when the storm hit.

Lesson 3 Comparison of Adjectives

Comparison is the change that adjectives undergo to express different degrees of quality, quantity, or value.

Most adjectives have three degrees of comparison: positive, comparative, and superlative.

> This is a *large* apple. (*Positive degree*)
> This is a *larger* apple than yours. (*Comparative degree*)
> This is the *largest* apple in the basket. (*Superlative degree*)

The positive degree denotes quality.

The comparative degree denotes quality in a greater or a lesser degree.

The superlative degree denotes quality in the greatest or the least degree.

Methods of Comparison

1. Most adjectives of one syllable and some adjectives of two syllables (generally those ending in *ow, y,* and *e*) form the comparative degree by adding *er* to the positive, and the superlative degree by adding *est* to the positive.

POSITIVE	COMPARATIVE	SUPERLATIVE
noble	nobl*er*	nobl*est*
merr*y*	merri*er*	merri*est*
narr*ow*	narrow*er*	narrow*est*

2. Adjectives of three or more syllables, and some of two syllables, form the comparative and the superlative degrees by prefixing *more* and *most* or *less* and *least* to the positive form of the adjective.

POSITIVE	COMPARATIVE	SUPERLATIVE
industrious	*more* industrious	*most* industrious
thoughtful	*less* thoughtful	*least* thoughtful

3. Certain adjectives are compared irregularly. Those used frequently are:

POSITIVE	COMPARATIVE	SUPERLATIVE
little	less	least
bad, ill, evil	worse	worst
good	better	best
many, much	more	most
late	later, latter	latest, last
far	farther	farthest
old	older, elder	oldest, eldest
near	nearer	nearest, next
_____	*further	furthest
_____	*inner	innermost, inmost
_____	*outer	outermost, outmost
_____	*upper	uppermost, upmost

*These adjectives have no positive degree.

4. Some adjectives cannot be compared, such as *dead, perpendicular, eternal, supreme,* and so forth.

Exercise 54

Identify the adjectives and give the degree of comparison.
1. Chicago gets more snow than Los Angeles does.
2. Nadine had a small radio clipped to her belt.
3. The population of Moscow is greater than that of New York.
4. Oliver wore his newest shirt.
5. Isabel is taller than her sister.
6. Derek thought they were his worst enemies.
7. Georg Solti is one of the greatest living orchestra conductors.
8. The red wallet contains more money.
9. Loraine left a few apricot cookies in the box.
10. Much iron is mined in Scandinavia.

Correct Use of Comparative and Superlative Degrees

The comparative degree of the adjective is used when two are compared. The superlative degree is used when more than two are compared.

Which river is *longer*, the Ohio or the Mississippi? (*Comparative*)
The Mississippi is the *longest* river in North America. (*Superlative*)

Mississippi River barge

Exercise 55

Select the correct degree of the adjective to complete each sentence.

1. Which is (more useful, most useful), copper or silver?
2. The Pacific is the (larger, largest) ocean.
3. Ralph knew a (safer, safest) way home than Paula.
4. Which of the two buildings is (more modern, most modern)?
5. Ginny is (faster, fastest) than Greg.
6. Which are the (more precious, most precious) gems, diamonds, or rubies?
7. Was the hare or the tortoise the (faster, fastest)?
8. Of the two, the hare was the (better, best) runner.
9. Who did the (better, best) work, Joe, Maureen, or Kenny?
10. They rented the (newer, newest) model of VCR.

Correct Use of *Fewer* and *Less*

> Use *fewer* when number is indicated. Use *less* when quantity is indicated.

There are *fewer* players than spectators.
We have had *less* snow this winter than last winter.

Exercise 56

Choose the correct word, *fewer* or *less*, to complete each sentence.
1. _____ people go camping in the winter than in the summer.
2. This farmer has _____ cherry trees and _____ corn than that one.
3. This test allows _____ time and has _____ questions than the one you took last week.
4. Carol had _____ books in the bookcase than on her bedroom floor.
5. _____ students chose to attend the senior prom this year than last.
6. Roberto found _____ worms in the garden today than yesterday.
7. _____ guests than expected came to the wedding.
8. Greater diligence results in _____ mistakes.
9. Midge had _____ opportunity to practice than she needed.
10. As many jobs become automated, _____ workers are needed.
11. Idaho has _____ large cities than Ohio.
12. Horses have _____ offspring than dogs.
13. _____ people eat rice every day in the United States than in most Asian countries.
14. The shortstop made _____ errors today than she did yesterday.
15. Cindy spends _____ time cooking than Bob.

You Are the Author

Choose one.
1. Choose a person who has been a major influence in your life—a parent or other relative, a teacher, a coach, or a friend. Tell how he or she has contributed to your understanding of your own character. In your description use as many different kinds of adjectives as you can.
2. Write a paragraph in which you discuss why you agree or disagree with the decision made by Martha's grandfather *or* the decision made by the principal.

Chapter Challenge

Read the paragraph very carefully and then answer the questions that follow it.

¹Have you ever considered what would happen to us if our American bird life became extinct? ²To appreciate the dire consequences of such a misfortune, we must consider the many ways in which birds help us. ³The destruction of harmful insects is perhaps their most important work. ⁴This constant war on one natural enemy of humankind makes the farmers' task easier. ⁵The seed diet of some birds helps to keep the weed crop under control, while many of the larger birds prevent mice and rats from becoming intolerable pests. ⁶What good reasons we have for valuing these small creatures! ⁷They are among our greatest benefactors.

1. What kind of adjective is *our* in the first sentence?
2. Find a proper adjective in the first sentence.
3. How is the adjective *extinct* in the first sentence used?
4. What is the comparative form of the adjective *extinct?*
5. Name the definite and indefinite articles in the second sentence.
6. What kind of a pronominal adjective is *their* in the third sentence?
7. Give the comparative form of *harmful* found in the third sentence.
8. Give the positive and the comparative forms of *most important* found in the third sentence.
9. Select a numeral adjective in the fourth sentence.
10. What is the syntax of *easier* in the fourth sentence.
11. Find a singular and a plural demonstrative adjective in the fourth and sixth sentences.
12. Name an indefinite adjective in the fifth sentence.
13. Name the adjective that modifies the subject of the fifth sentence. Can this word be used as any other part of speech?
14. Give the positive and superlative forms of *larger* found in the fifth sentence.
15. In the sixth and the seventh sentences, name the adjectives in the positive degree and the superlative degree.

Chapter 4

Verbs

The Tiger, the Brahman, and the Jackal

as retold by Flora Annie Steel

from *Tales of the Punjab*

Once upon a time a tiger was caught in a trap. He tried in vain to get out through the bars, and rolled and bit with rage and grief when he failed.

By chance a poor **Brahman** came by. "Let me out of this cage, O pious one!" cried the tiger.

"Nay, my friend," replied the Brahman mildly, "you would probably eat me if I did."

"Not at all!" swore the tiger with many oaths; "on the contrary, I should be for ever grateful, and serve you as a slave!"

Now when the tiger sobbed and sighed and wept and swore, the pious Brahman's heart softened, and at last he consented to open the door of the cage. Out popped the tiger, and, seizing the poor man, cried, "What a fool you are! What is to prevent my eating you now, for after being cooped up so long I am just terribly hungry!"

In vain the Brahman pleaded for his life; the most he could gain was a promise to abide by the decision of the first three things he chose to question as to the justice of the tiger's action.

So the Brahman first asked a **pipal** tree what it thought of the matter, but the pipal tree replied coldly, "What have you to complain about? Don't I give shade and shelter to every one who passes by, and don't they in return tear down my branches to feed their cattle? Don't whimper—be a man!"

Then the Brahman, sad at heart, went farther afield till he saw a buffalo turning a well wheel, but he fared no better from it, for it answered, "You are a fool to expect gratitude! Look at me! While I gave milk they fed me on cotton-seed and oil-cake, but now I am dry they yoke me here, and give me refuse as fodder!"

Sedona by Beth Van Hoesen

The Brahman, still more sad, asked the road to give him its opinion.

"My dear sir," said the road, "how foolish you are to expect anything else! Here am I, useful to everybody, yet all, rich and poor, great and small, trample on me as they go past, giving me nothing but the ashes of their pipes and the husks of their grain!"

On this the Brahman turned back sorrowfully, and on the way he met a jackal, who called out, "Why, what's the matter, Mr. Brahman? You look as miserable as a fish out of water!"

Then the Brahman told him all that had occurred. "How very confusing!" said the jackal, when the recital was ended. "Would you mind telling me over again, for everything seems so mixed up?"

The Brahman told it all over again, but the jackal shook his head in a distracted sort of way, and still could not understand.

"It's very odd," said he sadly, "but it all seems to go in at one ear and out at the other! I will go to the place where it all happened and then perhaps I shall be able to give a judgment."

So they returned to the cage, by which the tiger was waiting for the Brahman, and sharpening his teeth and claws.

"You've been away a long time!" growled the savage beast, "but now let us begin our dinner."

"*Our* dinner!" thought the wretched Brahman, as his knees knocked together with fright. "What a remarkably delicate way of putting it!"

"Give me first minutes, my lord," he pleaded, "in order that I may explain matters to the jackal here, who is somewhat slow in his wits."

The tiger consented, and the Brahman began the whole story over again, not missing a single detail, and spinning as long a yarn as possible.

"Oh, my poor brain! Oh, my poor brain!" cried the jackal, wringing his paws. "Let me see! How did it all begin? You were in the cage, and the tiger came walking by—"

"Pooh!" interrupted the tiger. "What a fool you are! I was in the cage."

"Of course!" cried the jackal, pretending to tremble with fright. "Yes! I was in the cage—no, I wasn't. Dear, dear! Where are my wits? Let me see—the tiger was in the Brahman, and cage came walking by. No, that's not it either! Well, don't mind me, but begin your dinner, for I shall never understand!"

"Yes, you shall!" returned the tiger, in a rage at the jackal's stupidity. "I'll *make* you understand! Look here—I am the tiger—"

"Yes, my lord!"

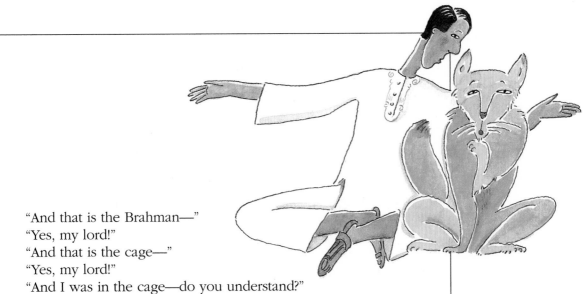

"And that is the Brahman—"

"Yes, my lord!"

"And that is the cage—"

"Yes, my lord!"

"And I was in the cage—do you understand?"

"Yes—no. Please, my lord—"

"Well?" cried the tiger, impatiently.

"Please, my lord! How did you get in?"

"How! Why, in the usual way, of course!"

"Oh dear me! My head is beginning to whirl again! Please don't be angry, my lord, but what is the usual way?"

At this the tiger lost patience, and jumping into the cage, cried, "This way! Now do you understand how it was?"

"Perfectly!" grinned the jackal, as he **dexterously** shut the door. "And if you will permit me to say so, I think matters will remain as they were!"

Illustrations by Mary Jones

The Writer's Craft

1. Even though this story is not realistic fiction, its characters exhibit true-to-life human traits. Do they remind you of people you know? Choose one character from the fable and describe the type of person it resembles.
2. Some fables have a moral, or saying, at the end that illustrates a main point of the story. (For example, the moral of Aesop's famous fable about the tortoise crossing the finish line before the hare is "Slow and steady wins the race.") Write a moral for this tale.
3. In describing the tiger's frantic efforts to free himself, the author uses attention-grabbing verbs. Find another action in the story that is described effectively with verbs.
4. Flora Annie Steel's choice of action verbs helps us visualize the story. Find three sentences that you especially like and change the verbs to convey a different meaning.

Recalling What You Know

1. A verb's principal parts are the present, past, and past participle. What parts of the verbs are underlined? *The tiger <u>was</u> cruel after the Brahman had <u>released</u> him.*
2. Irregular verbs do not form the past or past participle by adding *d* or *ed*. Give the past participles of *run, swim, sink.*
3. What other linking verbs could be substituted for *is* in this sentence? *The kind-hearted Brahman is sad.*

Lesson 1 Regular and Irregular Verbs

A verb is a word used to express action, being, or state of being.

    The Brahman *opens* the cage. *(Action)*
    The jackal *is* a clever animal. *(Being)*
    The tiger *stays* in the cage. *(State of being)*
Without a verb there can be no sentence.

The principal parts of the verb are the present, the past, and the past participle, because all other forms of the verb are determined from these.

A regular verb forms its past and its past participle by adding *d* or *ed* to the present form.

An irregular verb does not form its past and its past participle by adding *d* or *ed* to the present form.

	PRESENT	PAST	PAST PARTICIPLE
REGULAR VERBS:	walk	walked	walked
	love	loved	loved
IRREGULAR VERB:	rise	rose	risen

Review the principal parts of the following irregular verbs:

PRESENT	PAST	PAST PARTICIPLE
am (is, be)	was	been
awake	awoke, awaked	awaked
beat	beat	beat, beaten
begin	began	begun
bend	bent	bent
bet	bet	bet
bind	bound	bound
bite	bit	bitten
blow	blew	blown
break	broke	broken
bring	brought	brought
build	built, builded	built, builded
burn	burned, burnt	burned, burnt
burst	burst	burst
catch	caught	caught
choose	chose	chosen
come	came	come
creep	crept	crept
do	did	done
draw	drew	drawn
dream	dreamed, dreamt	dreamed, dreamt
drink	drank	drunk
drive	drove	driven
dwell	dwelt, dwelled	dwelt, dwelled
eat	ate	eaten
fall	fell	fallen
find	found	found
flee	fled	fled
fly	flew	flown
forget	forgot	forgotten
freeze	froze	frozen
give	gave	given
go	went	gone
grow	grew	grown
hang	hung	hung
have	had	had
hide	hid	hidden, hid
hold	held	held
hurt	hurt	hurt
keep	kept	kept

PRESENT	PAST	PAST PARTICIPLE
kneel	knelt, kneeled	knelt, kneeled
knit	knit, knitted	knit, knitted
know	knew	known
lay	laid	laid
lead	led	led
leave	left	left
lend	lent	lent
let	let	let
lie (recline)	lay	lain
light	lighted, lit	lighted, lit
lose	lost	lost
make	made	made
mean	meant	meant
meet	met	met
read	read	read
ride	rode	ridden
ring	rang	rung
rise	rose	risen
run	ran	run
say	said	said
see	saw	seen
seek	sought	sought
set	set	set
shake	shook	shaken
show	showed	shown, showed
sing	sang	sung
sink	sank	sunk
sit	sat	sat
sleep	slept	slept
slide	slid	slid, slidden
smell	smelled, smelt	smelled, smelt
sow	sowed	sown, sowed
speak	spoke	spoken
spend	spent	spent
spill	spilled, spilt	spilled, spilt
stand	stood	stood
steal	stole	stolen
stick	stuck	stuck
sting	stung	stung
stride	strode	stridden
swim	swam	swum

PRESENT	PAST	PAST PARTICIPLE
swing	swung	swung
teach	taught	taught
tear	tore	torn
throw	threw	thrown
wake	waked, woke	waked, woken
wear	wore	worn
weave	wove	woven
win	won	won
wind	wound	wound
wring	wrung	wrung
write	wrote	written

Exercise 57

Copy these sentences and fill in the blanks with the past tense or the past participle of the irregular verbs at the left.

can
1. In fables people often _____ see themselves and their shortcomings.

hide
2. The lesson in some fables is _____ .

read
3. Have you _____ any fables of Aesop?

take
4. This tale was _____ from *Tales of the Punjab*.

come
5. Many of the Indian folktales have _____ to us from the *Panchatantra*.

know
6. The *Panchatantra* is _____ as a collection of old Indian fables.

write
7. The *Panchatantra* was _____ in Sanskrit.

find
8. Some Indian fables are _____ in Greek literature.

be
9. La Fontaine _____ a French poet who wrote his fables in poetry.

dream
10. La Fontaine _____ many dreams as a youth that greatly influenced him later.

Troublesome Verbs

The verbs *lie* and *lay*, *sit* and *set*, *rise* and *raise*, *let* and *leave*, *borrow* and *lend*, *learn* and *teach*, *bring* and *take* are sometimes confused. Give special attention to these verbs when they are used in sentences.

Lie, lay, lain

This verb means to *rest* or *recline*. It is always intransitive.

> I like to *lie* on the beach.

Lay, laid, laid

The meaning of this verb is to *put* or *place* in position. It is always transitive.

> The company will *lay* our wall-to-wall carpeting today.

Sit, sat, sat

This verb means to *have* or *keep* a seat. It is always intransitive.

> Janie always *sits* in that big, overstuffed chair.

Set, set, set

The meaning of this verb is to *place* or *fix* in position. It is always transitive.

> *Set* the plant by a window that faces south.

Rise, rose, risen

This verb means to *ascend*. It is always intransitive.

> Smoke *rose* lazily from the chimney.

Raise, raised, raised

This verb means to *lift*. It is always transitive.

> *Raise* the window to let in some fresh air.

Let, let, let

This verb means to *permit* or *allow*.

> Please *let* me go to the movies tonight.

Leave, left, left

This verb means to *abandon* or *depart from*.

> I *left* my glasses at school.

Borrow, borrowed, borrowed

This verb means to *obtain* something from another person with the intention of returning it. It is often followed by *from*.

> Dale hasn't paid back the money he *borrowed from* me.

Lend, lent, lent

This verb means to *let* another person *have* or *use* something for a time.

> I think Dale *lent* the money to his sister.

Learn, learned, learned

This verb means to *receive* instruction or to *acquire* knowledge.

> Do you want to *learn* how to knit?

> ### Teach, taught, taught

This verb means to *give* instruction or to *impart* knowledge.

> My mother *taught* me how to knit.

> ### Bring, brought, brought

This verb means to *come* with some person or thing from another place. The verb denotes motion toward the speaker.

> Annie *brought* her dog to my house.

> ### Take, took, taken

This verb means to *go* with a person or something to another place. The verb denotes motion away from the speaker.

> Tom, *take* your little brother with you.

Exercise 58

Choose the correct verb form.
1. The clerk (lay, laid) the package on the counter.
2. The golf ball (lay, laid) just a foot from the hole.
3. The customer had been (sitting, setting) patiently.
4. The burglar (brought, took) our color TV.
5. My father (let, left) my sister drive the car.
6. She (rose, raised) her head and watched him go.
7. After a few minutes, she (rose, raised) slowly.
8. She asked a friend to (borrow, lend) her some money to take the bus home.
9. Please (let, leave) Mary go with you.
10. Did she (rise, raise) when addressed?
11. Vegetables are (risen, raised) on truck farms.
12. The baby has (lain, laid) there gurgling for hours.
13. We shall (let, leave) him know our answer soon.
14. (Let, Leave) Bill do the work in his own way.
15. The dog has (lain, laid) under the tree all day.

16. Mark (sit, set) the table for breakfast.
17. Mary (sat, set) at the table for breakfast.
18. Gay said she would (let, leave) the order at the door.
19. The carpet has been (lain, laid) on the stairs.
20. Do not (let, leave) the child alone in the yard.
21. Workers have (lain, laid) concrete for the foundation.
22. Carol (learned, taught) Gene how to read.
23. My ring (lay, laid) hidden in the grass.
24. Sue doesn't (let, leave) the cat go outside.
25. The cat (lay, laid) on the pink blanket in the sun.

Exercise 59

Insert an appropriate troublesome verb to complete each sentence.

1. _____ me show you the penguins.
2. The books _____ on the library tables where we left them.
3. Neil's doctor would not _____ him swim.
4. Our class _____ many poems.
5. Dianna _____ me how to swim.
6. Banks _____ money to people.
7. The waiter _____ me a clean glass.
8. Ricardo _____ me his bicycle for an hour.
9. If you come, be sure to _____ your record albums.
10. _____ this file to the mayor's office.

Sharpening Your Skills

Write a short paragraph about a special event you have attended. Use the irregular verbs in the list on pages 324–326. Underline the verbs and then label them as auxiliary or main verbs.

Lesson 2 Transitive, Intransitive, and Linking Verbs

Transitive Verbs

> A transitive verb expresses an action that passes from a
> doer to a receiver.

DOER	ACTION	RECEIVER
Joel	opened	the door.

Opened is a transitive verb because the action passes from the doer,
Joel, to the receiver, the *door.*

To determine the receiver of the action, ask the question *whom* or
what after the verb. Joel opened what? The answer to this question
determines the receiver of the action.

The action may pass from the doer to the receiver in two
different ways:

> The team *enjoyed* the trip.
> The trip *was enjoyed* by the team.

Team is the doer of the action in both sentences, and *trip* is the
receiver. Since the action passes from the doer to the receiver
in each case, the verb *enjoyed*, whether in the form of *enjoyed*
or *was enjoyed*, is a transitive verb.

The doer is not always expressed when a transitive verb is used in
the passive voice.

> News *is broadcast* by many commentators. (*Doer expressed*)
> News *is broadcast* every hour. (*Doer not expressed*)

Intransitive Verbs

An intransitive verb has no receiver of its action.

DOER	ACTION	(NO RECEIVER)
The general	hastened away.	_____

The action of the verb *hastened* begins and ends with the doer, or the subject of the verb. The question *whom* or *what* after the verb will receive no answer because there is no receiver.

Intransitive verbs are always in the active voice since a verb is in the active voice when its subject is the doer of the action.

Some verbs may be transitive or intransitive according to their use in the sentence.

> Experience *develops* character. (*Transitive verb*)
> Manufacturing *developed* rapidly in England. (*Intransitive verb*)
> The sun *melted* the ice. (*Transitive verb*)
> The ice *melted* slowly. (*Intransitive verb*)

Cognate Verbs

A cognate verb is a verb whose object repeats the meaning implied by the verb itself.

> Walter *dreamed* a pleasant *dream*.

A cognate verb is usually an intransitive verb that becomes transitive by taking an object derived from the verb itself.

Exercise 60

Name the verbs and tell whether they are transitive, intransitive, or cognate. For each transitive verb, name the receiver of the action and tell whether it is the subject or the object of the verb.

1. Joseph Lister introduced antiseptics into surgery.
2. What movies are shown at that theater?
3. Sidney Hillman established the American Labor Party.
4. British control of India started in Bombay, Madras, and Calcutta.
5. Betsy washes inside the cabinets.
6. Workers paved the road three times last summer.
7. Alice purchased a summer cottage.
8. Every group member helped an older person in some way.
9. The leaves were raked into a huge pile.
10. The performance bored the hot, tired audience.
11. The elves danced a dance of boundless glee.
12. The rabbits scattered in all directions.
13. Multicolored shells were tossed up on the beach.
14. Nothing remains of the old temple.
15. Edna St. Vincent Millay wrote lyrical, romantic poems.

Linking Verbs

> **A linking verb couples or links the subject with a noun, a pronoun, or an adjective.**

A word or group of words used to complete the meaning of a linking verb is called a *subjective complement*. The complement may be a noun, pronoun, or adjective.

SUBJECT	LINKING VERB	COMPLEMENT
His name	is	Paul (*Noun*)
I	am	she (*Pronoun*)
The room	seems	cold (*Adjective*)

The verb *be* in its various forms is the most common linking verb. Some other verbs that may be used as linking verbs are *appear, become, continue, feel, grow, look, remain, seem, smell, sound,* and *taste*.

Exercise 61

Name the linking verbs in each of the following sentences. Tell whether the verb links the subject with a noun, a pronoun, or an adjective.

1. Betsy's new car is green.
2. We are competitive swimmers.
3. Paul grew restless during the lecture.
4. The optic nerve is the nerve of sight.
5. The captain seemed eager to set sail before the seas got too rough.
6. Red and yellow were the leaves on the trees in Michigan.
7. Samantha always remains cool, calm, and collected.
8. A tome is a large, scholarly book.
9. Carl's latest plan sounds exciting.
10. King Richard and King John were brothers.
11. Skin feels drier in the winter.
12. Kevin remained the person with the highest score.
13. Who is that?
14. The snake meat tasted bitter.
15. Liz's perfume smells wonderful.

Sharpening Your Skills

Using the linking verbs *appear*, *feel*, *look*, *seem*, *smell*, *sound*, and *taste*, write five sentences describing one of the following: pizza, popcorn, fried chicken, spaghetti.

Lesson 3 Active and Passive Voice

Voice is the quality of a verb that shows whether the subject is the doer or the receiver of the action.

In the *active voice,* the subject is the doer of the action. In the *passive voice,* the subject is the receiver of the action.

> Alexander Graham Bell *invented* the telephone.
> The telephone *was invented* by Alexander Graham Bell.

In the first sentence the subject, *Alexander Graham Bell*, is the doer of the action, *invented*; therefore, *invented* is the active voice. The receiver of the action is the direct object, *telephone.* In the second sentence the subject, *telephone*, is the receiver of the action, *was invented*; therefore, *was invented* is in the passive voice.

Only transitive verbs are used in the passive voice. Intransitive verbs have no receivers of the action.

Formation of the Passive Voice

The passive voice is formed by using some tense of the verb *be* as an auxiliary with the past participle of the verb. Therefore the verb *be* (and its tenses), used before a past participle, is generally the sign of the passive voice.

> was + called = passive voice

Two sentences may convey the same idea, the one expressing it by a verb in the *active voice*, and the other by a verb in the *passive voice.* When a verb in the active voice is changed to the passive voice, the subject of the active verb is usually made the object of a preposition, and the object of the active verb becomes the subject of the passive verb.

> The brain *keeps* the body under control. (*Active voice*)
> The body *is kept* under control by the brain. (*Passive voice*)

In each of these sentences, the *brain* performs the action, and the *body* receives the action. In the first sentence *brain* is the subject of the verb *keeps*; in the second sentence it becomes the object of the preposition *by.*

Body, the receiver of the action, is the direct object of the active verb *keeps*, but in the second sentence it becomes the subject of the passive verb *is kept*.

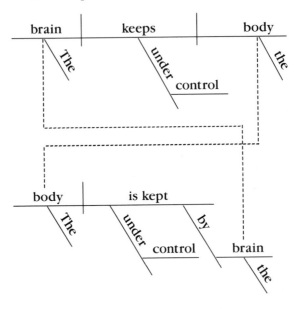

Exercise 62

Change the verbs in the first set of sentences from active to passive voice. In the next set, change the verbs from passive to active voice.

1. Cliff walked his dog in the park.
2. The dog snapped the leather leash.
3. Cliff frantically called the dog.
4. The park guard would close the gate at sunset.
5. Cliff and his dog left the park just in time.

1. The mouse is killed by the cat.
2. The cat is eaten by the snake.
3. The snake is attacked by the mongoose.
4. The mongoose is destroyed by the hunter.
5. The hunter is fined by the government.

Exercise 63

Rewrite the following sentences, changing active verbs to passive voice and passive verbs to active voice.

1. Terry wrote a very simple word processing program.
2. The incandescent lamp was invented by Edison.
3. The teacher sent cards to all of her students.
4. Canadian wood pulp is exported to the United States.
5. The Panama Canal connects the Atlantic and the Pacific Oceans.
6. Exercise strengthens the heart and lungs.
7. The president is guarded by Secret Service agents.
8. Jackie lost a moon-shaped earring.
9. Frank's car was put into the body shop.
10. The Greeks established many colonies in Italy.

Sharpening Your Skills

Model your own passive voice poem after the one below.

The tree is
    planted by the gardener
    strengthened by the sun
    nourished by the rain
    bent by the wind
    uprooted by the storm

Lesson 4 Simple and Compound Tenses

Tense is the quality of a verb that denotes the time of the action, the being, or the state of being.

Simple Tenses

Present tense signifies action, being, or state of being in present time.

Past tense signifies action, being, or state of being in past time.

Future tense signifies action, being, or state of being in future time.

PRESENT: Lorrie *studies* diligently.
PAST: Lorrie *studied* diligently.
FUTURE: Lorrie *will study* diligently.

In the passive voice the tense is shown by the *auxiliary verb.*

PRESENT: The lesson *is studied.*
PAST: The lesson *was studied.*
FUTURE; The lesson *will be studied.*

Exercise 64

Give the tense and voice of each verb.
1. Our class will study some poems by Gerard Manley Hopkins.
2. The drowning of five nuns in an 1875 shipwreck was memorialized by Hopkins in his poem "The Wreck of the Deutschland."
3. The nuns left Germany as exiles under the Falk Laws.
4. Hopkins was inspired by their courage.
5. Many people study his poem.
6. They will be moved by his emotional appeal.
7. I read the poem several years ago.
8. I still find it poetically pleasing.
9. Hopkins is studied as part of the Victorian period.
10. His poetry will be read for years to come.

Use of *Shall* and *Will*

To express simple futurity or expectation, use *shall* in the first person and *will* in the second and the third persons.

> I *shall* go tomorrow.
> You *will* go tomorrow.
> He *will* go tomorrow.

Exercise 65

Fill in each blank with the correct form, *shall* or *will*, to express future time.
1. My friends _____ not be home this evening.
2. All the nations _____ be represented at the meeting.
3. My little sister _____ be three years old tomorrow.
4. The swimming meet _____ be moved to another pool.
5. I must hurry or I _____ be late for class.
6. We _____ study the causes of the war.
7. The peace talks _____ start again tomorrow.
8. The doctor _____ be here soon.
9. I _____ be glad to help you.
10. Susan's parents _____ pick her up at the park.

Shall and *Will* in Questions

To ask a question, use *shall* when the subject is in the first person. In the second and the third persons use the same word, either *shall* or *will,* that is expected in the reply.

QUESTION	EXPECTED REPLY
Shall we help him?	We *shall.*
Shall you see him?	Yes, I *shall.*
Will you help me?	Yes, I *will* help.
Will the concert begin soon?	It *will.*

Exercise 66

Choose the correct form, *shall* or *will,* to complete each sentence. Give a response to the question that fits your verb choice.

1. _____ somebody please carry this chair?
2. _____ I meet you at the corner?
3. _____ he show us how to configure the system?
4. Where _____ I find the information?
5. When _____ the next bus leave?
6. _____ you give me a ride to the circus?
7. _____ we walk there together?
8. _____ anyone see us?
9. _____ Christmas be on a Sunday this year?
10. Who _____ create a better theory?

Compound Tenses

Present perfect tense signifies action, being, or state of being completed or perfected in present time.

Past perfect tense signifies action, being, or state of being completed or perfected before some definite past time.

Future perfect tense signifies action, being, or state of being that will be completed or perfected before some specified time in the future.

	ACTIVE VOICE
PRESENT PERFECT:	Lorrie *has* always *studied* diligently.
PAST PERFECT:	Lorrie *had studied* diligently before the examination.
FUTURE PERFECT:	Lorrie *will have studied* diligently before the examination.

	PASSIVE VOICE
PRESENT PERFECT:	The lesson *has been studied.*
PAST PERFECT:	The lesson *had been studied.*
FUTURE PERFECT:	The lesson *will have been studied.*

Exercise 67

Give the tense and voice of each verb.

1. Carlos has purchased a new camera.
2. The check will have been mailed before the payment is due.
3. I shall have completed this grammar exercise before class tomorrow.
4. The laundry had been left out in the rain.
5. That solution has been tried.
6. Have you read *The Once and Future King*?
7. Louise had trained hard before the race.
8. The act will have been performed by the time you get there.
9. Wendy has told us her view of the subject.
10. The results had been announced.
11. Heavy fog has shrouded the little town.
12. The bicycle has been repaired.

Sharpening Your Skills

Your mom tells you that you must complete certain chores before you can go to your class party this evening. Write your mom a note and tell her in the first paragraph what you *had* already *completed* before she even told you about the chores, in the second paragraph what you *have completed* this morning, and in the third paragraph what you *will have completed* by this evening.

Lesson 5 Mood

Mood or mode is the attribute or quality of a verb that denotes the manner in which the action, the being, or the state of being is expressed.

Indicative Mood

The indicative mood is used to state a fact, to deny a fact, or to ask a question.

STATES A FACT: The population of Alaska *has increased* in recent years.

DENIES A FACT: It *is* not always cold in Alaska.

ASKS A QUESTION: When *was* the Alcan Highway *completed*?

All the six tenses are found in the indicative mood.

PRESENT: She *writes* letters.

PAST: She *wrote* the letters yesterday.

FUTURE: She *will write* the letters today.

PRESENT PERFECT: She *has written* many letters today.

PAST PERFECT: She *had written* the letters before noon.

FUTURE PERFECT: She *will have written* the letters before tomorrow.

Progressive Form of the Indicative Mood

The progressive form of the verb denotes an action as going on or in progress. In the active voice the various tenses of the verb *be* are used with the present participle of the main verb to form the progressive verb phrases.

PRESENT TENSE: She *is writing* letters.

PAST TENSE: She *was writing* letters yesterday.

FUTURE TENSE: She *will be writing* letters today.

PRESENT PERFECT TENSE: She *has been writing* letters this morning.

PAST PERFECT TENSE: She *had been writing* letters before noon.

FUTURE PERFECT TENSE: She *will have been writing* letters before the end of the day.

The present and the past tenses of the progressive form are the two tenses most frequently used in the passive voice.

PRESENT: The letter *is being written*.

PAST: The letter *was being written*.

Exercise 68

Find the progressive verb phrases and give the tense and the voice of each.

1. Cory is teaching his dog a new trick.
2. Five purple airplanes were flying over the field.
3. Hot chocolate was being served in the lodge.
4. Harriet was hiking when the snake bit her.
5. We had been talking for hours before the show.
6. Those people have been fishing all night.
7. The fish they caught are being displayed at the pavilion.
8. Mark has been observing the student teachers.
9. Where is your new home being built?
10. As of tomorrow, horses will have been training a week for the derby.
11. Helen has been feeding the tigers.
12. She will be combing the monkey tomorrow.

Emphatic Form of the Indicative Mood

Use the emphatic form to give emphasis to the verb.

Moral support *does lend* encouragement.
High ideals *did lead* him to the nobler things of life.

Use the emphatic form only in the present and the past tenses of the active voice. The auxiliaries *do* and *does* before the present part of the verb form the present tense, and the auxiliary *did* before the present part of the verb forms the past tense.

NOTE: In questions and in negative statements, *do, does,* and *did* are not used emphatically.

Exercise 69

Find the emphatic verb phrases and identify their tenses.

1. I do see my mistake now.
2. She does love me.
3. Matthew and Clare do work well together.
4. He did think he had done the right thing.
5. Lucy does jog every night.
6. Vernon did return the tapes.
7. I did try my key in the lock.
8. The secretary did submit the report on time.
9. I did enjoy the first book, but I did not like the second.
10. You did receive the award this morning.
11. They did not want you to know in advance.
12. My brother does play in the band.

Potential Form of the Indicative Mood

The potential form of the indicative mood is used to express permission, possibility, ability, necessity, or obligation.

PERMISSION: You *may begin* the lecture, Robert.
POSSIBILITY: Sheila *might return* tomorrow.
ABILITY: My sister *can play* the violin.
NECESSITY: You *must wind* this clock every night.
OBLIGATION: We *should do* the work now.

The auxiliary verbs *may, might, can, could, must, should,* and *would* are used in the potential form.

Tenses of the Potential Form

The potential form is used in the present, the past, the present perfect, and the past perfect tenses, but not in the future tenses.

ACTIVE VOICE

PRESENT TENSE:	We *must complete* the work.
PAST TENSE:	I *could* not *find* the paper.
PRESENT PERFECT TENSE:	He *may have broken* the chair.
PAST PERFECT TENSE:	You *should have packed* the lunch last night.

PASSIVE VOICE

PRESENT TENSE:	All the work *must be completed.*
PAST TENSE:	The paper *could* not *be found.*
PRESENT PERFECT TENSE:	The chair *may have been broken.*
PAST PERFECT TENSE:	The lunch *should have been packed* last night.

Exercise 70

Identify the potential verb phrases and tell what form of expression they represent (permission, possibility, ability, necessity, or obligation).

1. Marty can swim faster than anyone in the state.
2. We should contribute to charity.
3. Katherine should have prepared her lesson.
4. Karl can speak German.
5. The campers may have lost their tent.
6. They could not find the trail.
7. You may borrow my guitar.
8. Tax forms must be filed by April 15.
9. You should have answered my question sooner.
10. Brad must get more outdoor exercise.
11. Oranges cannot grow in Alaska.
12. Tiffany may bring her friend along.

Outline for Drill on Special Forms of the Indicative

	PROGRESSIVE	EMPHATIC	POTENTIAL
USE:	Denotes action in progress.	Lends emphasis to a statement.	Expresses permission, possibility, ability, necessity, obligation.
SIGN:	*ing* (present participle of the principal verb)	*Do, does,* or *did* used as auxiliaries	*May, can, must, might, could, should, would*
TENSE:	Present, past, future, present perfect, past perfect, future perfect	Present, past	Present, past, present perfect, past perfect
VOICE:	Active, passive	Active	Active, passive

Exercise 71

Name the special form, the tense, and the voice of each verb.
1. The sharks are being fed.
2. Gretchen may have sent the package to your old address.
3. She did come to the party last night.
4. No one can disgrace me but myself.
5. The window must have been broken during the night.
6. Everyone did comment on his new hat.
7. Daniel should have combed his hair before they took the picture.
8. He has been wearing those yellow shoes every day.
9. Renaldo does work hard.
10. Betty has been working at the hamburger stand.
11. Who could help her get a better job?
12. Randi is interviewing her tomorrow.
13. I do wash the dishes every night.
14. Their apartment is being painted.
15. Too much sun does burn skin.

Imperative Mood

Use the imperative mood to express a command in the
second person. A mild command often takes the form
of an entreaty or a request.

COMMAND: (you) *Present* arms!
ENTREATY: (you) *Have* pity on the man, my friends.
REQUEST: (you) *Close* the door quietly, Rose.

The present tense is the only tense in the imperative mood.
The subject of a verb in the imperative mood is always in the
second person, either singular or plural, and it is usually
not expressed.

Subjunctive Mood

The subjunctive mood generally expresses a wish or
desire, an uncertainty, or a condition contrary to fact.

The subordinate conjunctions *if, as if, provided, though, lest,
whether, unless,* and some of the potential auxiliaries, are
sometimes used to introduce a verb in the subjunctive mood.
A subordinate conjunction or an auxiliary verb, however, is not
always necessary when the verb is in the subjunctive mood.

WISH: Peace *be* to all! (*No conjunction or
auxiliary verb*)
UNCERTAINTY: Whether that *be* true or not, we have not changed
our plans. (*With the subordinate conjunction
whether*)
CONTRARY TO FACT: If she *were* a queen, she could not be more
gracious. (*With the subordinate conjunction* if)

In the subjunctive mood there are four tenses: the present, the past,
the present perfect, and the past perfect. Study the subjunctive
mood in the conjugations of the verbs *be* and *teach* on pages
362–367.

Exercise 72

Name the verbs in the imperative and the subjunctive moods.
Explain what each verb expresses.

1. Take off your boots.
2. Long live the Cubs!
3. My sister would play the piano if she were here.
4. May she be happy in her new job!
5. Heaven help you!
6. Whether he be honest or not, we have to trust him.
7. We wish someone else were available.
8. Move to the rear of the elevator, please.
9. May the queen grant us this favor.
10. He looks as if he just swallowed a sock.
11. Kindly complete this exercise quickly.
12. Run to the gym with me today, Leslie.
13. May all of your dreams come true.
14. Remember to brush your teeth, son.
15. If I were you, I would read the assignment.

Sharpening Your Skills

Copy each sentence and supply the verb form called for in
parentheses. All verbs are in the indicative mood except
where indicated.

write
1. The monks ____ books on sheepskin. (*Past tense, active voice*)

consume
2. The pizza _____ in a very short time. (*Past tense, passive voice*)

build
3. A modern bridge _____ over the lagoon. (*Present perfect tense, passive voice*)

beware
4. ____ of the fiendish monster. (*Imperative mood, present tense, active voice*)

visit
5. Mount Rushmore in South Dakota ____ by many tourists. (*Present tense, passive voice*)

redecorate
6. We _____ the bedroom as soon as the check comes. (*Future tense, active voice*)

aid
7. Christopher Columbus ____ by Queen Isabella. (*Past tense, passive voice*)

have	8. Ever since they moved to Key West, they _____ many visitors during the winters. (*Present perfect tense, active voice*)
shine	9. The moon _____ on the magic circle. (*Progressive form, present tense, active voice*)
finish	10. I _____ this assignment before dinner. (*Future perfect tense, active voice*)
plan	11. __ your trip carefully, Kate. (*Imperative mood, present tense, active voice*)
enjoy	12. May you __ a long life! (*Subjunctive mood, present tense, active voice*)
present	13. *Julius Caesar* _____ by the community theater. (*Future tense, passive voice*)
destroy	14. Pompeii _____ by an eruption of Mt. Vesuvius in A.D. 79. (*Past tense, passive voice*)
consent	15. Erik's parents _____ to his attending the dirt bike race. (*Future tense, active voice*)
break	16. The first Atlantic cable ___ in mid-ocean. (*Past tense, active voice*)
hear	17. __ you __ the news? (*Present perfect tense, active voice*)
sit	18. Adam _____ there all morning looking at the broken cup. (*Progressive form, present perfect tense, active voice*)
be	19. Current news stories _____ about issues affecting many politicians. (*Present perfect tense*)
be	20. If I __ you, I would learn to type. (*Subjunctive mood, past tense*)

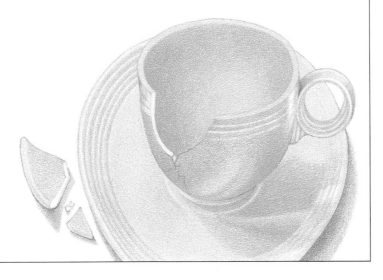

Lesson 6 Agreement of Verb with Subject Part I

Person and Number

> The verb must always agree with its subject in person and number.

A verb may be in the first, second, or third person, and either singular or plural in number. What person and number it is depends upon the subject.

	SINGULAR NUMBER	PLURAL NUMBER
FIRST PERSON	I draw.	Lanette and I draw. (we)
SECOND PERSON	Keith, draw an apple. (you)	Students, draw an apple. (you)
THIRD PERSON	Leona draws well. (she)	Henry and Jake draw well. (they)

Note that in the example, the verb keeps the same form except in the third person, singular number, when it ends in *s*. All verbs in the present tense take the *s* form in the third person, singular number.

The verb must agree with the subject even when the subject *follows* the verb, as in the case of a sentence beginning with the expletive *there*.

There *are* your *books*.

One exception to agreement is the use of the forms *you are* and *you were*. These forms are used whether the subject is singular or plural.

Sara, *you are* a wonderful cook!
Children, *you are* not to play with matches.

Exercise 73

Give the person and number of each subject; then select the correct form of the verb to complete each sentence.

1. There (is, are) twenty puppies in the kennel.
2. Mr. DiMartino (was, were) not home when I called.
3. In the garden (is, are) many bright flowers.
4. There (was, were) only one person in the car.
5. Morris (give, gives) us moral support.
6. Native Americans (was, were) fine hunters and riders.
7. Smooth roads (make, makes) driving easy.
8. You (is, are) a comical magician.
9. His friends (was, were) all amused.
10. The grocer (sell, sells) paper goods as well as food.
11. (Is, Are) you going to camp this summer?
12. (Was, Were) you on the honor roll this month?
13. Where (was, were) you this morning?
14. Why (is, are) crop rotation necessary?
15. There (is, are) large sulfur deposits in Texas and Louisiana.
16. *Silent Spring* (explain, explains) how chemicals affect wildlife.
17. They (read, reads) the computer magazines every day.
18. The old chest (belong, belongs) to the museum.
19. The curators (think, thinks) the chest (contain, contains) ancient treasures.
20. She (worry, worries) about the consequences of her actions.

Doesn't and *Don't*

If a sentence's subject is in the third person, *doesn't* is the correct form in the singular, and *don't* is the correct form in the plural.

> The *coach doesn't* want us for practice today.
> The *clocks don't* have the correct time.

In the first and second persons the correct form is *don't*, whether the subject is singular or plural.

> *I don't* know whether alligators are in this swamp.
> *We don't* remember which path we took to the berry patch.

> *Dave, don't* mix those chemicals.
> *Class,* please *don't* forget to write the directions clearly.

Exercise 74

Select the correct form, *doesn't* or *don't*, to complete each sentence.

1. _____ it seem quiet since Franco went away?
2. Marsha _____ look very healthy.
3. Our plane _____ leave until after lunchtime.
4. _____ you understand the problem?
5. They _____ want to help push the car.
6. Julia _____ care whether she sees the play.
7. You _____ seem to notice the cold.
8. The sun _____ rise in the west.
9. The teacher _____ want Antonio to get hurt.
10. _____ he realize the value of close friends?
11. I _____ know who invented the submarine.
12. Michael _____ like tuna and banana sandwiches.

Phrases and Parenthetical Expressions

A phrase or a parenthetical expression between the subject and the verb does not change the number of the verb. If the subject is singular, the verb must be singular; if plural, the verb must be plural.

One of my sisters *goes* to college.

Exercise 75

Name the subject of each sentence and select the correct form of the verb to complete the sentence.

1. Several members of the team (practice, practices) here on Saturday mornings.
2. The delightful climate of the Hawaiian Islands (account, accounts) for the extensive tourist trade.
3. A stack of hot pancakes (was, were) placed on the table.
4. Jacqueline's description of her travels (was, were) thrilling.
5. This statue of Martin Luther King, Jr., together with its pedestal, (was, were) donated to the city.
6. Melody, as well as her sisters, (is, are) very shy.
7. A shipment of oranges (is, are) expected soon.
8. The construction of new houses (seem, seems) shoddier than that of old ones.

9. The reference books, including a dictionary, (was, were) on the table.
10. The legends of Camelot (provide, provides) source material for the fiction and poetry of many generations.
11. The second game of the series (was, were) played in San Francisco.
12. Tuition, as well as the cost of books, (has, have) increased.

Sharpening Your Skills

Complete each thought below. Make sure that the verb agrees with the subject. Use only action verbs in your sentences.

1. The bus that passes my house...
2. My picture taken last year...
3. The redwood trees of California...
4. Books about science fiction...
5. Rob, as well as his friends...
6. A meeting of foreign diplomats...
7. The sun shining through my window...
8. People living in France...

Paris from the balcony of Notre-Dame de Paris

353

Lesson 7 Agreement of Verb with Subject Part II

Compound Subjects Connected by *And*

Compound subjects connected by *and* require a plural verb unless the subjects refer to the same person or thing, or express a single idea.

> Ken and Cheryl *were* at the game.
> The writer and publisher of this book *is* well known.

Exercise 76

Select the correct form of the verb. Give the reason for your choice.
1. Christine and Nancy (work, works) together.
2. The president and manager (was, were) not in her office.
3. (Was, Were) your father and mother at the meeting?
4. Ramona and her friend (is, are) expected soon.
5. Racquetball and soccer (is, are) fast-moving sports.
6. What (do, does) your parents and friends think about your haircut?
7. Just bread and water (seem, seems) a Spartan diet.
8. Oranges and limes (is, are) both citrus fruits.
9. My friend and classmate (write, writes) to me weekly.
10. Here (come, comes) the president and the treasurer together.
11. Purebred dogs and cats (is, are) registered.
12. His purpose and aim (is, are) to succeed.
13. The electricians and plumbers (agree, agrees) to strike in sympathy.
14. My dictionary and encyclopedia (is, are) out of date.
15. Eggs and toast (was, were) served.

Compound Subjects Preceded by *Each* and *Every*

Two or more singular subjects connected by *and* but preceded by *each*, *every*, *many a*, or *no* require a singular verb.

> *Has* every pen and pencil been placed on the desk?

Exercise 77

Select the correct form of the verb. Give the reason for your choice.
1. Many a man and woman (buy, buys) foolish things at times.
2. Every aunt and uncle (was, were) at the family reunion.
3. Every town and borough (was, were) represented.
4. Many a cat and dog (has, have) tried to do that trick.
5. Every window and door in the house (was, were) blown open.
6. Almost every plate and glass (was, were) in the sink.
7. Each lion and tiger (is, are) dangerous when angry.
8. Many a fireman and policeman (save, saves) lives.
9. Every house and store (was, were) covered with mud.
10. Many a puppet and beanbag (was, were) made by Cynthia.
11. Each day and hour (bring, brings) new trials.
12. Many a boy and girl (know, knows) how to play checkers.
13. Each senator and representative (was, were) present at the peace march.
14. No fortune and no position in life (make, makes) a guilty person happy.
15. Every nut and bolt (was, were) rusted tight.

Compound Subjects Connected by *Or* or *Nor*

When compound subjects are connected by *or* or *nor*, the verb agrees with the subject closer to it.

> Neither the lion nor the <u>tiger</u> *is* hungry.
> Neither the lion nor the <u>tigers</u> *are* hungry.
> Neither he nor <u>I</u> *am* hungry.

Exercise 78

Select the correct form of the verb. Give the reason for your choice.
1. Neither math nor science (is, are) hard for me.
2. (Is, Are) either Anne or Eileen going?
3. Neither the letter nor the postcard (was, were) for me.
4. Lillian or her sister (is, are) going parachuting.
5. Neither the pilot nor the copilot (like, likes) to watch people jump.
6. Neither the horse nor the cows (was, were) warm enough during the blizzard.
7. Neither Dolores nor I (was, were) prepared for the test.
8. Either this cake or those candies (was, were) eaten by Claudia.
9. Either the vice president or her secretary (answer, answers) the angry questions.
10. Neither the tulips nor the daffodils (has, have) bloomed yet.
11. Neither I nor he (think, thinks) the woman is guilty.
12. Neither the trunk nor the box (has, have) arrived.
13. Either the door or the windows (was, were) not closed.
14. Neither wind nor waves (deter, deters) Rachel from swimming in the lake.
15. Neither the computer nor the printer (work, works) properly.

Sharpening Your Skills

Write a complete sentence for each of the compound subjects. In parentheses are the conjunctions and/or adjectives that should be used. Be sure to keep the verbs in the present tense.
1. cucumbers/radishes (either, or)
2. pen/pencil (each, and)
3. soccer/football (and)
4. airplane/space shuttle (and)
5. package/letters (neither/nor)
6. spaghetti/meatballs (and)
7. musician/artist (many a, and)
8. players/coach (either, or)

Lesson 8 Agreement of Verb with Subject Part III

Collective Nouns

A collective noun requires a singular verb if the idea expressed by the subject is thought of as a unit. A plural verb may be used if the idea expressed by the subject denotes separate individuals.

A flock of sheep *was* seen on the mountainside. (*Unit*)
The flock of sheep *were* grazing. (*Sheep in the flock*)

Exercise 79

Name the subject and select the correct form of the verb.
1. The choir (rehearse, rehearses) on Sunday evenings.
2. A bevy of sheep and goats (stop, stops) traffic here every afternoon.
3. The committee (was, were) divided on the proposal to collect trash every ten days.
4. That team (display, displays) good spirit.
5. (Has, Have) the group submitted their reports?
6. The flock of birds (was, were) chased away by the squirrel.
7. The jury (has, have) reached a verdict.
8. The orchestra (offer, offers) a reward for the return of the violinist.
9. (Has, Have) the crew sailed together before?
10. The drove of horses (was, were) sold to the farmer.

Whaling Off the Coast of California by Coleman

Distributive and Indefinite Pronouns

The distributive pronouns *each*, *either*, *neither*, and the indefinite pronouns *one*, *anyone*, *no one*, *anybody*, *nobody*, *everyone*, *everybody*, *someone*, *somebody* are always singular and require singular verbs.

> *Each* of the brothers *has* a new car.

Exercise 80

Name the subject of each sentence and give the correct form of the verb in parentheses.

1. Somebody always (call) when I am asleep.
2. No one (want) to talk to those men.
3. Anyone who can think that way (frighten) me.
4. One of her favorite beverages (come) from Brazil.
5. Neither of the men (want) to go to prison.
6. Each of the clowns (ride) a unicycle.
7. (Have) anyone taken my ticket?
8. (Be) either of your brothers going on the hike?
9. Everyone in the parade (carry) a banner.
10. Each of the bakers (wear) an apron.
11. Someone (keep) asking me your name.
12. Nobody except Margaret (know) what happened.
13. Everyone (like) to see the sun after weeks of rain.
14. (Do) anyone help those refugees?
15. Neither of the recruiters (be) finding many interested students.

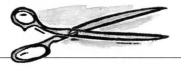

Special Singular and Plural Nouns

Some nouns that are plural in form, but usually singular in meaning, require singular verbs. These include *aeronautics*, *athletics* (training), *civics*, *economics*, *mathematics*, *measles*, *molasses*, *mumps*, *news*, *physics*.

Other nouns are usually considered plural and require plural verbs. These nouns include *ashes*, *clothes*, *eaves*, *glasses*, *goods*, *pincers*, *pliers*, *proceeds*, *scales*, *scissors*, *shears*, *suspenders*, *tanks*, *tongs*, *trousers*, *tweezers*.

> Measles *is* a disease of the young.
> My scissors *have* been lost.

Exercise 81

Choose the correct verb form.
 1. Athletics (develop, develops) the muscles.
 2. Molasses (is, are) sweet and sticky.
 3. His trousers (is, are) at the cleaners.
 4. Measles (require, requires) careful treatment.
 5. The ashes (is, are) still hot.
 6. Tongs (is, are) used to remove the cinders.
 7. Physics (is, are) a class with interesting experiments.
 8. (Does, Do) these pliers belong to you?
 9. The proceeds from the candle sale (was, were) enough to buy some new instruments.
10. News (is, are) sometimes very upsetting.
11. The scales (was, were) weighted wrong.
12. Sarah's glasses (has, have) a small butterfly on them.
13. The eaves (is, are) sagging under the weight of the snow.
14. The goods (was, were) not delivered on time.
15. Civics (is, are) required in some high schools.

You Are the Author

Choose one.
 1. In your own words rewrite this fable or another that you know.
 2. In small groups write an original fable that teaches a lesson. Base the fable on a lesson learned from ignoring good advice, from being unkind or rude to someone you care about, or from a situation of your choice.

Exercise 82 (Review)

Name the subject of each sentence and choose the correct verb form to complete the sentence.

1. (Doesn't, Don't) my brother drive his car well?
2. Each candidate (is, are) preparing for the campaign.
3. Today's news (bring, brings) joy to many people.
4. (Has, Have) everyone made a donation?
5. Everyone (was, were) happy when peace was declared.
6. Either Colleen or she (is, are) sure to be there.
7. Coal and iron (is, are) mined from the earth.
8. Measles (cause, causes) skin eruption.
9. *The Adventures of Tom Sawyer* (is, are) very humorous.
10. Henry (doesn't, don't) like mushrooms.
11. Their home, as well as their possessions, (was, were) destroyed in the fire.
12. The band (is, are) marching into the stadium.
13. There (is, are) two motorboats on the river.
14. Several Hockney paintings (was, were) exhibited at the gallery.
15. Both my father and my brother (like, likes) fire trucks.

Pool and Steps
by David Hockney

Chapter Challenge

Read this selection carefully and then answer the questions that follow:

[1]"Look out!" screamed half a dozen voices as a boy old enough to know better dashed into the street from between two parked cars. [2]What followed was a medley of screeching brakes, frightened screams, and confused shouts. [3]The noise died to an awed hush as a doctor pushed his way through the crowd and knelt beside the injured lad. [4]Was the boy beyond help? [5]Luckily, he was not, for it is that same boy who is writing this story from a wheel chair, where he will spend several months repenting of one moment's folly. [6]Why I did such a foolish thing I will never know! [7]Sure, I was intent on catching the ball, but I should have stopped once I came to the street. [8]I might have died if that doctor hadn't arrived so quickly. [9]May I never forget this painful experience and the lesson it taught me!

1. What mood and tense is the first verb in this paragraph?
2. Is the verb *screamed* in the first sentence regular or irregular?
3. Is the verb *dashed* in the first sentence transitive or intransitive?
4. In the first sentence *parked* is a verb functioning as what other part of speech?
5. Name the three verbs in the third sentence.
6. In what mood and tense are these three verbs?
7. Name the linking verb in the fifth sentence.
8. Find a progressive verb phrase in the fifth sentence.
9. In what tense is *will spend* in the fifth sentence?
10. What voice is *will know* in the sixth sentence? Give the parts of the verb *know*.
11. Name the potential verb phrase in the seventh sentence and give its tense and voice.
12. Name the potential verb phrase in the eighth sentence that expresses possibility. In what tense is it?
13. Name the verb in the ninth sentence that is in the subjunctive mood and explain what it expresses.
14. Give the parts of the verb *taught* in the ninth sentence.

Conjugation

Conjugation is the orderly arrangement of a verb
according to voice, mood, tense, person, and number.

Conjugation of the Verb *be*

	PRESENT	PAST	PAST PARTICIPLE
PRINCIPAL PARTS:	be	was	been

Indicative Mood

Singular	*Plural*
PRESENT TENSE	
I am	We are
You are	You are
He (she, it) is	They are

PAST TENSE	
I was	We were
You were	You were
He was	They were

FUTURE TENSE	
I shall be	We shall be
You will be	You will be
He will be	They will be

PRESENT PERFECT TENSE	
I have been	We have been
You have been	You have been
He has been	They have been

PAST PERFECT TENSE	
I had been	We had been
You had been	You had been
He had been	They had been

FUTURE PERFECT TENSE	
I shall have been	We shall have been
You will have been	You will have been
He will have been	They will have been

Subjunctive Mood

Singular	*Plural*

PRESENT TENSE

If I be	If we be
If you be	If you be
If he be	If they be

PAST TENSE

If I were	If we were
If you were	If you were
If he were	If they were

PRESENT PERFECT TENSE

If I have been	If we have been
If you have been	If you have been
If he have been	If they have been

PAST PERFECT TENSE

If I had been	If we had been
If you had been	If you had been
If he had been	If they had been

Imperative Mood

PRESENT TENSE

Be (be you)	Be (be you)

INFINITIVES

PRESENT: To be   PRESENT PERFECT: To have been

PARTICIPLES

PRESENT: Being   PAST: Been   PERFECT: Having been

Conjugation of the Verb *teach*

	PRESENT	PAST	PAST PARTICIPLE
PRINCIPAL PARTS:	teach	taught	taught

Indicative Mood *Active Voice*

Singular   *Plural*

PRESENT TENSE

Singular	Plural
I teach	We teach
You teach	You teach
He teaches	They teach

PAST TENSE

Singular	Plural
I taught	We taught
You taught	You taught
He taught	They taught

FUTURE TENSE

Singular	Plural
I shall teach	We shall teach
You will teach	You will teach
He will teach	They will teach

PRESENT PERFECT TENSE

Singular	Plural
I have taught	We have taught
You have taught	You have taught
He has taught	They have taught

PAST PERFECT TENSE

Singular	Plural
I had taught	We had taught
You had taught	You had taught
He had taught	They had taught

FUTURE PERFECT TENSE

Singular	Plural
I shall have taught	We shall have taught
You will have taught	You will have taught
He will have taught	They will have taught

Indicative Mood *Passive Voice*

Singular | *Plural*

PRESENT TENSE

I am taught	We are taught
You are taught	You are taught
He is taught	They are taught

PAST TENSE

I was taught	We were taught
You were taught	You were taught
He was taught	They were taught

FUTURE TENSE

I shall be taught	We shall be taught
You will be taught	You will be taught
He will be taught	They will be taught

PRESENT PERFECT TENSE

I have been taught	We have been taught
You have been taught	You have been taught
He has been taught	They have been taught

PAST PERFECT TENSE

I had been taught	We had been taught
You had been taught	You had been taught
He had been taught	They had been taught

FUTURE PERFECT TENSE

I shall have been taught	We shall have been taught
You will have been taught	You will have been taught
He will have been taught	They will have been taught

Subjunctive Mood *Active Voice*

Singular	*Plural*
PRESENT TENSE	
If I teach	If we teach
If you teach	If you teach
If he teach	If they teach

PAST TENSE	
If I taught	If we taught
If you taught	If you taught
If he taught	If they taught

PRESENT PERFECT TENSE	
If I have taught	If we have taught
If you have taught	If you have taught
If he have taught	If they have taught

PAST PERFECT TENSE	
If I had taught	If we had taught
If you had taught	If you had taught
If he had taught	If they had taught

Subjunctive Mood *Passive Voice*

Singular	*Plural*
PRESENT TENSE	
If I be taught	If we be taught
If you be taught	If you be taught
If he be taught	If they be taught

PAST TENSE	
If I were taught	If we were taught
If you were taught	If you were taught
If he were taught	If they were taught

PRESENT PERFECT TENSE	
If I have been taught	If we have been taught
If you have been taught	If you have been taught
If he have been taught	If they have been taught

PAST PERFECT TENSE	
If I had been taught	If we had been taught
If you had been taught	If you had been taught
If he had been taught	If they had been taught

Imperative Mood

PRESENT TENSE

Active Voice

Teach (teach you)

Passive Voice

Be taught (be you taught)

INFINITIVES

PRESENT: To teach   To be taught

PERFECT: To have taught   To have been taught

PARTICIPLES

PRESENT: Teaching   Being taught

PAST: Taught   Taught

PERFECT: Having taught   Having been taught

Synopsis of a Verb

A synopsis is an abbreviated conjugation. It is made by giving the form for one person and number of each tense in a designated mood or moods.

Synopsis of the Verb *teach*

(Indicative mood, third person, singular number)

	Active Voice	Passive Voice
PRESENT TENSE:	He teaches	He is taught
PAST TENSE:	He taught	He was taught
FUTURE TENSE:	He will teach	He will be taught
PRESENT PERFECT TENSE:	He has taught	He has been taught
PAST PERFECT TENSE:	He had taught	He had been taught
FUTURE PERFECT TENSE:	He will have taught	He will have been taught

Chapter 5

Verbals: Participles, Gerunds, Infinitives

Stopping by Woods on a Snowy Evening

by Robert Frost

Whose woods these are I think I know.
His house is in the village, though;
He will not see me stopping here
To watch his woods fill up with snow.

My little horse must think it queer
To stop without a farmhouse near
Between the woods and frozen lake
The darkest evening of the year.

He gives his harness bells a shake
To ask if there is some mistake.
The only other sound's the sweep
Of easy wind and downy flake.

The woods are lovely, dark, and deep,
But I have promises to keep,
And miles to go before I sleep,
And miles to go before I sleep.

Winter Moonlight by Charles Burchfield

A Minor Bird

by Robert Frost

I have wished a bird would fly away,
And not sing by my house all day;

Have clapped my hands at him from the door
When it seemed as if I could bear no more.

The fault must partly have been in me.
The bird was not to blame for his key.

And of course there must be something wrong
In wanting to silence any song.

The Writer's Craft

1. At first "Stopping by Woods on a Snowy Evening" seems like a simple poem. Describe the events that occur. Can you find a place in the poem where you think the action becomes symbolic of something other than a man's journey home on a winter evening? What does the action symbolize?
2. Do you agree with the poet's final statement in "A Minor Bird"? Discuss why or why not.
3. Compare the rhyme patterns of the two poems. Why does the pattern work well in each poem? Why do you think the rhyme scheme changes in stanza four of "Stopping by Woods"?
4. What action verbs or words derived from verbs does the poet use to support the idea of a journey in "Stopping by Woods"?

Recalling What You Know

1. An infinitive is a verb form that has not been conjugated and is usually preceded by *to*. Identify the infinitives in both poems.
2. A gerund is a verb form that ends in *ing* and is used as a noun. Find a gerund in "A Minor Bird."
3. In the second stanza of "Stopping by Woods on a Snowy Evening," find a word that is derived from a verb but is used to describe a noun.

Lesson 1   Participles

A participle is a word that does the twofold work of a verb and an adjective.

After graduation from high school, Frost spent some time *assisting* his mother in her classroom.

Frost, *born* in California, is known as a poet of New England.

Assisting and *born* are participles. Both words are derived from verbs, for they express action. *Assisting* has a direct object, *mother,* and *born* is modified by the adverbial phrase *in California.* The participles resemble adjectives in that they modify nouns or pronouns: *assisting* modifies *time*, and *born* modifies *Frost.*

A participle is a type of *verbal,* a word derived from a verb and functioning as another part of speech. You will also study the other two types of verbals—gerunds and infinitives—in this chapter.

Properties of the Participle

A participle has the properties of a verb and an adjective.

PROPERTIES OF A VERB
1. It is derived from a verb.
2. It may take an object.
3. It may be modified by an adverb or an adverbial phrase.

PROPERTIES OF AN ADJECTIVE
It limits a noun or a pronoun.

Forms of the Participle

A participle has voice and tense, but it does not have person and number.

	ACTIVE	PASSIVE
PRESENT:	seeing	being seen
PAST:	seen	seen
PERFECT:	having seen	having been seen

Position of the Participle

The participle may be placed after the noun or the pronoun it limits, or it may be used in an introductory phrase.

> Samuel Morse, *having invented* the telegraph, asked
> the aid of Congress.
> *Having invented* the telegraph, Samuel Morse asked
> the aid of Congress.

In both sentences, the participle *having invented* modifies *Morse*. In the first sentence, this participle follows the noun; in the second sentence, it is used in the introductory phrase.

Note that *having invented the telegraph* is a *nonrestrictive* phrase in both sentences. It is not a necessary part of the sentences and could be omitted. Participial phrases that are *restrictive* are essential to the meaning of a sentence. Commas set off nonrestrictive phrases but do not set off restrictive phrases.

> The man *asking aid from Congress* is Samuel Morse.

The phrase *asking aid from Congress* limits the word it modifies to a particular man. No commas are needed. A participial phrase consists of the participle and its complement and modifiers.

Samuel Morse
(self-portrait)

372

Exercise 83

Name each participle and tell which noun or pronoun it modifies.
1. After the death of Frost's father, the family moved to the East, settling in Lawrence, Massachusetts.
2. Frost, aspiring to write poetry, began writing at age sixteen.
3. His grandfather, concerned about Frost's economic future, bought his grandson a farm.
4. The grandfather, knowing Frost's love for writing, questioned the would-be farmer.
5. Unknown as a poet at age thirty-eight, he left for England.
6. Eventually, he met some English and American poets, including Ezra Pound.
7. Frost was among the writers liked by Pound.
8. Frost sought to grasp the sound of common speech in his poems, lifting it to a rare, exquisite eloquence.
9. Frost, honored by two English universities, won four Pulitzer Prizes.
10. The rivers flowing into the Pacific Ocean have little inland transportation.
11. The pictures hanging on the walls are photographs of their ancestors.
12. Finding themselves hopelessly lost in the dark, Tomás and Todd decided to sleep in the woods until morning.
13. Jumping into the water, she caught the small boy as he was struck by the waves.
14. The lifeguard watched the children playing on the beach.
15. The great oak, broken by the wind, fell against the building.

Complete each sentence with an appropriate thought. Draw an arrow from the participle to the word it modifies.
16. Shouting joyfully, _____.
17. Having discovered the hiding place, _____.
18. _____ grown in California _____.
19. _____ sitting on the bench _____.
20. _____, being very shy, _____.

Sharpening Your Skills

Compose five sentences that show the correct use of the participial phrase.

Participial Adjectives

Do not make the mistake of thinking that all words derived from verbs and ending in *ing* or *ed* are participles. Note the use of the word *running* in the following sentence:

> The *running* water wore away the stone.

Running is descriptive in character and has the usual position of an adjective—before the noun. This participial form is one of the types of descriptive adjectives; it is called a *participial adjective*. The following characteristics will help you to recognize a participial adjective:

1. It is descriptive in character.
2. It does *not* have the force of a verb.
3. It may *not* take an object.
4. It has the usual position of an adjective—before the noun or after a linking verb.

Exercise 84

Identify each participial adjective and the noun it modifies.
1. The neighbors watched the burning building with dismay.
2. An unopened letter lay on the desk.
3. Emmanuel's blazing eyes revealed his anger.
4. Mr. Mazzenga is a traveling paper sales representative.
5. The visiting professor had gone back to Detroit.
6. Experience is a trying teacher.
7. Drifting snow blocked the highway.
8. The doctor knelt over the injured calf.
9. Mom seems pleased with the news.
10. Running water is a luxury enjoyed by most people in the United States.
11. The harried waiter raced back to the kitchen.
12. Brazil is one of the strongest developing countries in the world.
13. The wailing siren continued for hours.
14. Sue likes raised bread.
15. Baking day is Tuesday.

The Nominative Absolute

A participle may be used with a noun or a pronoun in an independent adverbial phrase to express the time, the condition, the cause, or the circumstances of the action expressed by the main verb in the sentence. The noun or the pronoun used in this absolute construction is in the nominative case, and the participle modifies it.

> *The game being over*, the winning team returned joyfully to the school.

The introductory phrase in this sentence expresses the circumstances or the time when the team returned. The participle *being* modifies *game*, the noun in the nominative absolute.

The noun in a nominative absolute is not the subject of any verb. It is part of an independent adverbial phrase and is modified by the participle.

Compare these sentences:

> *Having thrown* the rider, the bull dashed madly across the field.
> *The rider having been thrown*, the bull dashed madly across the field.

In the first sentence the participle modifies *bull*, the subject. In the second sentence the participle *having been thrown* is part of the nominative absolute. The participle in this sentence modifies *rider*, the noun in the nominative absolute.

Exercise 85

Write out the nominative absolute in each sentence. Identify the participle and the noun it modifies.

1. The lifeguard having jumped into the water, the child's mother came running.
2. The concert having started, the doors were closed.
3. The armistice having been signed, fighting ceased.
4. The cars returned to the highway, the blizzard having finally ended.
5. The parade approaching, the crowd cheered wildly.
6. The balloon having risen, the spectators watched it fly away.
7. Years having passed, no one could remember what the argument had been about.
8. The tickets being so expensive, we decided not to attend.

The Correct Use of Participles

Tense of Participles

The present participle generally denotes action taking place at the same time as the verb.

The perfect participle denotes action completed before the action of the verb.

> The chorus, *singing* the song, entered the hall.
> (*Present participle*)
> *Having finished* their work, the employees were dismissed.
> (*Perfect participle*)

Exercise 86

Choose the correct form of each participle.

1. (Waving, Having waved) banners in front of the embassy for some time, the demonstrators moved on.
2. (Reading, Having read) the novel, Joan wrote a review of it for the school paper.
3. (Running, Having run) beside the car, the dog barked continuously.
4. Andrea spent three weeks (writing, having written) a paper about the Harlem Renaissance.
5. (Walking, Having walked) to school every morning, I see the sun rise.
6. (Eating, Having eaten) breakfast, Melinda packed a lunch to take with her.
7. (Feeding, Having fed) the fish, we watched them chase one another around the aquarium.
8. (Riding, Having ridden) fifty miles on his bicycle, Tony could barely walk.
9. (Crying, Having cried) for her mother, the lost child wandered down the aisles of the store.
10. (Drinking, Having drunk) the juice, I rinsed the glass in the sink.

Dangling Participles

A participle does the work of a verb and an adjective. As an adjective, the participle modifies a noun or a pronoun. A dangling participle is one that modifies no other word in the sentence. Avoid writing sentences with *dangling participles*.

> *Walking* to school, the horse ran away.

In this sentence *walking* does not modify any noun. Who is walking to school? It is not the horse. The participle *walking* must have a word that it limits. To correct a dangling participle, supply the missing noun or pronoun.

> Walking to school, *Becky* saw the horse run away.

Adding the noun *Becky* makes the meaning clear.

Exercise 87

The following sentences contain dangling participles. Rewrite them correctly.

1. Whistling loudly, the taxi sped away.
2. Having worked all morning, the job still was not finished.
3. Keeping my promise, the room was left in order.
4. Sitting on the porch, the storm passed.
5. Reading a book, the bus passed my stop.
6. Skipping down the street, the car arrived first.
7. Holding the child's hand, the elephant looked so big.
8. Folding one load of laundry, the dryer stopped.
9. Being suspended from school, Dad was very angry.
10. Opening the window, the robin flew away.

Exercise 88 (Participle Review Exercise)

Name each participle and tell which noun it modifies.
1. Francis, whistling quietly, learned the tune.
2. The Spanish gained wealth from mines worked by Indians.
3. Conquistadores having made the initial explorations, the Crown quickly claimed authority.
4. *Common Sense* is a pamphlet written by Thomas Paine during the American Revolution.
5. Urging separation from England, Paine captured the imagination of the colonial rebels.
6. The fire, spreading rapidly, caused great alarm.
7. We enjoyed a delicious Japanese meal, prepared by a trained chef.
8. Afflicted by allergies, Connie sneezed and sneezed.
9. The road leading to the lake has been washed away.
10. Ground having been broken, construction began immediately.
11. We heard Jill singing in the next room.
12. The team, having been defeated, congratulated the winners.
13. The map drawn by Carl was the most accurate one available.
14. A sentence expressing sudden emotion is called an exclamatory sentence.
15. Expressing emotion, Mr. Brumlik addressed the small group.

Complete each sentence with an appropriate participial phrase.
16. The house _____ began to deteriorate.
17. _____, the guests departed.
18. The Jacksons own the sailboat _____.
19. The baby _____ was not injured.
20. The doctor _____ asked some questions.
21. _____, they set out for a day's ride.
22. _____, the company made a generous offer.
23. New Orleans, _____, controls much river trade.
24. _____, the governor climbed onto the stage.
25. _____, she left home.

Sharpening Your Skills

Use the participles listed below in sentences of your own. Choose five to write as participial phrases and five to write as participial adjectives.

criticized   marked
cruising   remembering
discovered   rewriting
having pretended   rewritten
imagining   searching

Lesson 2 Gerunds

A gerund is a verb form ending in *ing* that has the properties of a verb and a noun.

Properties of the Gerund

A gerund has the properties of a verb and a noun. For this reason it is sometimes called a verbal noun.

PROPERTIES OF A VERB

1. It is derived from a verb.
2. It may take an object.
3. It may be modified by an adverb or an adverbial phrase.

PROPERTIES OF A NOUN

It is used as a noun.

Uses of the Gerund

As a noun, a gerund may be used as the subject or the object of a verb, as a subjective complement, as the object of a preposition, or as an appositive.

Traveling to distant places is a joy. (*Subject*)
She enjoyed *skating* on the lake. (*Direct object*)
His favorite pastime is *reading* biographies. (*Subjective complement*)
He began by *speaking* to the jury. (*Object of preposition*)
My appointed task, *washing* the car, kept me busy. (*Appositive*)

Name the verb from which each of these gerunds is derived and point out the adverbial modifier or the object of each gerund.

Exercise 89 (Gerunds Used as Subjects)

Identify the gerunds and name any direct objects or adverbial modifiers that follow them.

1. Sleeping in the park is forbidden.
2. Reading in the dark can hurt your eyes.
3. During a rainstorm, driving can be difficult.
4. Building sand castles is not my idea of a good time.
5. Watching the birth of the calf moved him to tears.
6. Finding dry firewood after the rain may be impossible.
7. Holding the sleeping child in one arm left her other arm free to open the door.
8. Riding a bicycle on the sidewalk is illegal in many places.
9. Jumping the boxes in the hallway caused Melanie to twist her ankle.
10. Playing baseball every afternoon keeps Jerri from doing homework.

Complete each sentence with an appropriate gerund phrase used as a subject.

11. _____ is dangerous work.
12. _____ is fun for me.
13. _____ helps increase your vocabulary.
14. _____ is a good health habit.
15. _____ takes courage.

Exercise 90 (Gerunds Used as Direct Objects)

Identify the gerunds and name any direct objects or adverbial modifiers that follow them.

1. City ordinance forbids swimming in the lagoon.
2. Molly has just finished painting a picture of her canary.
3. Does Jeremy prefer taking the train?
4. Lillian hates seeing violence on television.
5. The gardener has finished mowing the lawn.
6. The computer monitor began flashing on and off.
7. The printer stopped running.
8. Mr. Lavell stood waiting in the freezing rain.
9. The small brown animal keeps scratching at the tree.
10. Maura enjoys reading the newspaper.

Complete each sentence with an appropriate gerund phrase used as a direct object.

11. Our opening exercises include _____.
12. Do you enjoy _____?
13. Jessica proposed _____.
14. We should avoid _____.
15. Have they begun _____?

> **A gerund phrase consists of the gerund and its complements and modifiers.**

Protecting the forests is the work of forest rangers.
Courtesy demands *answering an invitation promptly*.

Exercise 91 (Gerunds Used as Complements)

Name each gerund phrase, and then rewrite the sentence substituting the gerund phrase for the subject and the subject for the gerund phrase.
The first one is done for you.

1. An important industry in Australia is raising sheep.
   Raising sheep is an important industry in Australia.
2. Lucy's work is teaching reading.
3. My favorite kind of vacation is camping in the mountains.
4. The problem is finding the owner.
5. Leon's duty is answering the telephone.
6. The most dangerous part of the trip was crossing the foaming river.
7. Perjury is lying under oath.
8. Their responsibility is keeping the goats out of the backyard.
9. The task is completing this exercise.
10. Helen's chore today is doing the dishes.

Complete each sentence with an appropriate gerund phrase used as a subjective complement.

11. The lifeguard's job is _____.
12. The guide dog's duty was _____.
13. Bernard's greatest pleasure is _____.
14. Kelly's goal is _____.
15. Members of both clubs were _____.

Exercise 92 (Gerunds Used as Objects of Prepositions)

Name the gerund and the preposition in each sentence. Give the verb from which the gerund is derived.

1. Do you have any objections to building the garage now?
2. She carefully followed the directions for assembling the bike.
3. Dino keeps in shape by running five miles every morning.
4. Tricia earned money for her vacation by mowing lawns.
5. He was commended for answering in a clear voice.
6. By pressing that button, you clear the screen.
7. Lauren's family was surprised by her taking a job in Japan.
8. By exercising daily, physical fitness can be maintained.
9. Jasper got the job by calling the office every day.
10. The band prepared for the contest by practicing every afternoon.

Complete each sentence with an appropriate gerund phrase used as the object of a preposition.

11. Do you find pleasure in _____?
12. What is the most effective way of _____?
13. Jermain excels in _____.
14. This will be a good reward for _____.
15. Lila got the party going by _____.

Exercise 93 (Gerunds Used as Appositives)

Name each gerund phrase used as an appositive and tell which word it explains.

1. One of the major agricultural activities of the Midwest, raising corn, can rob the soil of its minerals.
2. Renata's problem, learning the language, was a difficult one.
3. The programmer's task, creating a simple data base, took longer than expected.
4. Izzie continues to pursue his lifelong ambition, becoming an acrobatic tightrope walker.
5. Their current activity, planting new shrubs, may take several hours.
6. Her favorite recreation, playing horseshoes, does not appeal to many people.

7. Eli likes his assignment, guarding the cupcakes.
8. The most important part of the lesson, making an outline, involves careful thought.
9. The third race, jumping the hurdles, is expected to be close.
10. The architects enjoyed their assignment, designing an inner city police station.

Complete each sentence with an appropriate gerund phrase used as an appositive.
11. A thrilling winter sport, _____, is enjoyed by our family.
12. My task, _____, is always fun.
13. Debbie's favorite activity, _____, occupies much of her time.
14. Marcus enjoys his daily exercise, _____.
15. His summer job, _____, gave him good experience.

Exercise 94 (Gerund Review Exercise)

Name each gerund and tell how it is used in the sentence.
1. Ramona has considered taking a trip to Africa.
2. Raising the lid was a difficult task.
3. Irrigation is a means of converting desert land into fertile fields.
4. Bringing water down from the mountains is a common irrigation method.
5. Ralph's appointed task, directing traffic at the fair, was pleasant for him.
6. They enhanced their presentation by showing slides.
7. Exploring the attic is rainy day fun.
8. I remember writing that letter.
9. Wondering what you had done with it kept me anxious for weeks.
10. You could help by returning the letter to me.
11. Saying those things was very unkind of me.
12. Joe's job, tracing unclaimed packages, is interesting.
13. Your singing the new song inspired everyone.
14. Eating is one of Manuel's favorite activities.
15. The latest trend, wearing two pairs of socks at one time, was stretching the shoes into odd shapes.

Complete each sentence with an appropriate gerund phrase and tell how the gerund phrase is used.

16. _____ gives us a knowledge of our world.
17. Windmills are used for _____.
18. _____ requires special skill.
19. The students enjoyed _____.
20. _____ is a fun and inexpensive form of recreation.
21. The clerk's job, _____, was made easier by the new computer.
22. Paul tried _____.
23. The process of _____ is taught by the career guidance counselor.
24. _____ can be fun.
25. Maureen jogs around the campus before _____.

Sharpening Your Skills

Locate pictures in your social studies or science textbooks. Write a sentence for each picture, using a gerund phrase. Vary the use of the gerund phrase with each new sentence.

Market stall in Oaxaca, Mexico

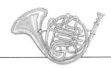

Nouns and Pronouns
Modifying Gerunds

A noun or a pronoun that modifies a gerund is usually in the possessive case.

Cormack approves of *our* joining the club.
Cormack approves of *Wendy's* joining the club.

Exercise 95

Select the correct word to complete each sentence.
1. (Me, My) playing the French horn at midnight upsets my neighbors.
2. Joan would not approve (Bill, Bill's) attending the conference.
3. There is no doubt about (she, her) being the best candidate.
4. (Them, Their) being transferred to another school made us angry.
5. She was upset by (him, his) looking at the old photographs.
6. The (cat, cat's) purring soothed the baby.
7. There was some question about (Marilyn, Marilyn's) being able to pass the test.
8. (Duane, Duane's) making the team was cause for celebration.
9. Miles was afraid of the (company, company's) being robbed.
10. The coach noted (Darlene, Darlene's) jumping ability.

Ing Nouns

Many nouns end in *ing*. Some of these are formed from verbs and others are not.

The *barking* of the dog aroused our attention.

Barking is a noun used as the subject of the verb *aroused*. It is modified by the article *the* and by an adjectival phrase, *of the dog*. The following characteristics will help you to recognize an *ing* noun:
1. It may not take an object.
2. It may not be modified by an adverb.
3. It is often preceded by the article *the* and followed by the preposition *of*.
4. It may have a plural form.

Exercise 96

Name the *ing* nouns and give their syntax.

1. We could hear the sighing of the wind in the trees.
2. He gave parts of his earnings to charity.
3. The baby was awakened by the crashing of the waves.
4. We were frightened by the owl's screeching.
5. Have the Impressionist paintings gone on exhibit yet?
6. Confucius had many wise sayings.
7. The harvesting of the corn was hard work.
8. In all games, the feelings of the players must be remembered.
9. Scott's father had misgivings about his decision.
10. Our attention was attracted by the flashing of the lights on the sign.
11. The exercising of our freedoms requires good judgment.
12. Her timing was perfect.
13. Did Tim attend the meeting?
14. The writing of William Faulkner depicts life in the South.
15. The paying of the bills is a monthly ritual for my mother.

Recognizing Nouns, Gerunds, Participles

Remember that words ending in *ing* may be participles, participial adjectives, gerunds, *ing* nouns, or the progressive verb forms. Note the use of the word *singing* in the following sentences:

The *singing* of the birds brought joy to the hikers. (Ing *noun*)
The boy *singing* the solo is my cousin. (*Participle*)
Clare takes *singing* lessons. (*Participial adjective*)
We enjoyed *singing* that song. (*Gerund*)
The choir has been *singing* for an hour. (*Progressive verb form*)

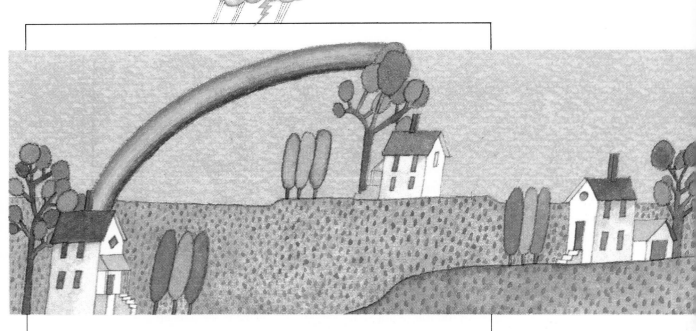

Exercise 97

Name the *ing* words and identify each as a participle, a participial adjective, a gerund, an *ing* noun, or a verb in the progressive form.

1. We were watching a broken fragment of rainbow after the storm.
2. The girls took whatever was necessary for the camping trip.
3. Studying a foreign language helps us understand our own.
4. The neighborhood pranksters kept ringing our doorbell.
5. The school bell has been ringing every five minutes for the last hour.
6. Philip has a ringing in his ears.
7. The handbell ringing at the wrong pitch is that one.
8. The ringing bells bothered people all over town.
9. The field being plowed, the farmer planted the seeds.
10. Jerome, listening intently to the radio headset, did not hear the approaching tornado.
11. Jacklyn was making a musical instrument as a science project.
12. Fearing a dead battery in the cold weather, he kept starting his car.
13. Her endearing personality does not excuse this behavior.
14. Harold keeps losing his house keys.
15. Tying garlic on a string around his neck didn't help his cold.

Lesson 3 Infinitives

An infinitive is a verb form, usually preceded by *to*, that has the properties of a verb, a noun, an adjective, or an adverb.

To read good books improves the mind.
I have planned *to leave* early.

The infinitives *to read* and *to leave* have the force of verbs because *to read* has the object *books* and *to leave* is modified by the adverb *early*. They are used as nouns, for the infinitive phrase *to read good books* is the subject of *improves* and the phrase *to leave early* is the object of *have planned*.

In the following sentences the infinitive is used as an adjective and as an adverb.

The florist has flowers *to sell*. (*Limits the noun* flowers)
The star sang *to please* the audience. (*Modifies the verb* sang)
I was pleased *to receive* your invitation. (*Modifies the adjective* pleased)

Properties of the Infinitive

An infinitive has the properties of a verb and those of a noun, an adjective, or an adverb.

PROPERTIES OF A VERB

1. It is derived from a verb.
2. It may take an object.
3. It may be modified by an adverb or an adverbial phrase.

OTHER PROPERTIES

1. It may be used as a noun.
2. It may limit a noun or a pronoun.
3. It may modify a verb, an adjective, or an adverb.

Forms of the Infinitive

The infinitive is used in the present and the perfect tenses, active and passive voices.

	ACTIVE	PASSIVE
PRESENT:	to write	to be written
PERFECT:	to have written	to have been written

Uses of the Infinitive

In a sentence the infinitive may do the work of a noun, an adjective, or an adverb.

> **An infinitive phrase consists of the infinitive and its complements and modifiers.**

Juan likes *to write poetry.*
To paint beautifully is Janet's dream.

Infinitives Used as Nouns

The infinitive is used as a noun when it does the work of a noun. It may be used as the subject or the object of a verb, as the object of a preposition, as a subjective complement, or as an appositive.

To win was their only thought. (*Subject*)
I should like *to live* in Boston. (*Direct object*)
He was about *to write* the letter. (*Object of preposition*)
The duty of every citizen is *to vote.* (*Subjective complement*)
She had one desire, *to win* the race. (*Appositive*)

An infinitive is considered to be an appositive when it is used after the expletive *it.*

It is a police officer's duty *to enforce* the laws. (*Appositive*)

The infinitive is in apposition with *it.* In this sentence the infinitive phrase *to enforce the laws* is the logical, or real, subject. The infinitive phrase can be read in place of the expletive *it.*

To enforce the laws is a police officer's duty.

Exercise 98 (Infinitives Used as Subjects)

Name the infinitive and the infinitive phrase in each sentence.
1. To refuse aid was out of the question.
2. To achieve honors requires much study.
3. To feed the hungry is a serious responsibility.
4. To find housing for poor people in the city is difficult.
5. To organize the assembly-line workers is Leonora's job.
6. To speak in public requires skill.
7. To hope for success is not enough.
8. To practice daily requires discipline.
9. To study law is Luke's desire.
10. To cross the river on horseback took a long time.

Complete each sentence with an appropriate infinitive or infinitive phrase used as the subject.
11. _____ is an accomplishment.
12. _____ is a good feeling.
13. _____ can be dangerous.
14. _____ requires a lot of studying.
15. _____ makes me happy.

Exercise 99 (Infinitives Used as Direct Objects)

Name the infinitive and the infinitive phrase in each sentence.
1. Frieda tried to skate backwards.
2. Ramon told me to give the monkey a bath.
3. The drummer upstairs likes to practice early in the morning.
4. Monica intends to hike from Canada to Mexico through the mountains.
5. Have you decided to move to the country?
6. Nikki has been wanting to read *The Adventures of Huckleberry Finn*.
7. Terri, try to be more careful.
8. We have planned to save coupons for free gifts.
9. Polly wanted to watch the meteor shower.
10. Willie wanted to study medicine.

Complete each sentence with an appropriate infinitive or infinitive phrase used as a direct object.

11. Ursula intended _____.

12. Joel promised _____.

13. Do you want _____?

14. The water continued _____.

15. We should try _____.

Exercise 100 (Infinitives Used as Objects of Prepositions)

Name the infinitive and the infinitive phrase in each sentence.
Give the preposition that introduces the phrase.

1. Linda wanted nothing but to preserve the peace.
2. The president is about to speak.
3. She had no choice but to change the flat tire.
4. Miles is about to open the mail.
5. Little was possible but to apologize.
6. Lydia is about to call the police.
7. Hank seemed about to cry.
8. No action can be taken but to suspend the students involved.
9. Olivia had no choice but to wait for the tow truck.
10. The concert is about to begin.

Complete each sentence with an appropriate infinitive or infinitive phrase used as the object of a preposition.

11. The astronauts had no choice but _____.

12. About _____, Wally behaved very politely.

13. The doctors had no other aim but _____.

14. Kale has no motive except _____.

15. I can think of no way to afford that bike except _____.

Exercise 101 (Infinitives Used as Complements)

Name the infinitive and the infinitive phrase in each sentence.
1. Tillie's habit is to tip her head to the left when reading.
2. The job is to give everyone at least three choices.
3. Leo's task was to paint scenery for the play.
4. The main function of the safety patrol is to prevent accidents.
5. Her desire is to learn German.
6. The goal of that group is to end racism.
7. The work of a prospector is to search for minerals.
8. The scout's mission was to find a safe pass through the mountains.
9. Molly's only choice was to sell her home.
10. The worst fault is to be conscious of none.

Complete each sentence with an appropriate infinitive or infinitive phrase used as a complement.
11. The governor's duty is ⎯⎯⎯⎯⎯⎯⎯⎯⎯⎯⎯⎯⎯⎯⎯⎯ .
12. The joy of many parents is ⎯⎯⎯⎯⎯⎯⎯⎯⎯⎯⎯⎯⎯⎯ .
13. A driver's responsibility is ⎯⎯⎯⎯⎯⎯⎯⎯⎯⎯⎯⎯⎯⎯ .
14. The best plan is ⎯⎯⎯⎯⎯⎯⎯⎯⎯⎯⎯⎯⎯⎯⎯⎯⎯⎯ .
15. Her most difficult problem was ⎯⎯⎯⎯⎯⎯⎯⎯⎯⎯⎯⎯ .

Exercise 102 (Infinitives Used as Appositives)

Name the infinitive and the infinitive phrase in each sentence. Tell what word the appositive explains.
1. David's job, to cut the grass, must come first.
2. Liv's plan, to organize a ski trip, succeeded.
3. The pilot's duty, to fly the plane safely, is a great responsibility.
4. Mom objected to Steve's proposal, to paint his room red with black stripes.
5. It is a smart thing to save some money.
6. The researcher's goal, to cure cancer, may be reached soon.
7. It was a great feat of medicine to conquer smallpox.
8. Theo's ambition, to sing the lead in the school play, was defeated when she got sick.
9. The contract to build the new bridge went to Fox Construction Company.
10. It is often a difficult task to locate oil deposits.

Complete the following sentences with an appropriate infinitive or infinitive phrase used as an appositive.

11. Mr. Turner gave the final instructions, _____.
12. Their desire _____ seemed funny to us.
13. The gardener's job, _____, was nearly impossible.
14. My plan _____ will take only two weeks.
15. Margo's hope _____ failed.

Exercise 103

Identify the infinitives used as nouns and tell their function in each sentence.

1. To reach the finish line at all was reward enough for Ted.
2. He tried to run at an even pace.
3. He seemed about to collapse at the halfway point.
4. Lauren's job was to pace him through the last three miles.
5. Karl's task, to bring water along, seemed simple enough.
6. To get water, however, was a problem.
7. The local water supply was about to go dry.
8. Lauren decided to find some juice.
9. We hope to see the finish on the television news report tonight.
10. To find the hotel took three hours.
11. Ted refused to accept help.
12. His desire to finish kept him going.
13. Race officials promised to mail the results.
14. Will you try to run the race next year?
15. To be intent on winning is not the goal.

Complete each sentence with an appropriate infinitive or infinitive phrase. Give the syntax of the added word(s).

16. The parachutists dared _____.
17. Would you like _____.
18. _____ was impossible.
19. _____ was her desire.
20. _____ required time.
21. That jet is about _____.
22. It is a privilege _____.
23. Ben plans _____.
24. My little brother likes _____.
25. Sometimes it is not enough _____.

393

Sharpening Your Skills

Try writing two sentences for each type of infinitive. Use information from your other subjects to help make your sentences interesting.

Infinitives Used as Adjectives

An infinitive is used as an adjective when it does the work of an adjective; that is, when it modifies a noun or a pronoun.

> This is a good place *to have* a picnic.
> Every citizen has the right *to vote*.
> She seems *to be* happy.

Exercise 104

Name the infinitives used as adjectives and the nouns they modify.
1. The lost kitten had no food to eat.
2. Marla is a person to be trusted.
3. An artist must have an ability to work with color.
4. Color blindness is the inability to distinguish certain colors.
5. Cherries to preserve are on sale here.
6. Actors have many lines to memorize.
7. Failure to observe traffic regulations can be fatal.
8. Sylvia had several checks to write.
9. This is an occasion to be remembered.
10. My aunt received a summons to serve on a jury.

Infinitives Used as Adverbs

Infinitives are used as adverbs when they express the purpose, the cause, or the result of an action. An infinitive used as an adverb may modify a verb, an adjective, or an adverb.

> Rosa went *to see* the circus. (*Modifies the verb* went)
> The apprentice was quick *to learn*. (*Modifies the adjective* quick)
> We arrived too late *to gain* admission. (*Modifies the adverb* late)

Exercise 105

Name the infinitives used as adverbs and tell whether each modifies a verb, an adjective, or an adverb.

1. We eat to live.
2. The players are ready to start.
3. Marco came to feed his turtle.
4. That pitcher is used to hold orange juice.
5. The farmer went out to plant her crops.
6. To write a good paragraph, you must organize your ideas.
7. The Masons were anxious to return to Brazil.
8. The goats came to greet us.
9. No mountain is easy to climb for the inexperienced.
10. The snow was too heavy to shovel.

The Correct Use of Infinitives

Tense of Infinitives

The present infinitive is used when the action expressed by the infinitive takes place at the same time as the action of the main verb or after the time expressed by the main verb. The perfect infinitive is used only when the action has been completed at the time of the main verb.

> I like *to write* letters. (*Same time as main verb*)
> I had intended *to write* to you yesterday. (*Same time as main verb*)
> I shall come *to see* you. (*After time of main verb; the* seeing *will take place after the* coming)
> She seems *to have succeeded* in her work. (*Action completed before time of main verb*)

Both the present and the perfect infinitive may be used with the verb *ought*. The present infinitive indicates obligation or necessity; the perfect infinitive indicates that the action did not take place.

> Joan ought *to call* immediately. (*Indicates duty or necessity*)
> Joan ought *to have called*. (*Indicates that she did not call*)

Exercise 106

Choose the correct tense of each infinitive.

1. We are eager (to see, to have seen) your new home.
2. The train was scheduled (to leave, to have left) early in the morning.
3. I will be happy (to give, to have given) you the ten-cent tour tomorrow.
4. Does Milton intend (to come, to have come) to the party?
5. That woman is said (to see, to have seen) every important city in Europe.
6. Did Lana mean (to do, to have done) that?
7. Ronny seems (to play, to have played) the piano every afternoon this week.
8. Gladys will be pleased (to receive, to have received) your letter.
9. Wanting (to meet, to have met) the principal, Ms. Tipson requested an interview.
10. You ought (to finish, to have finished) yesterday.

Omission of the Infinitive Sign

The infinitive is used without *to,* often called the sign of the infinitive, in the following cases:

1. After verbs of perception, such as *hear, see, behold, know, feel,* and so forth.

   We watched the great tree *fall.*
   The campers heard the bear *pass.*
   The doctor felt the patient *move.*

2. After the verbs *let, dare, need, make, bid,* and so forth.

   The dean made the student *study.*
   The swimmers dared not *jump* into the shallow pool.
   You need not *go* to the library.

3. Frequently after the preposition *but* and the subordinate conjunction *than.*

   The lions did nothing but *roar* for food.
   It is more like him to write than *visit.*

Exercise 107

Identify the hidden infinitives.
1. Marshall saw Halley's Comet appear in the sky.
2. He dared not show his fear.
3. People will not see that comet blaze again until 2061.
4. We watched the astronomer look at it through a telescope.
5. Seeing the comet streaking through the sky made us feel small.
6. The commuters heard the whistle blow.
7. I felt something sting me.
8. The puppies did nothing but play all day.
9. Doug let her borrow his chemistry book.
10. The computer instructor's advice helped us fix the program.
11. Olga bade him come quickly.
12. Sis heard the baby cry.
13. Patricia is more likely to call than write.
14. Fear made Kelly weep.
15. Fred need not take this class.

Split Infinitives

A split infinitive occurs when a word or a group of words comes between *to* and the rest of the infinitive. Take care to avoid split infinitives.

> I went *to merely see* the picture.

Exercise 108

Tell where in the sentence the adverb at the left belongs.

not	1. Victor seemed to care very much.
already	2. The snow appears to have begun falling.
soon	3. They want you to announce the test date.
thoroughly	4. Denise seemed to enjoy the play.
not	5. Nat expected to see you today.
quickly	6. Don't expect to sweep the chimney.
justly	7. To speak of others is our duty.
smoothly	8. Sandra learned to land the plane.
eventually	9. Gail hopes to become a professional folk singer.
correctly	10. Bill planned to answer all the questions.

Exercise 109 (Check on Uses of Infinitives)

Name each infinitive and its function: subject, direct object, complement, object of preposition, appositive, adjective, or adverb.

1. Learn to ski properly.
2. To break your leg is not the goal.
3. Hallie tried to fit into my boots.
4. The idea, to have fun, got lost in the details.
5. To read silently by the fire is his greatest delight.
6. Lonnie was about to jump on the train when the police arrived.
7. David arrived too early to be admitted to the play.
8. Phoebe likes to read about the history of women.
9. The cold made Mike shiver.
10. The farmer had baskets of green peppers to sell.

You Are the Author

Choose one.

1. Frost claimed that a poem should "begin in delight and end in wisdom!" Does "Stopping by Woods on a Snowy Evening" illustrate his claim? Write a brief composition in which you use different kinds of verbals to agree or disagree with him.
2. Write a paragraph about stopping at, and then going on from, a place to which you were attracted. Use three types of verbals.

Chapter Challenge

Read this selection very carefully and then answer the questions that follow.

> ¹Standing in the raw winter wind had not been pleasant for the huge throng gathered before the Capitol to view the inauguration of a new president. ²The prospect of witnessing so historic an event, however, compensated the waiting crowd for the many hours of discomfort.
>
> ³A sudden burst of applause announced that the proceedings were about to begin. ⁴A prayer having been offered, the president-elect stepped forward and, placing his hand upon the Bible, repeated in a firm voice the oath administered by the chief justice. ⁵In the inaugural address that followed, the president assured the people of his determination to labor untiringly to justify the confidence they had placed in him.

1. Name a participle in the first sentence.
2. What noun does the participle in the first sentence modify?
3. The word *waiting* in the second sentence is what part of speech?
4. Name the participles in the fourth sentence.
5. Why is the noun *prayer* in the fourth sentence in the nominative case?
6. What part of speech is *proceedings* in the third sentence?
7. Find a gerund in the first sentence.
8. How is the gerund in the first sentence used?
9. In what respects does the word *witnessing* in the second sentence resemble a verb?
10. What is the syntax of the word *witnessing* in the second sentence?
11. Find an infinitive in the third sentence.
12. Is the infinitive in the third sentence used as a noun, an adjective, or an adverb?
13. Find an infinitive in the last sentence that is used as an adjective and name the noun that it modifies.
14. What word does the infinitive *to justify* in the last sentence modify?
15. Name an infinitive in the first sentence.
16. How is the infinitive in the first sentence used?

Chapter 6

Adverbs

Don't Ride the Bus on Monday

by Kai Friese

from *Rosa Parks: The Movement Organizes*

It was Thursday, December 1, 1955. The workday was over, and crowds of people boarded the green-and-white buses that **trundled** through the streets of Montgomery. Rosa Parks was tired after a full day of stitching and ironing shirts at the Montgomery Fair Department Store. She thought she was lucky to have gotten one of the last seats in the rear section of the Cleveland Avenue bus that would take her home.

Soon the back of the bus was full, and several people were standing in the rear. The bus rolled on through Court Square, where African Americans had been auctioned off during the days of the Confederacy, and came to a stop in front of the Empire Theatre. The next passenger aboard stood in the front of an aisle. He was a white man.

When he noticed that a white person had to stand, the bus driver, James F. Blake, called out to the four black people who were sitting just behind the white section. He said they would have to give up their seats for the new passenger. No one stood up. "You'd better make it light on yourself and let me have those seats," the driver said threateningly. Three men got up and went to stand at the back of the bus. But Rosa Parks wasn't about to move. She had been in this situation before, and she had always given up her seat. She had always felt insulted by the experience. "It meant that I didn't have a right to do anything but get on the bus, give them my fare and then be pushed around wherever they wanted me," she said.

By a quirk of fate, the driver of the bus on this December evening was the same James F. Blake who had once before removed the troublesome Rosa Parks from his bus for refusing to enter by the back door. That had been a long time ago, in 1943. Rosa Parks

Rosa Parks on a bus in Montgomery, Alabama

didn't feel like being pushed around again. She told the driver that she wasn't in the white section and she wasn't going to move.

Blake knew the rules, though. He knew that the white section was wherever the driver said it was. If more white passengers got on the bus, he could stretch the white section to the back of the bus and make all the blacks stand. He shouted to Rosa Parks to move to the back of the bus. She wasn't impressed. She told him again that she wasn't moving. Everyone in the bus was silent, wondering what would happen next. Finally Blake told Rosa Parks that he would have her arrested for violating the racial **segregation** codes. In a firm but quiet voice, she told him that he could do what he wanted to do because she wasn't moving.

Blake got off the bus and came back with an officer of the Montgomery Police Department. As the officer placed Rosa Parks under arrest, she asked him plainly, "Why do you people push us around?"

With the eyes of all the passengers on him, the officer could only answer in confusion. "I don't know. I'm just obeying the law," he said.

Rosa Parks was taken to the police station, where she was booked and fingerprinted. While the policemen were filling out forms, she asked whether she could have a drink of water. She was told that the drinking fountain in the station was for whites only. Then a policewoman marched her into a long corridor facing a wall of iron bars. A barred door slid open. She went inside. The door clanged shut, and she was locked in. She was in jail.

The Writer's Craft

1. In what ways was Rosa Parks a victim of racial discrimination? How would you have felt in her place? Why?
2. The title of the selection refers to a protest organized by African-American community members as a result of Rosa Parks's arrest. Parks's refusal to give up her seat was itself an act of protest. How does the author help us to understand Parks's reasons for doing what she did?
3. How does the adverb *threateningly* in the third paragraph serve to reinforce the injustice of Parks's experience?

Recalling What You Know

1. Most adverbs answer a question: *when, where, why, how, how much,* or *how little.* In *"Move," he said angrily,* what is the adverb? What question does it answer?

2. In the sentence *That night Rosa met with a group of ministers,* the phrase *that night* is used as an adverb. What word does *that night* modify? What part of speech is the modified word?

Lesson 1 Classification and Comparison of Adverbs

An adverb is a word that modifies a verb, an adjective, an adverb, a participle, a gerund, or an infinitive.

Rosa Parks *wearily* boarded the bus.
(*Wearily* modifies the verb *boarded.*)

She was *very* tired.
(*Very* modifies the adjective *tired.*)

Her feet ached *too* much.
(*Too* modifies the adverb *much.*)

Parks, believing *firmly* that she was right, refused to move.
(*Firmly* modifies the participle *believing.*)

After *politely* refusing to move, Rosa was arrested.
(*Politely* modifies the gerund *refusing.*)

The people sought to reverse the verdict *peacefully.*
(*Peacefully* modifies the infinitive *to reverse.*)

Classification of Adverbs

Classification According to Meaning

Adverbs of time answer the question *when* or *how often*. They include such adverbs as *again, before, early, frequently, now*.

Adverbs of place answer the question *where*. These are adverbs of place: *above, away, below, down, forward, overhead, upward*.

Adverbs of degree answer the question *how much* or *how little*. They include the following adverbs: *almost, barely, little, merely, quite, rather, very*.

Adverbs of manner answer the question *how* or *in what manner*. *Easily, fervently, quickly, thoroughly* are adverbs of manner.

Adverbs of affirmation and negation tell whether a statement is true or false. They include the adverbs *yes, no, indeed, doubtless, not*.

Exercise 110

Identify each italicized adverb according to time, place, degree, manner, affirmation, or negation.

1. Jim Crow laws *unjustly* restricted African Americans.
2. One of these laws required African Americans on public buses to ride *only* in the back.
3. Rosa Parks, *rightfully* refusing to obey these laws, was arrested.
4. She reacted *quite calmly* to her arrest.
5. She felt *very* bad while in jail, however.
6. The police fingerprinted Rosa and *then* locked her in a cell.
7. *First,* the people who went to church prayed.
8. Several ministers, including Martin Luther King, Jr., spoke *honestly* to achieve justice *peacefully*.
9. After the service, the people *quickly* elected Dr. King president of the *newly* organized Montgomery Improvement Association.
10. After the election, the people continued their protest *daily* by *not* riding the buses.

Classification According to Use

Simple Adverbs

> **A simple adverb is an adverb used merely as a modifier.**

Slowly the clouds moved across the blue sky.

Interrogative Adverbs

> **An interrogative adverb is an adverb used in asking questions. The interrogative adverbs are *how, when, where,* and *why.* They usually modify the verb.**

Why is carbon monoxide dangerous?
Where is Yosemite National Park?
How can I identify this rock?

Exercise 111

Identify the adverbs in each sentence. Tell whether they are simple or interrogative adverbs.
1. The rusty car rolled forward slowly.
2. When did the car start to approach the corner?
3. It barely scraped Tom's car.
4. He quickly jumped out and started angrily shaking his fist.
5. He yelled loudly at the offending driver.
6. How long did he chase the empty car?
7. When did he realize his mistake?
8. The car kept rolling away from him.
9. The police finally stopped it.
10. Where will they take the old car?

Relative Adverbs

> **A relative adverb is a word that does the work of an adverb and a relative pronoun. The principal relative adverbs are *when, where,* and *why.***

Rick returned to the room *where* he had left his jacket.

Where explains the place of the action; hence it is an adverb.
Where also does the work of a relative pronoun, for it joins the clause *where he had left his jacket* to the principal clause.

NOTE: A relative adverb usually follows a noun of time, place, or reason. The test of a relative adverb is that you may replace it with a prepositional phrase containing a relative pronoun.

Rick returned to the room *in which* he had left his jacket.

Exercise 112

Identify the relative adverbs and tell whether they explain the reason for the action, its time, or its place.
1. Winter is the time when the flowers sleep.
2. That is the reason why I like the story of Galileo.
3. This is the house where the author lived.
4. San Antonio is the city where the battle of the Alamo was fought.
5. September is the month when the autumn season begins.
6. They drove past an orchard where many peach trees were in bloom.
7. There are moments when all wish to be alone.
8. We discovered a field where beautiful violets grow.
9. Paris is the place where we shall meet.
10. There are mornings when it is difficult to wake up.
11. I ran to the corner where the bus stop is.
12. Do you know the reason why the bus is late?
13. We do not know the hour when the bus will arrive.
14. I have no idea why we begin work so early.
15. This is the stop where I get off.

Adverbial Objectives

> **An adverbial objective is a noun that expresses time, distance, measure, weight, value, or direction and performs the function of an adverb.**

James has attended this school two *years*.

The word *years* is a noun. In this sentence it indicates time, a function usually performed by an adverb, by telling how long James has attended school.

Because an adverbial objective resembles an adverb, it may modify a verb, an adjective, or an adverb. Because it is a noun, the adverbial objective may be modified by an adjective. In the sentence above, the adverbial objective *years* modifies the verb *has attended*, and it is modified by the adjective *two*.

Exercise 113

Name the adverbial objectives and tell whether each expresses time, distance, measure, weight, value, or direction.
1. The meeting lasted three hours.
2. Moira spent a month in the hospital.
3. Brent waited all day for you.
4. This photograph costs fifty dollars.
5. Troy went home.
6. Each lane measures eight feet.

7. The Puccios live five kilometers from Venice.
8. My brother hopes to grow seven feet tall.
9. That package weighs eleven ounces.
10. The diving pool is four meters deep.

Complete the remaining five sentences with original adverbial objectives.

11. _____ my sister won the annual science fair award. (time)
12. Some people exercise _____. (time)
13. The antelope journeyed _____ from its home. (distance)
14. Mom used _____ of flour to make the cake. (measure)
15. The aircraft could carry _____ of food to the earthquake victims. (weight)

Comparison of Adverbs

Many adverbs are compared. Like adjectives, they have three degrees of comparison: positive, comparative, and superlative.

Regular Comparison

Some adverbs form the comparative degree by adding *er* to the positive, and the superlative degree by adding *est* to the positive. Adverbs ending in *ly* generally form the comparative degree by prefixing *more* or *less* to the positive, and the superlative degree by prefixing *most* or *least* to the positive.

POSITIVE	COMPARATIVE	SUPERLATIVE
fast	faster	fastest
hastily	more hastily	most hastily

Irregular Comparison

Some adverbs are compared irregularly.

POSITIVE	COMPARATIVE	SUPERLATIVE
well	better	best
badly	worse	worst

Many adverbs denoting time and place (*here*, *now*, *then*, *when*, *where*, *again*, *always*, *down*, *above*) and adverbs denoting absoluteness or completeness (*round*, *eternally*, *never*, *universally*) cannot be compared.

Exercise 114

Name each adverb and its degree of comparison.
1. The editor examined the manuscript closely.
2. The editor should have examined the manuscript more closely.
3. This is the most closely examined manuscript any writer has ever written.
4. The judge listened most attentively.
5. Are you adequately prepared for this test?
6. Is your grandmother feeling better now?
7. The wind blew more strongly as we entered open water.
8. The physics award went to the one who most deserved it.
9. Bud ran faster than any other horse.
10. Time passed more slowly as the anticipation grew stronger.

Sharpening Your Skills

Use a different adverb to modify each of the adjectives listed below. Then use both words together in a sentence. Do not use the overworked adverb *very*.

Example:
awkward
extremely awkward
Pam found herself in an *extremely awkward* situation.

sharp	sour
daring	strong
consistent	tall
beautiful	primitive

Lesson 2 The Correct Use of Adverbs

Distinguishing between Adjectives and Adverbs

> Adjectives modify nouns and pronouns. Adverbs modify
> verbs, adjectives, adverbs, participles, gerunds,
> and infinitives.

Adverbs and those adjectives that are used as complements are often confused. In order to determine whether a modifier is a complement or an adverb, study each sentence carefully and ask yourself if the writer is trying to tell something about the subject, the verb, or an adjective.

The candy tasted *good*. (Candy *was* good; an adjective)
You may taste the candy *now*. (Tells *when* you may
taste; an adverb)
Did the candy taste *exceptionally* good? (Tells *how*
good; an adverb)

Exercise 115

Select the correct form of the word and tell whether the word is an adjective or an adverb.
1. Trish will return the book (prompt, promptly).
2. The bell sounds (harsh, harshly).
3. This chair seems (comfortable, comfortably).
4. The dogwood trees smell (unusual, unusually) fragrant this year.
5. His velvet coat felt (smooth, smoothly) to the touch.
6. These cherries taste (sweet, sweetly).
7. Justin seated himself (comfortable, comfortably) beside the stereo.
8. Ruby is a (decided, decidedly) clever person.
9. The boxes fell (loud, loudly) to the floor.
10. The hikers appear (weary, wearily).

Words Used as Adjectives and Adverbs

An adjective describes or limits a noun or a pronoun. An adverb modifies a verb, an adjective, or an adverb.

Marcy had the *highest* mark in the class. (*Adjective*)
Of the three, John had tossed the football *highest*. (*Adverb*)

Exercise 116

Identify each italicized word as an adjective or an adverb.
1. The band marched *first*.
2. Is this the *first* day of the carnival?
3. *Little* acorns grow into towering oaks.
4. The sick puppy plays *little*.
5. What do you mean by the *near* future?
6. Sit *near*, please.
7. Celia will feel *well* soon.
8. This food is *well* cooked.
9. Follow the *above* directions.
10. The helicopter hovered *above*.

Farther and *Further*

Farther refers to distance. *Further* denotes an addition. Both of these words may be used as adjectives and as adverbs.

I live *farther* than you.
I have nothing *further* to say.

Exercise 117

Select the correct word, *farther* or *further*, to complete each sentence.
1. Raise your hand if you need _____ instructions.
2. Temperatures grew colder as we climbed _____ up the mountain.
3. Denver is _____ west than Kansas City.
4. _____ research will be necessary.
5. Monica declared _____ discussion useless.
6. Leave this room without _____ delay.

411

7. Angela lives _____ from the park than Dwight does.
8. He has no _____ use for that plow.
9. Call this number for _____ information.
10. The distance is _____ than either of us wants to walk.

Adverbs in Comparisons

Use *as... as* when making comparisons that denote equality between persons or things. Use *so... as* in negative comparisons that deny equality between persons or things.

Albert is *as* tall *as* Vic.

I am not *so* old *as* you.

Exercise 118

Select the correct word, *as* or *so*, to complete each sentence.
1. Cedric's bicycle is _____ good as mine.
2. San Francisco has _____ much fog as London.
3. Nanette is not _____ clever with her hands as Edie is.
4. In the middle of the morning, the sky turned _____ dark as night.
5. That end of the pool is not _____ deep as this end.

Equally as an Adverb

Equally means *as* when it modifies an adjective or an adverb. Practice using the correct forms *equally great*, *equally well*, *equally good*. Never use *as* between *equally* and the adjective or adverb.

The apples and the oranges are *equally* good.

Exercise 119

Select the correct adverb form.
1. Ava's parents are (equally pleased, equally as pleased).
2. Both are (equally qualified, equally as qualified) for the job.
3. Jogging and swimming are (equally effective, equally as effective) exercise.
4. Sitting and standing seem (equally painful, equally as painful) to my back.
5. Woody and Max play the tuba (equally as well, equally well).

You Are the Author

Choose one.
1. In a brief essay, discuss your feelings about Rosa Parks's refusal to give up her seat on the bus. Use different kinds of adverbs.
2. Think of some events taking place unjustly in our country today. Write a paragraph, using adverbs, in which you compare and/or contrast one of them with the Rosa Parks incident.

Chapter Challenge

Read the selection carefully and answer the questions.

¹The first astronauts had to be very brave. ²They ventured where none had ever been. ³Carefully trained in mind and body, they intrepidly began to explore parts of the universe previously seen only at a distance. ⁴As space activity pushes forward, inhabited earth-orbiting stations that were once idly dreamed about are being actively planned. ⁵Even now, people with much less training than the early astronauts are able to travel out of the earth's atmosphere on space shuttles. ⁶How people will feel about living far from earth is still a question.

1. Identify the adverb in the first sentence. Give its classification (time, place, degree, manner, affirmation, or negation).
2. Name the adverb in the second sentence and tell whether it modifies a verb, an adjective, or a participle.
3. What is the adverb of time in the third sentence?
4. Name the adverb in the third sentence that modifies a participle.
5. If you were going to add an adverb to the third sentence between the word *explore* and the word *parts*, would you choose *further* or *farther*? Why?
6. Name the adverbs of manner in the fourth sentence.
7. What word does the adverb *even* modify in the fifth sentence? What part of speech is that word?
8. Name the other adverb in the fifth sentence that modifies an adjective.
9. Name an adverb of place in the sixth sentence.
10. Name the adverb of time in the sixth sentence.

Chapter 7

Prepositions, Conjunctions, Interjections

The Shepherd and the Princess

told by Pura Belpré

from *The Tiger and the Rabbit and Other Tales*

Long ago the simple songs of a young shepherd, whose flock grazed near a king's palace, often brought a smile to the face of a lovely princess as she stood by her window. The king had announced that his daughter would marry the man who brought him three specific things—things impossible to find, so it seemed.

One day the shepherd heard of the king's announcement and decided to try his luck. He slung his guitar on his back and started on his way. When night fell he was in the middle of a forest. Far in the distance he saw a light. Inside a hut, near a fire, he saw a boy watching over a pit and laughing to himself.

"What are you doing?" asked the shepherd.

"Oh!" answered the boy, "I am picking up the ones that have risen and waiting for the ones that are to rise."

The shepherd thought for a moment, and then he, too, burst into laughter, for the boy was boiling beans, taking out those that rose to the top and waiting for those on the bottom to rise.

"Do you live alone?" asked the shepherd.

"No," answered the boy. "My father and mother are in the fields gathering yesterday's food."

The shepherd **pondered** over the answer before he said, "You must be wrong, for you must have eaten yesterday's food."

The boy winked and said, "My parents are picking the wool left in the briars as the sheep raced through. Whatever wool they gather

Portrait of Mademoiselle Violette Heymann by Odilon Redon

415

will be sold to pay for the food we ate yesterday. But who are you," asked the boy, "and what do you do here?"

The shepherd told the boy his story.

"I can help you," said the boy, "if you promise to do as I say."

Following the boy's directions, he soon had the glass of all waters, the bouquet of all flowers, and a basket full of Ay, Ay nuts. With them he arrived at the palace.

When the king heard that the shepherd was in court, he called the princess, and together they went in to meet him.

"Have you brought the three things?" asked the king. "Yes, Your Majesty," answered the shepherd, glancing at the princess.

"Here is a glass of all waters," said the shepherd. "It contains all the waters—waters from the rain, the mountains, the hills, the valleys, the brooks, the springs, and the rivers, for it comes from the sea where all the waters flow."

The shepherd presented the king with a bouquet of all flowers. "Here, Your Majesty, indeed, is the most beautiful bouquet I could find. It contains flowers of all kinds, put together by the bees in this honeycomb."

"Good, indeed!" shouted the king. "Now for the last one."

"Your Majesty," said the shepherd, "the last thing you must pick out yourself. Here in this basket are the Ay, Ay nuts."

The king took the basket and thrust a hand into it to pick out a handful. Something pricked his fingers. "Ay! Ay!" he cried.

"That is correct, Your Majesty," said the shepherd. "For those are the kind of nuts you told me to bring."

The boy and the shepherd had placed tiny crabs among the nuts, which now clung to the king's fingers. When the king shook off the last tiny crab, he finally drew out a handful of nuts.

"Ay, Ay nuts, indeed!" he cried.

The Writer's Craft

1. How do you think the princess reacted to her father's announcement and the outcome? How do members of contemporary royal families select their spouses?
2. Is the boy a believable character? Why or why not?
3. Sometimes few conjunctions are needed to ensure smooth writing, as in the conversation between the shepherd and the king. Find a paragraph in which conjunctions *are* needed to maintain the flow of the story. Prove your point by omitting the conjunctions and rewording the sentences.

Lesson 1 Prepositions

A preposition is a word or a group of words placed before a noun, pronoun, phrase, or clause to show its relation to some other word.

Pura Belpré told stories *about* Puerto Rico.

The most commonly used prepositions are

about	at	down	near	throughout
above	before	during	of	to
across	behind	except	off	toward
after	beside	for	on	under
against	between	from	over	until
among	beyond	in	past	up
around	by	into	through	with

Forms of Prepositions

The preposition may be a single word or a group of words used as one preposition.

This tale is one *of* her many stories.
Because of her background, Belpré is able to tell stories from Spanish and Latin American literature.

Groups of words that are considered one preposition include the following:

on account of	in regard to	because of
instead of	in spite of	by means of
in addition to	in front of	for the sake of

The Object of a Preposition

The object of a preposition is a noun, a pronoun, or a group of words used as a noun. These groups of words might be a prepositional phrase, gerund phrase, infinitive phrase, or a noun clause. Study the examples below.

Pura Belpré was born in *Puerto Rico*. (*Noun*)
New York was also a home to *her*. (*Pronoun*)
Pura arrived here from *across the sea*. (*Prepositional phrase*)
She kept Spanish tales alive by *the telling and retelling of them*. (*Gerund phrase*)
Sometimes Belpré felt she had little choice except *to write stories*. (*Infinitive phrase*)
We saw her collection from *where we stood*. (*Clause*)

Exercise 120

Name each preposition and identify its object.
1. The king was one of the most insistent kings on earth.
2. Because of the princess's beauty, many men fell in love with her at first sight.
3. These men traveled to strange lands to find the three things that the king demanded.
4. A shepherd living near the king's palace sang to the princess.
5. He sang his favorite songs on many moonlit nights.
6. The princess responded to his singing with smiles.
7. After the shepherd had fulfilled all of the king's demands, the princess laughed heartily.
8. On account of the princess's happiness and also because of the shepherd's cleverness, the king allowed the marriage.
9. When the king consented to the marriage, everyone rejoiced.
10. There was a fine wedding in the summer.

The Correct Use of Prepositions

Between and Among

When speaking of two persons, places, or things use *between*.
When speaking of more than two, use *among*.

> He divided the money *between* Helen and Joan.
> He divided the money *among* the four children.

Beside and Besides

Beside means *at the side of* or *next to. Besides* means *in addition to*.

> Carlo stood *beside* the barn.
> Pierre speaks French and Greek *besides* English.

In and Into

In denotes position within. *Into* denotes motion or change
of position.

> The papers are *in* the desk drawer.
> The robin flew *into* its nest.

From and Off

From indicates the person from whom something is obtained.
Off means *away from*.

> We secured this paper *from* the vendor.
> The farmer hopped *off* the truck.

Behind

Use *behind* to indicate location at the rear of.

> The barn is *behind* the house.

Differ From and Differ With

Differ with denotes disagreement of opinion. *Differ from* denotes
differences between persons or things.

> I *differ with* you about the scoring of the game.
> The ribbons *differ from* each other in width.

Different From

After the adjective *different* use *from*, not *than*.

> The writing is *different from* his.

Need Of

Use *need of*, not *need for*.

> We shall have no further *need of* your help.

Within

Use *within*, not *inside of*, to indicate the time within which something will occur.

> I shall call for you *within* an hour.

Angry With and Angry At

Use *angry with* a person; *angry at* a thing.

> I am *angry with* Sid.
> We were *angry at* the result.

At and To

At denotes presence in. *To* denotes motion toward.

> Jason was *at* the party.
> Jason walked *to* the gate.

Exercise 121

Choose the correct preposition.
1. The four girls had a secret (between, among) themselves.
2. They have a chauffeur and a gardener (beside, besides) a cook.
3. He sat (between, among) Raul and Eugene.
4. My sweater is different (than, from) yours.
5. Margie's idea differs (with, from) Kate's.
6. Eric threw the paper ball (in, into) the basket.
7. The candidates filed (in, into) the press room.
8. Miguel bought these tomatoes (off, from) our grocer.
9. We have no need (of, for) a car.
10. I am angry (at, with) that man.
11. Do you think he has need (of, for) a lawyer?
12. Irene was angry (with, at) the outcome of the election.
13. We shall be in the hall (inside of, within) an hour.
14. I differ (with, from) you about your choice in music.
15. We planted ivy (beside, besides) the wall.

Words Used as Adverbs and Prepositions

An adverb tells *how, when* or *where*. A preposition shows the relationship between its object and some other word in the sentence.

> Have you ever visited Ottawa *before*? (*Simple adverb*)
> Lee stood *before* the class. (*Preposition*)

Exercise 122

Identify each word in italics as a preposition or an adverb.
1. *Down* splashed the rain.
2. Inez piled the reports *on* my desk.
3. Sheila left the note *outside* your door.
4. Suddenly the door opened, and *in* rushed Michelle.
5. The gorilla stood *outside*.
6. Is that your hamster crawling *in* the dirt under the porch?
7. Jane is moving *away*.
8. The speaker proclaimed that the movement must carry *on*.
9. Move the baby *away* from the fire.
10. The snake crawled *down* the tree.

Sharpening Your Skills

With a partner, write fifteen to twenty prepositional phrases on a piece of paper. Compose a humorous short story using as many prepositional phrases as possible.

Lesson 2 Conjunctions

A conjunction is a word used to connect words, phrases, or clauses in a sentence.

Washington *and* Oregon are western states. (*Connects words*)
Sugarcane grows in the Philippines *and* in Hawaii. (*Connects phrases*)
Although we are tired, we are not discouraged. (*Connects clauses*)

Kinds of Conjunctions
Coordinate Conjunctions

A coordinate conjunction is a conjunction that connects words, phrases, *or* clauses of equal rank.

The most common coordinate conjunctions are *and, or, nor, but*, and *yet*.

Warren made one error, *but* André had a perfect score.

The words *however, moreover, nevertheless, also, therefore,* and *consequently* are also used to link independent clauses.

He was exhausted; *therefore* he went to sleep.

Exercise 123

Name the conjunctions and tell whether they connect words, phrases, or clauses.
1. Mexico, the United States, and Canada are in North America.
2. Shall I meet you in Sacramento or Reno?
3. They called us, but we did not hear them.
4. We cannot replace minerals, nor can we increase their amount.
5. The two have worked together for years; moreover, they are good friends.
6. Ken won both academic and athletic awards.
7. Jay left clues under the apple tree and next to the house.

8. Jennifer has been to Mexico twice, but I have never been there.
9. I am tired; nevertheless, I will finish this assignment.
10. The ship passed through the canal and into the ocean.
11. I try to spend wisely, yet I never seem to have enough money.
12. Which is a more important crop for Arkansas, rice or cotton?
13. Sherri and Kassie went to see that new movie together.
14. Larry wants you or me to go with him.
15. The water was deep enough, but he was afraid to jump in.

Correlative Conjunctions

> **Correlative conjunctions are coordinate conjunctions used in pairs.**

Neither corn *nor* wheat is grown in this state.

The most frequently used correlative conjunctions are:
neither…nor   not only…but also
either…or   both…and

Exercise 124

Name the correlative conjunctions in each sentence.
1. They traveled not only in Colombia but also in Brazil.
2. Alice reads both history and science fiction.
3. Steven plays either the piano or the violin.
4. Both hard coal and soft coal are mined in Pennsylvania.
5. Not only did she lend me her skirt, but she also offered her new blouse.
6. Leonardo da Vinci was both painter and inventor.
7. Neither Linda nor I would agree to talk with him.
8. Colette is both an athlete and a scholar.
9. Either his smile is painted on or he is happy all the time.
10. Both mail and telephone service were disrupted during the revolution.

Leonardo da Vinci
(self-portrait)

Subordinate Conjunctions

> **A subordinate conjunction is a conjunction that connects clauses of unequal rank.**

I will tell you *because* you ask me.

In this sentence there are two clauses. The first, *I will tell you*, is the principal, or independent, clause. It does not depend upon any other part of the sentence and forms a complete idea. The second clause, *because you ask me*, is a dependent clause answering the question *why* and modifying the verb *will tell*. The subordinate conjunction *because* joins the dependent or subordinate clause to the independent clause in the sentence.

The most common subordinate conjunctions are:

after	before	since	then	where
although	for	so	unless	while
as	if	than	until	
because	provided	that	when	

Very often groups of words are used as subordinate conjunctions. Learn these groups:

as soon as	in order that	provided that
as if	inasmuch as	so that

Exercise 125

Identify the principal clause, the subordinate clause, and the subordinate conjunction in each sentence.

1. If I knew how, I would install the new faucet.
2. Moving to Texas was a good decision, although we miss our old friends.
3. Marco gave me his turtle because I promised to feed it regularly.
4. Sylvia spoke only to Martha, as if I were invisible.
5. Since Minnesota is a border state, it has customs checkpoints along its northern boundary.
6. Lydia borrowed four dollars from me so that she could go to the movie.

7. Julio sings better than I do.
8. Inasmuch as he opposes violence, Nick turned off the television.
9. Holly offered us a ride provided we would bring some potato chips.
10. Although this is supposed to be a joyous event, some people are sad.
11. Sophia ran as if she were in a race.
12. Since that was her desire, everyone agreed.
13. We gathered at the park in order that Jerry could take a photograph.
14. I am allergic to fish, so I cannot eat with you.
15. Hugh cannot move the piano unless you help.

The Correct Use of Conjunctions and Prepositions

Prepositions are often carelessly used as conjunctions. The following prepositions and conjunctions require special study.

Without is a preposition and introduces a *phrase*. *Unless* is a conjunction and introduces a *clause*.

> Do not come *without your textbook*. (*Phrase*)
> Do not come *unless you bring your textbook*. (*Clause*)

Like is a preposition and introduces a *phrase*. *As* and *as if* are conjunctions and introduce *clauses*.

> John looks *like his father*. (*Phrase*)
> John writes *as his father writes*. (*Clause*)

Exercise 126

Select the correct word to complete each sentence.
1. I may not go (without, unless) I get permission.
2. Walking in this weather (without, unless) wearing a hat is foolhardy.
3. Willy did that job (like, as if) he were used to the work.
4. Elena will be unhappy (without, unless) her friends around.
5. Elena will be unhappy (without unless) her friends are around.
6. (Like, As) his father, David is very patient.
7. Build this cabinet (like, as) these instructions direct.
8. Theresa went walking in the rain (without, unless) her umbrella.
9. Sandy did (like, as) he was told.
10. Bianca looks very much (like, as) her brother.
11. (Like, As) her sister, Fran wants to be a dancer.
12. (Without, Unless) you canceled the appointment, Vera will arrive any moment.
13. We began (like, as) the sun was rising.
14. You will not finish this assignment (without, unless) you stop talking.
15. (Without, Unless) taking his keys, Phil stormed out of the house.

Sharpening Your Skills

Write three or four related sentences using a coordinate, correlative, and subordinate conjunction. The conjunctions may be used in any order.

Lesson 3 Interjections

An interjection is a word that expresses some strong or sudden emotion.

Hurrah! Here comes the champion.
Ouch! I hurt my arm.

An interjection may express *delight, disgust, contempt, pain, assent, joy, impatience, surprise, sorrow, wonder, regret.* It is generally set off from the rest of the sentence by an exclamation point. If the entire sentence is exclamatory, however, the interjection may be followed by a comma, and the exclamation point placed at the close of the sentence.

Ah, how beautifully that orchestra plays!

The most common interjections are:

Ah!	Hark!	Listen!	Shh!
Alas!	Hello!	Lo!	Ugh!
Beware!	Hurrah!	Oh!	What!
Bravo!	Hush!	Ouch!	Wow!
Good!	Indeed!	Pshaw!	

O and Oh

The interjection *O* is used before a noun in direct address and is not directly followed by an exclamation point. *Oh* expresses an emotion such as surprise, sorrow, or joy and *is* generally followed by an exclamation point. If the emotion continues throughout the sentence, however, *Oh* is followed by a comma, and the exclamation point is put at the end of the sentence.

O Marie! I wish I could go to the beach with you. (*Direct address*)
Oh! The player was injured. (*Emotion does not continue*)
Oh, how surprised I am! (*Emotion continues*)

427

Exercise 127

Name the interjections and tell what emotion is expressed by each.

1. Alas! I am sorry to hear that.
2. Quiet! The librarian looks angry with us.
3. Oh, how the sun is shining!
4. Wait! I'm almost ready to go.
5. Congratulations! You earned highest honors.
6. O Liz! I missed having you around.
7. Hurrah! I passed the test.
8. Ouch! That pin prick hurt.
9. What! Is everybody leaving?
10. Beware! Few return from that cavern.

You Are the Author

Choose one.

1. As a group, write and dramatize a play based on the story.
2. Do you believe that the incidents in the story could occur today? Write a brief composition to explain why or why not.

Chapter Challenge

Read the selection carefully and answer the questions that follow it.

[1]Less than a minute remained in the final Northern League basketball game of the season. [2]The contest had been an exciting, hard-fought battle between our Mayfair team and the Lincoln players. [3]Everything depended on what we did in the next few seconds, for Lincoln held a one-point lead. [4]In spite of close guarding, one of our players made a deft hook shot from under the basket. [5]Good! The spectators cheered loudly as two precious points put us in the lead. [6]Lincoln, now in possession of the ball,

made a desperate attempt to score. ⁷The ball, however, sailed harmlessly through the air and across the basket. ⁸It fell into eager hands as a loud blast from a horn announced not only the end of the game but also a glorious victory for Mayfair.

1. Name the prepositions in the first sentence.
2. Find a coordinate conjunction in the second sentence, and tell what words it connects.
3. Is the group of words used as the object of the preposition *on* in the third sentence a phrase or a clause?
4. Name a subordinate conjunction in the third sentence.
5. Find a phrase that is used as the object of the preposition in the fourth sentence.
6. Identify a group of words used as a single preposition in the fourth sentence.
7. What part of speech is the first word in the fifth sentence?
8. Name the prepositions in the sixth sentence.
9. Name two phrases that are connected by a coordinate conjunction in the seventh sentence.
10. Name a correlative conjunction in the eighth sentence.

Review of the Parts of Speech

Test your knowledge by identifying the part of speech of each italicized word.

1. The morning temperature was *below* zero again today.
2. *Advanced* cities have modern public transportation systems.
3. Can you *fashion* a castle out of the wet sand?
4. This recipe calls for *ground* corn.
5. Put the ball *down*, Tommy.
6. The president will *sign* the bill into law.
7. They waited *below* for an hour.
8. The tulip *blossoms* every spring.
9. Rose *blossoms* are beautiful.
10. *That* is my favorite television program.
11. Karl took down the *sign*.
12. The *ground* under the tent is cold and hard.
13. Canada exports a variety of *wood* products.
14. Dorothy served some delicious *peppermint* tea.
15. Touch the brakes as you go *down* the hill.

Chapter 8

Phrases, Clauses, Sentences

At the Mercy of the Breakers

by Thor Heyerdahl

from *Kon-Tiki: Across the Pacific by Raft*

On board the *Kon-Tiki* all preparations for the end of the voyage were being made. Everything of value was carried into the cabin and lashed fast. Documents and papers were packed into watertight bags, along with films and other things which would not stand a dip in the sea. The whole bamboo cabin was covered with canvas, and especially strong ropes were lashed across it. When we saw that all hope was gone, we opened up the bamboo deck and cut off with machete knives all the ropes which held the centerboards down. It was a hard job to get the centerboards drawn up, because they were all thickly covered with stout barnacles. With the centerboards up, the draught of our vessel was no deeper than to the bottom of the timber logs, and we would therefore be more easily washed in over the reef. With no centerboards and with the sail down, the raft lay completely sideways on and was entirely at the mercy of wind and sea.

We tied the longest rope we had to the homemade anchor and made it fast to the step of the **port** mast so that the *Kon-Tiki* would go into the surf **stern** first when the anchor was thrown overboard. The anchor itself consisted of empty water cans filled with used radio batteries and heavy scrap, and solid mangrove-wood sticks projected from it, set crosswise.

Order number one, which came first and last, was Hold on to the raft! Whatever happened, we must hang on tight on board and let the nine great logs take the pressure from the reef. We ourselves had more than enough to do to withstand the weight of the water. If we jumped overboard, we should become helpless victims of the suction, which would fling us in and out over the sharp corals. The rubber raft would capsize in the steep seas or, heavily loaded with

Photograph of Pacific wave by Bill Romerhaus

us in it, it would be torn to ribbons against the reef. But the wooden logs would sooner or later be cast ashore, and we with them, if we only managed to hold fast.

Those were anxious hours in which we lay drifting helplessly sideways, step after step, in toward the reef. It was noticeably quiet on board; we all crept in and out from cabin to bamboo deck, silent or **laconic**, and carried on with our jobs. Our serious faces showed that no one was in doubt as to what awaited us, and the absence of nervousness showed that we had all gradually acquired an unshakable confidence in the raft. If it had brought us across the sea, it would also manage to bring us ashore alive.

Entries in the *Kon-Tiki's* log ran:

—8:15: We are slowly approaching land. We can now make out with the naked eye the separate palm trees inside on the **starboard** *side.*

—8:45: The wind has veered into a still more unfavorable quarter for us, so we have no hope of getting clear. No nervousness on board, but hectic preparations on deck. There is something lying on the reef ahead of us which looks like the wreck of a sailing vessel, but it may be only a heap of driftwood.

—9:45: The wind is taking us straight toward the last island but one we see behind the reef. We can now see the whole coral reef clearly; here it is built up like a white-and-red-speckled wall which barely sticks up out of the water as a belt in front of all the islands. All along the reef white foaming surf is flung up toward the sky. Bengt is just serving up a good hot meal, the last before the great action!

It is a wreck lying in there on the reef. We are so close now that we can see right across the shining lagoon behind the reef and see the outlines of other islands on the other side of the lagoon.

As this was written, the dull drone of the surf came near again; it came from the whole reef and filled the air like thrilling rolls of the drum, heralding the exciting last act of the *Kon-Tiki*.

A few minutes later the anchor rushed overboard and caught hold of the bottom so that the *Kon-Tiki* swung around and turned her stern inward toward the breakers. It held us for a few valuable minutes, while Torstein sat hammering like mad on the key. He had got Rarotonga now. The breakers thundered in the air, and the sea rose and fell furiously. All hands were at work on deck, and now Torstein got his message through. He said we were drifting toward the Raroia reef. He asked Rarotonga to listen in on the same wave length every hour. If we were silent for more than thirty-six hours,

Rarotonga must let the Norwegian Embassy in Washington know. Torstein's last words were:

"O.K. Fifty yards left. Here we go. Good-by."

Then he closed down the station, Knut sealed up the papers, and both crawled out on deck as fast as they could to join the rest of us, for it was clear now that the anchor was giving way.

The swell grew heavier and heavier, with deep troughs between the waves, and we felt the raft being swung up and down, up and down, higher and higher.

Again the order was shouted: "Hold on. Never mind about the cargo, hold on!"

We were now so near the waterfall inside that we no longer heard the steady continuous roar from all along the reef. We now heard only a separate boom each time the nearest breaker crashed down on the rocks.

No one stood **aft**, for it was there the shock from the reef would come. Nor were the two firm stays which ran from the **masthead** down in the stern safe, for if the mast fell they would be left hanging overboard, over the reef. Herman, Bengt, and Torstein had climbed up on some boxes which were lashed fast forward of the cabin wall, and, while Herman clung onto the **guy ropes** from the ridge of the

Heyerdahl pulls in a large fish to supplement the crew's diet of canned food.

433

roof, the other two held onto the ropes from the mast-head by which the sail at other times was hauled up. Knut and I chose the stay running from the bow up to the masthead, for, if mast and cabin and everything else went overboard, we thought the rope from the bow would nevertheless remain lying inboard, as we were now head on to the seas.

When we realized that the seas had got hold of us, the anchor rope was cut, and we were off. A sea rose straight up under us, and we felt the *Kon-Tiki* being lifted up in the air. The great moment had come; we were riding on the wave back at breathless speed, our ramshackle craft creaking and groaning as she quivered under us. The excitement made one's blood boil. I remember that, having no other inspiration, I waved my arm and bellowed "Hurrah!" at the top of my lungs; it afforded a certain relief and could do no harm anyway. The others certainly thought I had gone mad, but they all beamed and grinned enthusiastically. On we ran with the seas rushing in behind us; this was the *Kon-Tiki's* baptism of fire. All must and would go well.

But our elation was soon dampened. A new sea rose high up astern of us like a glittering, green glass wall. As we sank down, it came rolling after us, and, in the same second in which I saw it high above me, I felt a violent blow and was submerged under floods of water. I felt the suction through my whole body, with such great power that I had to strain every single muscle in my frame and think of one thing only—hold on, hold on! I think that in such a desperate situation the arms will be torn off before the brain consents to let go, evident as the outcome is. Then I felt that the mountain of water was passing on and relaxing its devilish grip of my body. When the whole mountain had rushed on, with an ear-splitting roaring and crashing, I saw Knut again hanging on beside me, doubled up into a ball. Seen from behind, the great sea was almost flat and gray. As it rushed on, it swept over the ridge of the cabin roof which projected from the water, and there hung the three others, pressed against the cabin roof as the water passed over them.

We were still afloat.

In an instant I renewed my hold, with arms and legs bent round the strong rope. Knut let himself down and with a tiger's leap joined the others on the boxes, where the cabin took the strain. I heard reassuring exclamations from them, but at the same time I saw a new green wall rise up and come towering toward us. I shouted a warning and made myself as small and hard as I could where I hung. In an instant hell was over us again, and the *Kon-Tiki* disappeared completely under the masses of water. The sea tugged

and pulled with all the force it could bring to bear at the poor little bundles of human bodies. The second sea rushed over us, to be followed by a third like it.

Then I heard a triumphant sound from Knut, who was now hanging on to the rope ladder:

"Look at the raft—she's holding!"

After three seas only the double mast and the cabin had been knocked a bit crooked. Again we had a feeling of triumph over the elements, and the elation of victory gave us new strength.

Then I saw the next sea come towering up, higher than all the rest, and again I bellowed a warning aft to the others as I climbed up the stay, as high as I could get in a hurry, and hung on fast.

We must have hit the reef that time. I myself felt only the strain on the stay, which seemed to bend and slacken jerkily. But whether the bumps came from above or below I could not tell, hanging there. The whole submersion lasted only seconds, but it demanded more endurance than we usually have in our bodies. There is greater strength in the human mechanism than that of the muscles alone. I determined that, if I was to die, I would die in this position, like a knot on the stay. The sea thundered on, over and past, and as it roared by it revealed a hideous sight. The *Kon-Tiki* was wholly changed, as by the stroke of a magic wand. The vessel we knew from weeks and months at sea was no more; in a few seconds our pleasant world had become a shattered wreck.

I saw only one man on board besides myself. He lay pressed flat across the ridge of the cabin roof, face downward with his arms stretched out on both sides, while the cabin itself was crushed in, like a house of cards, toward the stern and toward the starboard side. The motionless figure was Herman. There was no other sign of life, while the hill of water thundered by, in across the reef. The hardwood mast on the starboard side was broken like a match, and the upper stump, in its fall, had smashed right through the cabin roof, so that the mast and all its gear slanted at a low angle over the reef on the starboard side. Astern, the steering block was twisted round lengthways and the crossbeam broken, while the steering oar was smashed to splinters. The splashboards at the bow were broken like cigar boxes, and the whole deck was torn up and pasted like wet paper against the forward wall of the cabin, along with boxes, cans, canvas, and other cargo. Bamboo sticks and rope ends stuck up everywhere, and the general effect was of complete chaos.

I felt cold fear running through my whole body. What was the good of my holding on? If I lost one single man here, in the run in, the whole thing would be ruined, and for the moment there was

only one human figure to be seen after the last buffet. In that second Torstein's hunched-up form appeared outside the raft. He was hanging like a monkey in the ropes from the masthead and managed to get onto the logs again, where he crawled up onto the debris forward of the cabin. Herman, too, now turned his head and gave me a forced grin of encouragement but did not move. I bellowed in the faint hope of locating the others and heard Bengt's calm voice call out that all hands were aboard.

The Writer's Craft

1. The sailors on the *Kon-Tiki* risked their lives trying to prove that ancient people could have traveled from South America to the South Pacific aboard primitive rafts. Would you like to have been a member of the *Kon-Tiki* crew? Why or why not?
2. This selection is a description of the end of a journey that lasted more than three months. Why do you think the men showed no panic despite their predicament?
3. In this excerpt the author has conveyed a sense of urgency. What do the phrase "in such a desperate situation," the clause "but it demanded more endurance than we usually have in our bodies," and the sentence "It *is* a wreck lying there on the reef" have in common?
4. In good writing, types of sentences vary. If stories contained only simple sentences or only compound sentences, for example, they would be boring to read. Reread the paragraph on page 434 that begins, "When we realized . . ." Identify the types of the first four sentences.

The *Kon-Tiki*, with flags flying, at the beginning of the voyage

Recalling What You Know

1. A complex sentence contains a principal clause and one or more subordinate clauses. Identify the principal and subordinate clauses in *As we sank down, it came rolling over us.*
2. In this sentence what is the infinitive? *He asked Rarotonga to listen in on the same wave length.*
3. A participial phrase is introduced by a participle. Identify the participial phrase: *Tapping furiously, he sent his message.*

Lesson 1   Phrases

A phrase is a group of related words used as a single part of speech.

Thor Heyerdahl sailed *from Callao, Peru.*

Types of Phrases

A *prepositional phrase* is a phrase that is introduced by a preposition. The phrase may be an adjectival, an adverbial, or a noun phrase.

Heyerdahl was a citizen *of Norway. (Adjectival phrase)*
He served *in the Free Norwegian Army. (Adverbial phrase)*
After the war was a time of great adventure. *(Noun phrase)*

Adjectival phrases modify nouns or pronouns. Adverbial phrases modify verbs, adverbs, adjectives, participles, gerunds, or infinitives. Noun phrases may serve as the subject of the sentence, the direct object, the complement, the object of a preposition, or an appositive.

> A *participial phrase* is a phrase introduced by a participle.
>
> An *infinitive phrase* is a phrase introduced by an infinitive.
>
> A *gerund phrase* is a phrase introduced by a gerund.

The person *riding the bicycle* lives in my neighborhood.
(*Participial phrase*)
To succeed in life is our aim. (*Infinitive phrase*)
Writing a poem is a pleasure. (*Gerund phrase*)

Exercise 128

Identify the prepositional, participial, infinitive, and gerund phrases.
Classify the prepositional phrases by type.

1. Thor Heyerdahl led the *Kon-Tiki* expedition from Peru
   to Polynesia on a raft made of balsa logs.
2. To reach the South Seas was his goal.
3. Worshipping the sun god Kon was a practice of some of the
   early South American Indians, according to legend.
4. Tiki was one of the leaders of this group.
5. The people believing Tiki a forefather of their race lived
   in Polynesia.
6. The purpose of the expedition was to prove that Inca Peruvians
   were the settlers of Polynesia.
7. The *Kon-Tiki* sailed from Peru with a watertight radio
   transmitter and other necessary provisions.
8. Each of the men was responsible for certain chores.
9. As the waves rushed the raft and hurled it into the air, the men
   prepared for the end of their voyage.
10. Losing contact with other radio operators alarmed them.
11. Before the landing was a period of severe endurance.
12. The *Kon-Tiki* was damaged on the reef, but the men survived.
13. Later they recovered some important provisions from the
    wrecked raft.
14. They also found empty pineapple cans that they had tossed
    into the sea from the *Kon-Tiki.*
15. In the end they saw that the wreck of the raft still floated.

Lesson 2 Adjectival Clauses

A clause is a part of a sentence containing a subject and a predicate.

A *principal clause* is one that expresses a complete thought.

A *subordinate clause* is one that does not express a complete thought and cannot stand alone.

Henry Ford, *who revolutionized the auto industry*, became immensely wealthy.
Henry Ford became immensely wealthy. (*Principal clause*)
who revolutionized the auto industry (*Subordinate clause*)

Subordinate clauses can be adjectival, adverbial, or noun clauses.

An *adjectival clause* is a subordinate clause used as an adjective.

An *ambitious* person usually succeeds.
A person *with ambition* usually succeeds.
A person *who has ambition* usually succeeds.

In the first sentence the adjective *ambitious* modifies the noun *person*; in the second sentence *person* is modified by the adjectival phrase *with ambition*; in the third sentence the modifier is a group of words, *who has ambition*. This group of words contains a subject and a predicate and is, therefore, a clause. Since the clause does the work of an adjective, it is an adjectival clause.

Some adjectival clauses are nonrestrictive; others are restrictive. A nonrestrictive clause is one that may be omitted from the sentence without changing its meaning. It is separated from the rest of the sentence by commas. A restrictive clause is one that is a necessary part of the sentence because it points out or identifies a particular person or object. No punctuation is required for restrictive clauses.

The players, *who practice long hours,* will be rewarded.
(Nonrestrictive clause)
The players *who practice long hours* will be rewarded.
(Restrictive clause)
Relative pronouns (*who, whom, whose, which, that*) or, sometimes, relative adverbs (*when, where, why*) introduce adjectival clauses.

Exercise 129

Identify the adjectival clauses and the noun or pronoun each modifies.

1. Wise is the person who keeps silent when ignorant.
2. Benjamin Franklin, who is credited with discovering electricity, was a printer as well as a statesman and inventor.
3. Pam is the person who taught us this technique.
4. The farm that provided our income is now deserted.
5. Philip is a man in whom I have great faith.
6. The idea that they could rest tomorrow gave the workers energy to finish the job today.
7. The girl who is last in line is the team captain.
8. The income that keeps our club going comes from projects like this.
9. Norway is a country where fjords abound.
10. That train, which leaves for New York in five minutes, is already full.

Exercise 130

Rewrite the following sentences, inserting an adjectival clause after the italicized word. Underline the adjectival clause, including the relative pronoun or relative adverb. The first one is done for you.

1. We went to see the *play*.

   We went to see the play <u>that had the best review</u>.

2. The *art* was displayed in the school library.
3. The antique *car* needed repair.
4. I bought a new computer *program*.
5. The *senator* was not re-elected.
6. *Greg* signed out two books fom the library.
7. The *panda bears* were not interested in our funny faces.
8. *Jean* tried out for the Olympic team.
9. Frankenstein created a *monster*.
10. I remember the *day*.

Sharpening Your Skills

Look up the following words in an encyclopedia or dictionary and complete each thought using an adjectival clause:

The Hoover Dam   Niagara Falls
The Gateway Arch   The Fountain of Youth
The Big Apple   Pyramids
The Great Wall of China   Mount Rushmore

Great Wall of China

Lesson 3 Adverbial Clauses

> **An adverbial clause is a subordinate clause used as an adverb.**

Tina acted *courageously*.
Tina acted *with courage*.
Tina acted *as if she had courage*.

In the first sentence the adverb *courageously* modifies the verb *acted*; in the second sentence the adverbial phrase *with courage* modifies the verb *acted*; in the third sentence the clause *as if she had courage* modifies the verb *acted*. Since this clause does the work of an adverb, it is an adverbial clause.

Adverbial clauses are usually introduced by *subordinate conjunctions*. These clauses may tell time, place, degree, manner, cause, or purpose.

In adverbial clauses of degree or comparison (those that answer the questions *how much* or *how little*) there is often an omission of words.

Peter jumped higher than he [*jumped*].
I admire him more than [*I admire*] her.

Exercise 131

Identify each adverbial clause and the word it modifies.
1. Strike while the iron is hot.
2. Go when you are told.
3. We saw the Mounties when we were in Ottawa.
4. Darlene learned the value of water when she lived in the desert.
5. The plant flowered, for it received good care.
6. The greyhound ran faster than the rabbit could.
7. An honest woman speaks as she thinks.
8. He saved his money that he might attend college.
9. Judy ran as if she were late for dinner.
10. Pat is more devoted to skiing than to swimming.
11. The computer program worked although some of the commands were wrong.

12. Lynne wanted me to come to the party because she hoped I would sing.
13. A sequoia is larger than an oak.
14. The Saint Bernard played outside all day as if she did not notice the bitter cold.
15. I will get a loan if you need more money.

Exercise 132

Complete each of the following sentences with an adverbial clause and underline the subject and verb in the clause. The subordinate conjunctions are given, and the first sentence is done for you as an example.

1. Because _____, the people panicked.

   Because the <u>earth began</u> to tremble, the people panicked.

2. The zookeeper let us watch when _____.
3. Since _____, the Indians decided to fight for their land.
4. The Eastwood Eagles were winning the game until _____.
5. While _____, the mountain climbers scaled Mt. Everest.
6. In order that _____, April studies harder than ever.
7. You can learn to play the guitar if _____.
8. So that _____, the Puritans came to America.
9. Although _____, we must still conserve our natural resources.
10. Pedro devoured the pie as if _____.

Sharpening Your Skills

Write a short paragraph about how to operate your newly-invented homework machine. Write complex sentences using the following subordinate conjunctions: *because, when, after, until, while.*

Lesson 4 Noun Clauses

> **A noun clause is a subordinate clause used as a noun.**

Jenner's *defeat* was unfortunate.
That Jenner was defeated was unfortunate.

In the first sentence the noun *defeat* is the subject; in the second sentence the clause *that Jenner was defeated* is the subject. Since this clause does the work of a noun, it is a noun clause.

Noun Clauses Used as Subjects

A noun clause may be used as the subject of a sentence. In sentences containing noun clauses, the entire sentence is considered the principal clause. The noun clause is the subordinate clause.

That the polio vaccine benefits many persons has been proved. (*Principal clause*)

That the polio vaccine benefits many persons (*Noun clause used as subject*)

Exercise 133

Identify the noun clause used as the subject in each sentence.
 1. That the magician was late for the party surprised me.
 2. What we should do next was the question.
 3. How to keep people entertained was an issue.
 4. That they could entertain themselves soon became clear.
 5. Whether they would pay attention to the magician was uncertain.
 6. Why she did not call to explain her lateness disturbed us.
 7. That she had lost the address and phone number did not occur to us.
 8. How she finally found us is a mystery.
 9. That our guests are enjoying her performance is obvious.
10. Whether they will ever want to leave is not certain.

Complete each of the remaining five sentences with an appropriate noun clause used as the subject.
11. _____ is my motto.
12. _____ was long remembered.
13. _____ was soon discovered.
14. _____ is an important piece of information.
15. _____ has always interested me.

Noun Clauses Used as Direct Objects

A noun clause may be used as the object of a verb.

> We know *that the polio vaccine benefits many persons.*

It is easy to recognize a subordinate clause, but it is important to remember that the entire sentence is the principal clause.

> We know that the polio vaccine benefits many persons. (*Principal clause*)
> that the polio vaccine benefits many persons (*Noun clause used as object*)

Quotations, both direct and indirect, are considered noun clauses in such sentences as these:

> Jim said, "*I have finished my essay.*" (*Direct quotation*)
> Katrina asked *who painted the picture.* (*Indirect quotation*)

Exercise 134

Identify the noun clause used as the object in each sentence.
1. Howard insisted that Andy eat the peas.
2. Janice wondered how he learned to water-ski.
3. Patrick Henry demanded that he be granted liberty.
4. Betsy announced that she would study only women writers.
5. Appoint whoever is capable.
6. The bylaws state that all members must vote.
7. Have you heard when the boat will dock?
8. The textbook explains how kidneys purify the blood.
9. Can you explain how this machine operates?
10. I knew that I had finished that exercise.

Complete each of the remaining five sentences with an appropriate noun clause used as the direct object.
11. Earl did _____.
12. Julie said, "_____."
13. I do not know _____.
14. The paper announced _____.
15. Senator Jackson declared _____.

Noun Clauses Used as Objects of Prepositions

A noun clause may be used as the object of a preposition.

> He spoke of *how the polio vaccine benefits many persons.*
> He spoke of how the polio vaccine benefits many persons.
> (*Principal clause*)
> how the polio vaccine benefits many persons (*Noun clause used as object of a preposition*)

Exercise 135

Identify the noun clause used as the object of the preposition in each sentence.

1. The raggedly dressed man addressed the crowd from where he stood.
2. Otto had no thought but that his pie would win first prize.
3. Lance cannot buy a car on what he earns.
4. Elected officials do not always get support for whatever they want to do.
5. The class is studying about how nuclear fission occurs.
6. Give the message to whoever arrives first.
7. The people were moved by what they saw in the film.
8. Did you hear about what Tiffany did on her vacation?
9. We know every detail of the plan except what you want us to do.
10. Professor Candor angered every student by what he said about today's news.

Complete each of the remaining five sentences with an appropriate noun clause used as the object of the preposition.

11. Nicole will give her tickets to _____.
12. We could not see the stage from _____.
13. Diego, work with _____.
14. We should make use of _____.
15. Megan is interested in _____.

Noun Clauses Used as Complements

A noun clause may be used as a complement. Remember that the complement follows a linking verb and completes its meaning.

> The fact is *that the polio vaccine benefits many persons.*
> The fact is that the polio vaccine benefits many persons.
> (*Principal clause*)
> that the polio vaccine benefits many persons (*Noun clause used as complement*)

Exercise 136

Identify the noun clause used as the complement in each sentence.
1. My hope is that we finish this work soon.
2. The fact is that Nathan is not qualified for the position.
3. The question was how we could earn enough money to pay for the broken window.
4. The truth is that the person who made the decision did not have all the facts.
5. The rule is that no one may smoke in this room.
6. The consensus is that we should provide a home for the refugees.
7. The story is that Aunt Sally wore five gold rings.
8. Gina's chief concern is what she can do to regain your confidence.
9. Steve's idea is that we join him for lunch at the firehouse.
10. One requirement for the position is that you speak Spanish.

Complete each of the remaining five sentences with an appropriate noun clause used as the complement.
11. The greatest attribute of the team is _____.
12. Jack's most admirable characteristic is _____.
13. Her favorite saying is _____.
14. The teacher's suggestion was _____.
15. What Candice wondered was _____.

Noun Clauses Used as Appositives

A noun clause may be used as an appositive. An appositive clause explains or describes the noun or the pronoun that precedes it.

> The fact *that the polio vaccine benefits many persons* cannot be denied.

A noun clause is considered an appositive when it follows and explains the expletive *it*.

> It is a fact *that the polio vaccine benefits many persons.*

Do not confuse appositive clauses with adjectival clauses. An appositive clause is a noun clause and takes the place of a noun; an adjectival clause modifies a noun or a pronoun.

> The notice *that we would have a holiday* caused great joy.
> (*Noun clause*)
> The notice *that she posted* was read by everybody.
> (*Adjectival clause*)

Exercise 137

Identify the noun clause used as the appositive in each sentence.
1. It was a mystery to us how the duck got in among the chickens.
2. The fact that the class president gave such an enthusiastic speech was encouraging to everyone.
3. Janet told the truth, that she had not accepted a bribe.
4. He forgot his promise that he would take us for a boat ride.
5. The saying that many hands make light work is familiar to everyone.
6. It is doubtful that Jeannette won first prize.
7. It is certainly a fact that cancer research requires a lot of time and money.
8. The rumor that the star would visit our school was received with much excitement.
9. The belief that good health promotes happiness may be correct.
10. Her wish that she might visit Paris was realized last summer.

Complete each of the remaining five sentences with an appropriate noun clause used as the appositive.
11. Have you heard the news _____?
12. It cannot be denied _____.
13. It was Colette's hope _____.
14. Do you believe the report _____?
15. Dan's dream, _____, seemed a possible reality.

449

Exercise 138

In each sentence, identify the noun clause and its use.

1. Kyle's fear that the air conditioner would fall out the window seemed unreasonable.
2. How such a thing might happen was not clear to us.
3. The fact was that the air conditioner had not been securely installed.
4. That it shook loose and fell on the car stunned us.
5. Kyle showed us that the screws were in the wrong places.
6. The car owner was angry about how the accident had occurred.
7. That the man was not hurt did not change his complaint.
8. He told the police that people should be careful about how they install air conditioners.
9. The driver decided that we would not have to pay for damages.
10. He hopes that insurance will pay for the repair.
11. How we will pay for a new air conditioner is another question.
12. Kyle insists that he will install it this time.
13. He does not think that we should trust anyone else.
14. The police officer suggested that we use window fans instead.
15. The news that insurance would cover all damages delighted us.

Sharpening Your Skills

Use the following noun clauses in sentences of your own. Tell how each clause is used.

1. that she was creative
2. how the team played the game
3. what she prized most
4. that the tourists arrived
5. why Craig won
6. what you bought
7. that the flights were canceled
8. that you would come
9. who stole the purse
10. that Greg was elected

Exercise 139 [Review of Clauses]

Name the clauses and identify each as an adjectival clause, an adverbial clause, or a noun clause.

1. Uneasy lies the head that wears the crown.
2. I was pleased when I heard the news.
3. Mr. Kunik, who visited us, promised me a ticket.
4. Lucy realized that she had made a mistake.
5. Bruce read a poem that Marietta had written.
6. The lawnmower, which was in the garage, needed repair.
7. Veronica was not home when we called.
8. The moon is visible to us because it reflects the sun's light.
9. It has one side that never faces the earth.
10. It is known that the moon's gravity is only a fraction of the earth's.
11. Kirsten practiced hard because she wanted to perform as well as she could.
12. The person who wrote that letter to the editor remained anonymous.
13. What we fail to understand is often what we need to do most.
14. That Sarah should pass the test is clear.
15. Baby William will not wander into the water if we stay on the grass.
16. Swim while the sun shines.
17. Can you tell me where the chief nurse's office is located?
18. Pablo proved in many ways that he was a good coach.
19. A barge is a flat vessel in which bulky materials are transported.
20. Do you know that they live in an old schoolhouse?

Lesson 5 Sentences

A sentence is a group of words expressing a complete thought.

Hieroglyphics is the ancient picture writing of the Egyptians.

Essential Elements of a Sentence

No sentence is complete without a *subject* and a *predicate*.

> **The subject of a sentence names a person, a place, or a thing about which a statement is made. The predicate tells something about the subject.**
>
> **The subject with all its modifiers is called the *complete subject*. The predicate with all its modifiers and complements is called the *complete predicate*.**

COMPLETE SUBJECT	COMPLETE PREDICATE
People	expect good service.
The team trainers	watch over us.
Bert, [you]	write the letter.

Exercise 140

Tell which of the following groups of words are sentences. Rewrite the sentence fragments as complete sentences.

1. Sitting on the floor.
2. Laughs heartily.
3. Stand.
4. Give it to me.
5. Knowledge is power.
6. The spectator who saw the boat race.
7. Riding a bicycle through the city streets.
8. Smooth seas make poor sailors.
9. Palaces beautifully constructed.
10. During the night the boat drifted out to sea.

11. Into the burning house.
12. Werner von Braun, who designed the first rocket.
13. Stood the guest speaker.
14. Beside the river stood a small cottage.
15. Where have you been?
16. As soon as I heard your voice.
17. Heavy footsteps made Tim start in surprise.
18. The people whom we know as friends.
19. The cry of the loon.
20. You may sit here.

Exercise 141

Copy each sentence and draw one line under the complete subject and two lines under the complete predicate.

1. Spanish conquistadores explored the New World.
2. There was a storm on the lake last evening.
3. Around the field galloped the excited horses.
4. Over the house flew the airplane.
5. The *Titanic* struck an iceberg.
6. Competition in the computer industry is keen.
7. In Italy was born Pirandello, a famous writer.
8. One of the most respected television personalities was Walter Cronkite.
9. Report at nine o'clock.
10. At the Centennial Exposition of 1876 the telephone was exhibited.
11. Mark Antony was defeated by Augustus at Actium.
12. Have you corrected all the errors in your essay?
13. Many semitrailer trucks have eighteen wheels.
14. The winning team autographed the baseball.
15. Always be prompt.

Natural and Inverted Order in Sentences

> Whenever the predicate verb follows the simple subject, a sentence is in the natural order.
>
> Whenever the verb or an auxiliary verb is placed before its subject, a sentence is in the inverted order.

Subject   Verb
<u>Wildflowers</u> <u>bloom</u> in the spring. (*Natural order*)

Verb   Subject
In the spring <u>bloom</u> <u>wildflowers</u>. (*Inverted order*)

Exercise 142

Identify the subject and the verb of each sentence. Tell whether the sentences are in the natural or the inverted order.

1. Have you read any books by the novelist Cynthia Voight?
2. She has written many fine stories for young adults.
3. They should go to the studio immediately.
4. The swimmers rushed to the lake at the sound of the whistle.
5. Does the small village lie beyond the distant mountains?
6. Milk flowed like a white waterfall from the overturned truck.
7. From behind the bushes came the rampaging rhinoceros.
8. Is the planet with rings around it called Saturn?
9. In the corner of the cab's back seat slumped the tired passenger.
10. Ten thousand people marched in the parade for civil rights.
11. From around the corner sprang the hungry kitten.
12. During the night the sky turned an eerie green.
13. Tom will give his acceptance speech at nine o'clock.
14. Before the news could reach her parents, Susan called them.
15. Behind a loose board in the old mansion was hidden a bundle of hundred-dollar bills.

Division of Sentences According to Use

A *declarative sentence* is a sentence that states a fact.

An *interrogative sentence* is a sentence that asks a question.

An *imperative sentence* is a sentence that expresses a command.

An *exclamatory sentence* is a sentence that expresses strong or sudden emotion.

The first satellite was Sputnik. (*Declarative*)
Who was the first cosmonaut? (*Interrogative*)
Read the history of space exploration. (*Imperative*)
How interesting it is! (*Exclamatory*)

Exercise 143

Classify each sentence according to use, and tell what punctuation mark should end the sentence.

1. With her help we designed a river raft
2. What beautiful flowers these are
3. What is "primogeniture"
4. Who are the painters of the American Gothic school
5. What an important inventor Edison was
6. Peking is one of the largest cities in the world
7. Bring the report to me at once
8. Betty was chosen secretary of the club
9. How was smallpox virtually eliminated
10. See the hydrofoil
11. Mail used to be delivered twice a day
12. Tokyo is the largest city in Japan
13. From whom were the tickets purchased
14. From Carol's house to mine is three miles
15. I can't believe it happened to me

Lesson 6 Simple and Compound Sentences

According to form, sentences are divided into simple, compound, complex, and compound-complex sentences.

Simple Sentences

> **A simple sentence is a sentence containing one subject and one predicate, either or both of which may be compound.**

Subject   Predicate
Leo Tolstoy wrote many fine novels.

> **If the subject of a sentence consists of more than one noun or pronoun, it is said to be a *compound subject*. If the predicate consists of more than one verb, it is said to be a *compound predicate*.**

A sentence may have a compound subject, a compound predicate, or a compound subject and a compound predicate.

Spain and *Portugal* are the countries of the Iberian peninsula. (*Compound subject*)
That line *owns* and *operates* ships in many waters. (*Compound predicate*)
Toby and *Louise sing* and *dance*. (*Compound subject and compound predicate*)

Exercise 144

Show that each sentence is simple by identifying its subject and predicate.

1. From the stage came the sound of the actor's voice.
2. Did Amanda and Louise invite you to the party?
3. Jill likes to swim and dive in the lake.
4. In October, the leaves change color and fall from the trees.
5. Terry and Roz are vegetarians.
6. Many people take vacations in the summer.
7. Singing and dancing, we celebrated the event.
8. Many varieties of fish are found in the aquarium.
9. Monique photographed the inspiring sunset.
10. The next day the hill was covered with snow.

Exercise 145

Complete each sentence by supplying a compound subject or compound predicate.

1. _____ and _____ are large cities in the United States.
2. _____, _____, and _____ are playing together in the hay.
3. The sprinters and hurdlers on our team _____ and _____ every day.
4. _____ and _____ brought flowers home.
5. Juan and Judy either _____ a letter or _____.
6. Darren _____ nuts and _____ them.
7. _____ and _____ hope to visit their cousins in Germany this summer.
8. The carpenter _____ and _____ the board.
9. The _____ and the _____ are large oceans.
10. The _____ and _____ live in the castle.

Sharpening Your Skills

Write five simple sentences using the elements suggested below.

1. a compound subject and compound predicate in natural order
2. a compound subject in transposed order
3. a compound predicate in transposed order
4. a compound predicate in an interrogative sentence
5. a compound subject and compound predicate in an interrogative sentence

Compound Sentences

> **A compound sentence is a sentence that contains two or more independent clauses.**

The United States is a large country, and it is rich in natural resources.

This sentence contains two complete statements (simple sentences) which are connected by the conjunction *and*.

The United States is a large country. It is rich in natural resources.

Exercise 146

Identify the subject and verb of each independent clause in these compound sentences.

1. Class was dismissed and the students went home.
2. I cannot talk with you right now; I will explain later.
3. Henry expected to get an excellent grade on the test; nevertheless, he waited nervously.
4. I read *The Adventures of Tom Sawyer*, but I did not see the movie version.
5. The water had been shut off; yet no one could understand why.
6. I studied very hard for this test; moreover, I have always done well on science tests.
7. I wanted to go running, but the weather was just too cold.
8. Snow and ice covered the streets, and the car was buried in front of the building.
9. Carla did not paint the mural, nor did she carve the statue.
10. The students listened eagerly to the lunchtime announcements, but the principal did not dismiss school for the day.

Exercise 147

Combine each pair of simple sentences into one compound sentence.

1. A lake is a large body of standing water. A pond is a small body of standing water.
2. I watched. I did not see the man again.
3. In the mountains, summer days are warm. Nights are cool.
4. The Mets and the Cubs play baseball in the National League. The Yankees and the White Sox play in the American League.
5. The man seemed to smile. He offered no help.
6. Anthracite is hard coal. Bituminous coal is soft coal.
7. Ichabod Crane was tall and lanky. His whole frame was loosely hung together.
8. Synonyms are words of similar meaning. Antonyms are words of opposite meanings.
9. Sun and wind sometimes burn skin. Water and harsh soaps can damage skin.
10. Erin will read a poem or sing a song at the wedding. Harvey will play a new guitar composition.

Sharpening Your Skills

Choose one specific topic to write about. Write your sentences according to the suggestions below. Your sentences may be in any order.

1. a compound sentence with a compound subject in either clause
2. a compound sentence with a compound predicate in either clause
3. a simple sentence
4. a compound sentence
5. a simple sentence with any compound element

Lesson 7 Complex and Compound–Complex Sentences

Complex Sentences

> A complex sentence is a sentence that contains one principal clause and one or more subordinate clauses.

Pennsylvania was settled by William Penn, who was the son of a wealthy English admiral.

This is a complex sentence because it contains one principal clause, *Pennsylvania was settled by William Penn*, and one subordinate clause, *who was the son of a wealthy English admiral.*

Subordinate clauses may be adjectival, adverbial, or noun clauses, according to their use in the sentence.

Adjectival clauses are generally introduced by relative pronouns (*who, whom, whose, which, that*) or relative adverbs (*when, where, why*). They are discussed on pages 439–441.

Penn's Treaty with the Indians by Edward Hicks

Adverbial clauses are generally introduced by subordinate conjunctions (*as, that, since, because, for, if, then, than, provided, unless, though, so, after, when, before, where, until, while*). An explanation of these clauses may be found on pages 442–443.

Noun clauses are usually introduced by the introductory words *how, whether, what, why,* and *that.* Refer to pages 444–451 for a discussion of the various types of noun clauses.

Exercise 148

Indicate the principal clause and the subordinate clause in each sentence. Tell whether the subordinate clause is adverbial, adjectival, or noun.

1. I get excited when I see a rainbow in the sky.
2. Monte Cassino was a famous monastery that was destroyed during World War II.
3. Although Paris and Berlin had their charms, Debbie longed for home.
4. The dog came when she called him.
5. If you drive slowly, stay in the right lane.
6. We think that they are lost somewhere in Africa.
7. The compass indicates that we are moving north.
8. The seismograph is an instrument that records the direction, the intensity, and the duration of earthquakes.
9. Until you have lived through a tornado, you cannot fully comprehend its strength.
10. The woman who taught him to play the trumpet lives down the street.

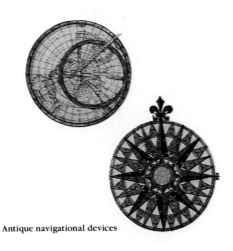

Antique navigational devices

Exercise 149

Complete the subordinate clauses and identify them as adjectival, adverbial, or noun clauses.

1. That_____ was no surprise to me.
2. Since_____ , the United States has been involved in a space race.
3. A monument now stands here because_____ .
4. Suzie's cello teacher, who_____ , encourages her to practice.
5. Dotty arranged the flowers that_____ .
6. Lester was talking about what_____ .
7. I always respond when_____ .
8. London, which_____ , is on the bank of the River Thames.
9. Molly admires people who_____ .
10. If_____ , I will not wait for you.

Exercise 150

Make one complex sentence from each of the following groups of simple sentences. Identify the introductory word of any subordinate clause.

1. Watch where you walk. Rusty nails are sticking out of the boards.
2. Leo Tolstoy was a Russian author. He wrote *War and Peace*.
3. President Monroe was concerned about the influence of other countries on countries in the western hemisphere. He issued the Monroe Doctrine.
4. The ancient Egyptians made paper from the papyrus plant. This plant grew along the banks of the Nile.
5. I studied the lesson. The lesson was assigned yesterday.
6. I looked up the river. I saw a beautiful boat sailing. The boat was sailing toward me. The boat was sailing swiftly.
7. Jim plowed the land. He planted the seeds. The seeds were for corn.
8. The sun was shining brightly. It melted the snow.
9. The waves washed a broken rowboat up onto the beach. The rowboat had been tied to a dock before the storm.
10. The plant drooped. It had not been watered in two weeks. It would have died. Tina watered it.

Compound–Complex Sentences

A compound–complex sentence is a sentence that
contains two or more principal clauses and one
or more subordinate clauses.

Napoleon had an austere manner, but he was always kind to the
soldiers who were under his charge.

*Napoleon had an austere manner, but he was always kind to the
soldiers* is a compound sentence connected by the coordinate
conjunction *but*. *Who were under his charge* is an adjectival clause
introduced by the relative pronoun *who*. A compound–complex
sentence must contain *two independent clauses* and *one dependent
clause*.

Exercise 151

Identify each of the following sentences as simple, compound, complex, or compound–complex.

1. Dolley Madison, the wife of President James Madison, was a Quaker.
2. She first married John Todd who was also a Quaker.
3. Her marriage to John lasted a short three years.
4. Dolley had two sons, but one died the same year as her husband [died].
5. In 1794, Dolley married James Madison.
6. Because her husband was not a Quaker, Dolley was rejected by the Society of Friends, and she could no longer attend Quaker meetings.
7. Dolley, who excited everyone with her style and charm, served as White House hostess for sixteen years.
8. Because Thomas Jefferson was a widower, Dolley assumed the role of First Lady during his administration.
9. Dolley was the first to serve ice cream in the White House.
10. When the British invaded Washington in 1814, Dolley fled the city.
11. She took with her many important documents, and she even managed to save a famous portrait of George Washington.
12. Dolley was anxious to return to the White House after it had been burned.
13. She wanted to resume her entertaining, but the restoration progressed slowly.
14. President Madison left office before the White House was ready to be occupied, but James Monroe was able to enjoy its new beauty.
15. The pirates sailed from their island home on a small ship called *The Jolly Roger*.
16. The World Trade Center towers, which are in New York City, are very tall, but the Sears Tower in Chicago is even taller.
17. The computer that we wanted to buy was on sale; nevertheless, it was out of our price range.
18. Claudia asked what I had done.
19. On the table near the tree were many packages wrapped in blue paper and tied with red ribbons.
20. The window was broken, but the picnickers who had been playing ball offered to fix it.

You Are the Author

Have you ever had a frightening experience on a bike or horse or in a car, bus, or boat? Write a composition describing how you felt. Use different kinds of phrases, clauses, and sentences.

Chapter Challenge

Read this selection very carefully and then answer the questions that follow.

[1]What are the factors that determine the occupations of those who live in certain localities? [2]To answer this question, consider carefully the physical features of the region. [3]If the climate, soil, and rainfall favor the raising of crops, the people turn to farming. [4]The fact that they live near the sea moves others to make fishing their work. [5]Inhabitants of districts having rich mineral deposits find employment in the mines. [6]In thickly populated areas many workers are available, and raw materials are easily transported. [7]If power resources are sufficient, manufacturing becomes important in such sections. [8]Since the other occupations are similarly controlled by natural environment, we see that an individual's choice of a life's work is limited greatly by the area in which he or she lives.

1. Name two adjectival clauses in the first sentence.
2. What kind of phrase is *to answer this question* in the second sentence?
3. Name the subordinate clause in the third sentence. Is it adjectival on adverbial?
4. Name the adverbial phrase in the fourth sentence.
5. What kind of a clause is *that they live near the sea* in the fourth sentence? Give the syntax of this clause.
6. Is the fifth sentence in natural or transposed order?
7. What kind of phrase is *having rich mineral deposits* in the fifth sentence?
8. Find a compound sentence in the paragraph.
9. Name a prepositional phrase in the seventh sentence.
10. Find an adverbial clause in the seventh sentence.
11. Is the phrase *of a life's work* in the last sentence adjectival or adverbial?

Chapter 9

Punctuation and Capitalization

The Strange Tale of King Midas
by Vernon Howard

from *The Complete Book of Children's Theater*

Ladies and gentlemen, welcome! We believe we have a treat for you this evening. Our class will act out for you one of the most famous of the ancient Greek myths. Perhaps you have read the strange story of King Midas, who ruled the kingdom of Phrygia. Tonight you will *see* his story. Our dramatic presentation is titled "The Strange Tale of King Midas."

There was one thing in life that King Midas treasured above everything else. It was an **obsession** with him; he craved it more and more—but I had better not give away the story!

(The scene is a royal room in the king's palace. Suitable furniture is set in the background. King Midas is seated upon his throne at upstage center. On a low table before him is a large box labeled "Treasure." The box is filled with a variety of riches, such as necklaces, rings, bracelets, gold and silver cups. King Midas eagerly holds them up, admires them.)

King Midas: Gold! Silver! Precious stones sparkling with light! They are mine, all mine! I am the richest king in all the kingdoms of the world. *(Clapping his hands)* Hasten, royal servants! *(First Servant quickly enters.)*

First Servant *(bowing deeply)***:** Yes, O royal king?

King Midas *(gesturing nervously)***:** Gold, more gold! Fetch me another royal treasure chest. Quickly!

First Servant: At once, your majesty. *(First Servant backs away while bowing, exits.)*

Second Servant *(entering, bowing)***:** O great King Midas, there is a weary traveler at the palace gate who begs for food and rest. Shall I send him on his way?

Photograph of Greek temple ruins by Erich Lessing

King Midas *(somewhat annoyed)*: Can't you see that I am counting my gold? *(Shrugging impatiently)* Ah, well, send him to me. *(Second Servant bows and exits as King Midas greedily continues to enjoy his treasure. The Weary Traveler enters, falls on his knees before King Midas.)*

Weary Traveler *(gratefully)*: May all good things come to you, O kindly king. I **beseech** but a dry crust of bread and a stone upon which to lay my weary head. *(First and Second Servants enter and set a heavy box labeled "Gold" before the king.)*

King Midas *(ignoring the Weary Traveler as he greedily digs both hands into gold coins and other golden objects)*: My precious gold! How it warms my hands! I shall spend the rest of the day counting my golden treasures!

First Servant *(coughing, to attract the king's attention)*: A-hum. . . a-hum!

King Midas *(looking up in annoyance)*: Yes, yes, what is it?

First Servant *(gesturing to the kneeling Weary Traveler)*: Pardon, your majesty, but . . .

King Midas *(sighing)*: Oh, yes. *(Briskly, but with kindness)* Take this weary fellow to the royal dining hall. Give him everything he needs. *(He again fondles his gold.)*

Weary Traveler *(backing away, bowing with upraised arms)*: The blessing of heaven upon your kindly majesty. *(He exits.)*

King Midas *(looking around suspiciously)*: I sense a stranger. Who is there? *(Standing, he angrily jerks his head about.)* Who dares to enter the royal chambers without permission?

Bacchus *(approaching King Midas slowly and with great dignity)*: I am no stranger to you, King Midas.

King Midas *(in astonishment)*: Bacchus! One of the gods come down from Mount Olympus! *(Bowing)* I am honored by the presence of mighty Bacchus!

Bacchus: I have observed your mercy and kindness to the weary traveler. That needy man was Silenus, my foster father. Because you have shown him compassion, I will grant you your fondest wish. Whatever you ask I will grant immediately.

King Midas *(tilting head, thinking deeply)*: My fondest wish! Hmmm. What shall I choose? *(Exclaiming, suddenly)* I know. Please, great Bacchus, I wish that everything I touch should turn to gold! I wish to have the golden touch.

Bacchus *(solemnly)*: I do not approve of your wish, King Midas, but it is hereby granted. *(Raising arms toward King Midas)* Henceforth, everything you touch shall turn instantly to gold! I leave you with your golden touch. *(Lowers arms and exits.)*

King Midas (*jubilantly holding up and admiring his hands*): My golden touch! (*Eagerly*) I must test it! (*He touches an apple in a fruit basket, holds up a golden apple.*) A golden apple! (*Racing to a potted plant he plucks off a twig, holds it up.*) Gold, gold, pure gold! Come, lords and ladies of the royal court! Witness the magic of King Midas!

First Princess: We await your majesty's pleasure.

King Midas (*shouting*): Then behold, as my royal chambers turn to pure gold! (*He races to two or three small objects, holding them up while ad-libbing:* Gold! . . . Look! . . . The golden touch! *The others gasp while also ad-libbing:* Amazing! . . . How can this be? . . . Look, it turned to gold!*)

First Prince: Congratulations, O king! Your fame will spread to the far corners of the earth!

First Servant (*bowing*): The royal dinner hour, your majesty.

King Midas (*annoyed by the interruption*): What's that? Oh, yes. Set them down. (*The servants set trays on a table and exit.*) Come, we must celebrate my good fortune.

Second Princess (*biting a small cake*): The baker has outdone himself with his sweetcakes. (*To King Midas*) Come, your majesty, the royal dinner awaits. (*As King Midas approaches, the Second Prince hands him a small cake.*)

Second Prince: Try this tasty sweetcake.

King Midas (*grimacing as he tastes*): What kind of a joke is this? (*Staring in horror at cake*) A cake of gold. My dinner itself has turned into gold!

Third Princess (*sympathetically*): Poor, poor King Midas. Everything you touch turns into hard, cold metal. What shall you do for your dinner?

Third Prince (*to others*): We must help our king.

First Princess (*gesturing hopelessly*): But how?

First Prince: Yes, how can we help him? He cannot eat his gold; neither can he drink it.

Second Princess: Nor can he ride throughout his kingdom upon a golden horse.

Second Prince (*as all gaze sympathetically at the dejected king*): It was a sorry hour when our king acquired the golden touch. (*Gesturing*) Come, perhaps we can devise some magic that will cure him of his curse. (*All except King Midas exit.*)

King Midas (*standing, after a brief pause, pleading as he sadly looks around*): Bacchus, god of Mount Olympus, hear my humble prayer. I beseech you to take away my grief. (*Nodding*) I have been a greedy man. (*Closing his eyes, he bows his head.*)

Bacchus (*entering, holding upraised hands over King Midas*)**:** Because you repent of your greed, I take pity upon you. (*King Midas hopefully raises his head.*) Go to the River Pactolus, plunge into its cleansing waters, and you will be healed! And may you always remember that there are far more precious treasures in life than gold. (*Bacchus exits.*)

Third Princess (*glancing about*)**:** We heard a strange voice. (*Brightly, as she sees a smile on the king's face*) Your majesty! Your face is bright with joy. What has happened?

King Midas (*nodding gratefully as he descends from throne*)**:** My golden curse will vanish as I bathe in the waters of the River Pactolus. Come, lords and ladies, this is a happy day for all of us. Your king has lost his golden touch . . . but has won a great deal of wisdom.

Third Prince: We rejoice with you, King Midas. Hail to our king, who is rich in peace and honor.

The Writer's Craft

1. Have you ever imagined being granted whatever you want most? What is your greatest wish? Why do you think it would be good for you—or not good for you— if you received it?

2. Bacchus said that he did not approve of King Midas's wish. Why do you think he granted it anyhow? Why did the king not think of the consequences before he made his request?

3. There are more exclamation points in this selection than you would normally expect to find in a piece of this length. Why do you think there are so many? Did the author overuse them? What might be the effect on a piece of writing if the exclamation point is too commonly used?

4. By following the rules for punctuation and capitalization, writers make their work understood more easily. Look at the capitalized words in this play. Find three words that illustrate different rules for capitalization.

Recalling What You Know

1. A comma separates the clauses of a compound sentence and words in a series. Place the commas in this sentence: *Did you feed the dog cat and fish and did you lock the door?*
2. Quotation marks enclose direct quotations. Place them in this sentence: *I am free, said the king, of the terrible curse.*
3. An apostrophe shows the omission of a letter or letters. Form a word with an apostrophe from: *he will, did not, she had.*

Lesson 1 Periods and Commas

The purpose of punctuation is to make clear the meaning of what is written. In speaking, the inflection of a person's voice helps to convey his or her message to a listener. In writing, different kinds of punctuation marks—the period, comma, semicolon, colon, exclamation point, interrogation point, quotation marks, apostrophe, hyphen, and dash—are used to clarify ideas for the reader. In this chapter, you will learn the basic rules for punctuation and capitalization that you will need in your writing.

The Period

Use a period
  1. at the end of a declarative or imperative sentence.

> King Midas is the main character in the play.
> Do enjoy the play.

  2. after an abbreviation and an initial.

> D.D.S.   James A. Longnose

The Comma

Use a comma

1. to separate words or groups of words used in a series.

> Some berries were red, unripe, and bitter.
> Mike searched for his lost dog on the streets, in the shops, and at the lake.

2. to separate independent elements and words of direct address.

> Yes, it is flying toward the river.
> Paul, can you see that plane?

3. to set off a short direct quotation and the parts of a divided quotation, unless an interrogation mark or an exclamation point is required.

> "I shall be glad to come," answered Linda.
> "Someday," said Leo, "I'll be a doctor."
> "Have you ever read *Call of the Wild?*" asked Sue.

4. to set off the parts of dates, addresses, or geographical names.

> The earthquake struck San Francisco, California, on April 18, 1906.

5. to separate nonrestrictive phrases and clauses from the rest of the sentence.

> The boat, crowded with people, sailed away.
> Brian, who has been to Boston, returned last night.

> NOTE: A *nonrestrictive* phrase or clause is one that may be omitted from a sentence without changing the meaning. Some phrases and clauses are necessary to the meaning of a sentence and cannot be omitted. They are called *restrictive* phrases or clauses and are not separated by commas.

> The whale that was beached drew much attention.

6. after long introductory phrases and clauses, and when needed to make the meaning clear.

> Seated in the midst of a group of enthusiastic spectators, Michael clapped and cheered.
> If you had stopped, Vince would have followed.

7. to set off an appositive that is not part of a proper name or that is not restrictive.

> Julius Caesar, the first Roman emperor, was a brilliant general.
> William the Conqueror became king of England in 1066.

8. to set off a parenthetical expression; that is, a word or a group of words inserted in the sentence as a comment or an explanatory remark, and one that is not necessary to the thought of the sentence.

> You are, indeed, an industrious worker.
> Copernicus was, without a doubt, an intelligent man.

9. to separate the clauses of a compound sentence connected by the conjunctions *and, but, or, nor, yet*. If the clauses are short and closely connected, the comma may be omitted.

> Your team won two games, but ours won three.
> The door opened and it closed quietly.

10. after the salutation in a social letter and after the complimentary close in all letters.

> Dear Maureen,   Dear Mrs. Thanopoulos,   Sincerely yours,

Exercise 152

Give the reason each period is used and the number of the rule that explains why each comma is used.

1. Myths, especially those of Greece and Rome, portray the way ancient people thought and felt.
2. The Greek myths deal with gods, goddesses, heroes, and creation.
3. The Titans were called the Elder Gods, and some of the important ones were Cronus, Atlas, and Prometheus.
4. Jon, do you know the Roman names for these Titans?
5. The main Greek gods were Zeus, Poseidon, and Hades.
6. In some of the well-known myths, Hera, who is the wife of Zeus, fights with the other gods and goddesses.
7. King Midas, whose name is synonymous with riches, regretted his desire for gold.
8. Bacchus, the god of wine, was called Dionysus by the Greeks.
9. Our teacher said, "Jon, please play the part of Midas."
10. Be sure to read more myths like this one, Andrea.

473

Exercise 153

Punctuate each sentence correctly.

1. It is time to eat children
2. Answer all questions truthfully completely and courteously
3. Frank parked his car a green Ford station wagon in front of the gym
4. Italy surrendered on September 8 1943 but Germany did not give up until May 8 1945
5. Come over Greg and see my new skates
6. The setting for example should be carefully arranged
7. Although Philip and Bill are no longer roommates they correspond regularly
8. If you had called Cecilia would have told you where I was
9. Sharon a friend of Kim's made David angry
10. We moved from Harrisburg Pennsylvania to Memphis Tennessee

Sharpening Your Skills

The following excerpt is taken from *Pilgrim at Tinker Creek* by Annie Dillard. Ms. Dillard has made excellent use of commas in this selection, but none appear below. Rewrite the paragraphs, inserting commas and periods where you feel they are appropriate.

When the muskrat went under the bridge I moved so I could face downstream comfortably He reappeared and I had a good look at him He was eight inches long in the body and another six in the tail Muskrat tails are black and scaled flattened not horizontally like beavers' tails but vertically like a belt stood on edge In the winter muskrats' tails sometimes freeze solid and the animals chew off the frozen parts up to about an inch of the body....

The muskrat clambered out on the bank across the stream from me and began feeding He chomped down on a ten-inch weed pushing it into his mouth steadily with his forepaws as a carpenter feeds a saw....Then he slid back into the water with the weed still in his mouth crossed under the bridge and instead of returning to his den rose erect on a submerged rock and calmly polished off the rest of the weed

Lesson 2 Other Types of Punctuation

The Semicolon

Use a semicolon
1. to separate the clauses of a compound sentence when they are not separated by a coordinate conjunction.

> Gary did not go to the football game; he went on a hike instead.

2. to separate the clauses of a compound sentence that are connected by such words as *nevertheless*, *moreover*, *therefore*, *then*, *thus*.

> She was a good worker; therefore, her name was added to the list.

3. before *as* and *namely* when these words introduce an example or an illustration.

> In the body there are two kinds of blood cells; namely, the red cells and the white cells.

4. to separate the members of a series when a comma alone would not separate them clearly.

> I am a farmer. For me democracy means the freedom to plant and harvest my own crops; to sell them or to use them to feed my cattle; to use the earth, the sun, and the rain for the well-being of all people.

Exercise 154

Insert semicolons and commas where they are needed.

1. The subway car seemed filled to capacity nevertheless four more people squeezed into it.
2. Leave the arrangements to me I'll take care of them.
3. The school newspaper has four reporters namely Scott Ellen Dan and Audrey.
4. To write a paragraph select and limit the subject build a vocabulary make an outline follow the outline in writing beginning middle and ending sentences.
5. I know how to play the guitar however my finger is broken.

The Colon

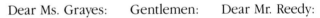

Use a colon

1. after the salutation of a business letter.

   Dear Ms. Grayes: Gentlemen: Dear Mr. Reedy:

2. before a list or enumeration of items.

   They ordered the following: a desk, a chair, a bookcase, and a table.

3. before a long direct quotation.

   The author wrote: "I have traveled a great distance and I am tired; I will go no farther until I am rested."

The Exclamation Point

Use an exclamation point

1. after an exclamatory sentence.

   What a magnificent scene lay before us!

2. after an exclamatory word, phrase, or clause.

   "Silence!" called the speaker.

The Interrogation Point

Use an interrogation point at the end of every question.

> Where is my camera?

Quotation Marks

Use quotation marks

1. before and after every direct quotation and every part of a
   divided quotation.

   > "Then you shall have it!" said the king.
   > "I would rather be right," said Henry Clay, "than
   > be president."

   NOTE: Sometimes a quotation includes another quotation. Such an
   included quotation is known as a *quotation within a quotation*
   and is marked with single quotation marks.

   > "When the crowd screamed, 'Watch out for the car!' I froze,"
   > confessed Neil.

2. to enclose titles of stories, poems, magazine articles, newspaper
   articles, television shows, and radio programs.

   > The best number on the program was Kilmer's "Trees."

   NOTE: Titles of books, magazines, movies, works of art, plays, and
   newspapers are printed in italics. In typing or handwriting, italics
   are indicated by underlining.

   > *The Call of the Wild* is an exciting book.
   > <u>The Call of the Wild</u> is an exciting book.

Exercise 155

Insert colons, exclamation points, interrogation points, and quotation marks where they are needed.

1. We will take these things with us on the camping trip a tent, sleeping bags, and food for two days.
2. Who ate my tangerine asked Madeline.
3. I did cried Karin.
4. Why do you think she did that
5. My, am I hungry
6. When looking to the future, consider these words Know what roads lie before you and make an intelligent choice. Don't be fooled by how narrow or how wide the path. If it leads to your goal, take it.
7. Flannery O'Connor wrote A Good Man Is Hard to Find.
8. Patrick Henry said, If this be treason, make the most of it.
9. What a thrilling play she wrote
10. Did Miguel promise to take us to the circus

Exercise 156

Practice using quotation marks by writing dialogue between two persons. Keep the following points in mind:

1. Each time you introduce a different speaker, you must indent the first line.
2. When your reader knows who is saying the next line, the speaker does not need mentioning.
3. Vary your quotations by naming the speaker first, last, or in the middle of the dialogue (divided quotation).

Now write four lines of dialogue for each situation below. The first one is done for you.

1. butcher to customer

> "How much ham would you like?" asked the butcher.
> Mrs. Robb answered, "Just slice me one pound, but give me a pound and a half of American cheese, please."
> "Anything else?"   **speaker not mentioned**
> "Not right now, thank you," said Mrs. Robb. "I'll make do with this."   **divided quotation**

2. driving instructor to new driver
3. coach to team member
4. teacher to student
5. babysitter to young child

The Apostrophe

Use an apostrophe
1. to show possession.

> Men's shoes are on sale.

2. with *s* to show the plural of letters when the omission of the apostrophe would lead to confusion.

> i's   t's   a's

3. to show the omission of a letter, letters, or figures.

> didn't   I'll   class of '80

The Hyphen

Use a hyphen
1. to divide a word at the end of a line whenever one or more syllables are carried to the next line.
2. in compound numbers from twenty-one to ninety-nine.

> She is twenty-five years old.

3. to separate the parts of some compound words.

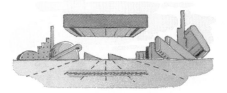

> self-respect   son-in-law

The Dash

Use a dash to indicate a sudden change of thought.

> I suddenly turned—I am still surprised at my action—and left the room.

Sharpening Your Skills

Indicate the correct punctuation.

1. Make your w s more plainly
2. Did John buy twenty five acres of land
3. When you play play hard when you study study hard
4. James laughed and said I ll stay home
5. Dante an Italian poet wrote many famous poems
6. Ouch I cut my finger
7. What is her name her age and her address
8. Oh what a beautiful baby exclaimed the lady in the blue coat
9. The library is open three days this week Monday Wednesday and Saturday
10. Jean asked Do you know who wrote that note
11. The letter was mailed from Lima Peru
12. Yes I will attend the party
13. A mouse cried Marsha
14. Good morning Susan called the doorkeeper
15. When Lil said You are wrong I decided to reconsider said Peter
16. It was early when we arrived the shops were not open
17. The work had to be done Anne was elected to do it
18. Shelley s poem To a Skylark begins with these words Hail to thee, blithe spirit
19. Gary s mother in law is very ill
20. We hoped we were always hoping that the outcome would be different

480

Lesson 3 Capital Letters

Use a capital letter for
1. the first word in a sentence.

> Tall trees shaded the park.

2. the first word of every line of most poetry.

> The day is ending,
> The moon is bending
> Over a star-studded sky
> Sprinking silver
> Where the pathways lie.

3. the first word of a direct quotation.

> Jane cried, "Come quickly!"

4. proper nouns and proper adjectives. These include particular persons or groups of persons, months of the year, days of the week, holidays, religious denominations, political parties, institutions, buildings, cities, states, and streets.

> Joseph, March, Armistice Day, Democrats, Mormon, Empire State Building, the Canadian flag, Republican party, Tuesday, Nevada, Catholic, Market Street, Tokyo

5. titles of honor and respect when preceding the name.

> Judge O'Hara   Queen Elizabeth

Do not capitalize any title not followed by a proper noun unless it is used in direct address as a substitute for the name.

> The judge has entered the courtroom.
> Not guilty, Your Honor.

6. *north*, *east*, *south*, and *west* when they refer to sections of a country.

> He comes from the West.

7. all names referring to the deity, the Bible, or parts of the Bible, and all other sacred books.

> The Koran is the collection of the sacred writings of Muhammad.

Queen Elizabeth I

481

8. the principal words in the titles of books, plays, poems, and pictures.

   Black Like Me

9. the pronoun *I* and the interjection *O*.

   O Mr. Barbera! See the meteor.

10. abbreviations when capitals would be used if the words were written in full.

    Gen.   St.

Do not capitalize

1. the seasons of the year.

   fall   winter

2. the articles *a*, *an*, *the*, conjunctions, or prepositions in titles, unless they are the first words.

   Two Years before the Mast   *The Time of Your Life*

3. the names of studies, unless they are derived from proper nouns.

   history   geography   English

4. the words *high school*, *college*, and *university*, unless they are parts of the names of particular institutions.

   My brother goes to high school in Dayton.
   My sister is a senior at the University of Southern California.

5. the word *god* or *gods* when referring to mythology.

   Who was the king of the gods?

Exercise 157

Choose the letter that contains the correct form.

1. a. heading northeast   b. heading Northeast
2. a. in the autumn   b. in the Autumn
3. a. Elementary School   b. Weber Junior High
4. a. June graduation   b. june Graduation
5. a. President of the Company   b. President Johnson
6. a. "the Raven"   b. "The Raven"
7. a. I'm enjoying math.   b. I'm enjoying Math.
8. a. God of War   b. god of war
9. a. living in the South   b. living in the south
10. a. Kingston road   b. Kingston Road

You Are the Author

Choose one.
1. Write a composition of about seven or eight sentences in which you describe a person or a country that possesses characteristics that are the opposite of those of King Midas.
2. Read a myth, for example one about Tantalus and Niobe, about Ceres and Proserpina, or about Atalanta, and then write a short play based on it. Choose other students for the roles and present the play in class. You may wish to be the narrator, introducing the play with a description of the setting.

Chapter Challenge

Divide the following two selections into sentences. Use the necessary capitals and insert the proper punctuation marks.

1. my father as i said was greatly delighted if my teacher had compared me to william shakespeare or had exclaimed he is a genius he could not have felt better he called me into the living room and with a beaming smile said

   there is no need for me to tell you i was pleased when your teacher said henry is a good student but even more he is a person of integrity who is respected by his peers i am not going to diminish the praise you ve been given by rewarding you materially as you are aware the best reward for being true to the moral values in which you believe is a clear conscience

2. a merry christmas uncle god save you cried a cheerful voice it was the voice of scrooges nephew who came upon him so quickly that this was the first intimation he had of his approach

   bah said scrooge humbug

   he had so heated himself with rapid walking in the fog and frost this nephew of scrooges that he was all in a glow his face was ruddy and handsome his eyes sparkled and his breath smoked again

   christmas a humbug uncle said scrooges nephew you don t mean that i am sure

   i do said scrooge merry christmas what right have you to be merry if i could work my will every idiot who goes about with merry christmas on his lips should be boiled with his own pudding and buried with a stake of holly through his breast

   —from *A Christmas Carol*, by Charles Dickens

Illustration from *A Christmas Carol*
by Charles Dickens

Chapter 10

Model Diagrams

Diagrams show in a graphic manner the relationships that exist among the various words that make up a sentence. As you have seen, there are simple, compound, and complex sentences. Since sentences of all types may contain modifiers, no one form of diagram will serve for every kind of sentence. The diagrams given here are those that should help you in your work. When asked to diagram a sentence, look here for one of the same kind and see how the diagram is made.

The diagraming of sentences serves a double purpose. First, it makes it easier for you to understand the complete meaning of every sentence you read. Secondly, it helps you to write effectively and to avoid the use of faulty sentences. If you keep these purposes in mind, diagraming will improve your English. It should not become merely a mechanical exercise, but instead should help you to read more intelligently and to write more correctly.

Simple Sentences

Nominative Case

Subject: Into the fort stumbled the exhausted *messenger.*

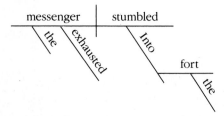

This painting uses lines and space in an abstract way. Diagrams use lines and space in a concrete way. How do diagrams help *you* see the relationships among words?

485

Subjective Complement: Five seventh-grade girls are the new *cheerleaders*.

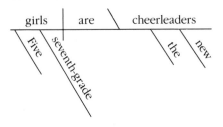

Apposition: Basil, the *soldier*, was the father of Gabriel.

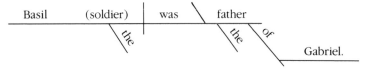

Address: *Jeb*, be our guide on this journey.

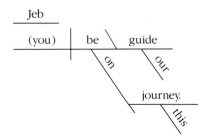

Exclamation: *Action!* The play needs action.

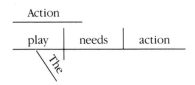

Absolute: The football *game* having ended, the spectators jumped to their feet.

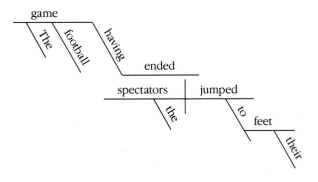

Objective Case

Direct Object: Squirrels collect *nuts*.

Squirrels	collect	nuts

Indirect Object: The teacher told the *class* a story.

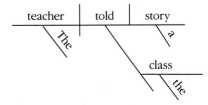

Apposition: We visited Tokyo, the *capital* of Japan.

Object of preposition: Washington performed his duties with great *courage*.

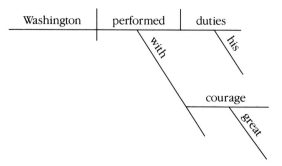

Adverbial Objective: This *morning* the ground was covered with frost.

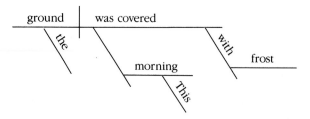

Objective Complement: The committee appointed Joseph *secretary*.

Compound Predicate: Rebecca *gathered* books and *read* them.

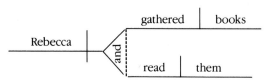

Compound Sentences

The tourists visited Independence Hall and they saw the Liberty Bell.

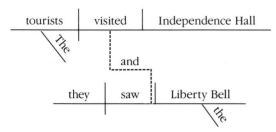

Complex Sentences

Adjectival Clauses

Molly gave her the picture *that she had brought from Rome.*

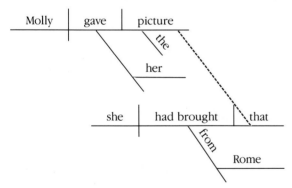

This is the man *whose horse won the prize.*

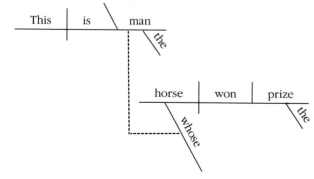

Adverbial Clauses

Connie came *because you sent for her.*

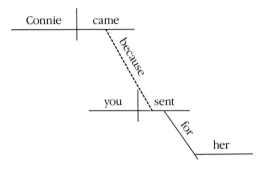

When snow falls the town presents a beautiful picture.

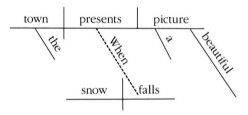

Noun Clauses

Subject: *That the ocean is large* is evident.

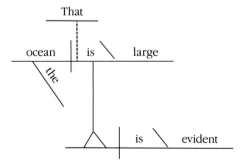

Subjective Complement: My hope is *that we finish the work soon.*

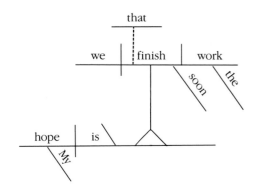

Direct Object: He realized *that he had made a mistake.*

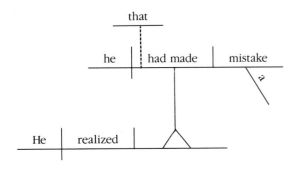

Object of Preposition: The hikers could see the town from *where they had camped.*

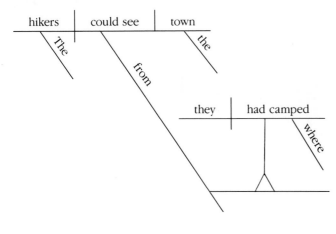

Apposition: The fact *that he was honest* could not be denied.

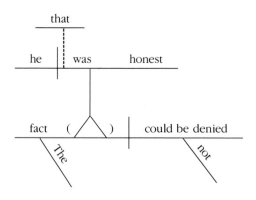

Infinitives

Subject: *To win* was their only thought.

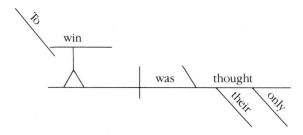

Subjective Complement: The boy's aim was *to rescue* his dog.

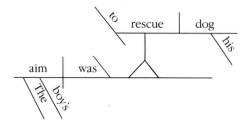

Object: I like *to see* good movies.

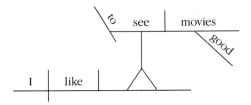

Object of Preposition: He was about *to write* the letter.

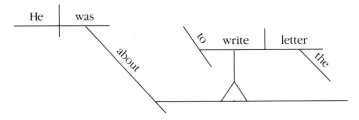

Apposition: It is the duty of a police officer *to enforce* the laws.

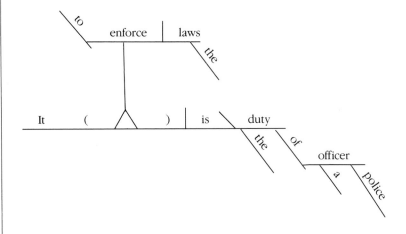

Adjective: They have many opportunities *to visit* the planetarium.

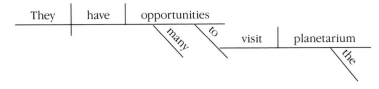

Adverb: Chrissy went *to buy* a new car.

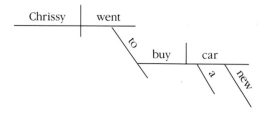

They were anxious *to return*.

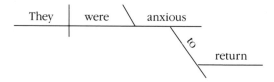

The king is powerful enough *to gather* an army.

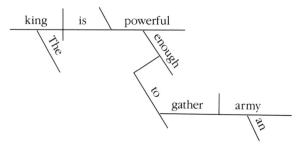

Subject: Whom do you expect *to rule* the country for the next four years?

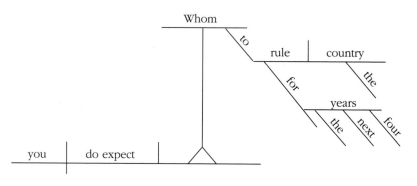

Participles

The protesters, *bearing signs,* marched into the square.

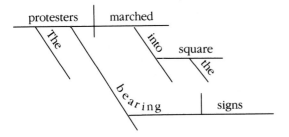

Shouting joyfully, they marched around the football field.

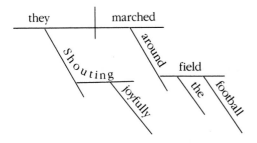

Participial Adjective

The *running* water wore away the stone.

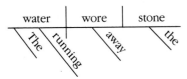

Gerunds

Subject: *Painting* pictures is my favorite hobby.

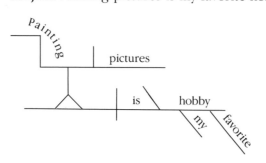

Direct Object: I remember *writing* that letter.

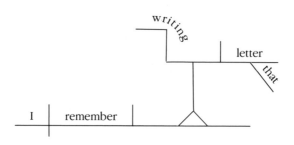

Object of Preposition: Windmills are used for *pumping* water.

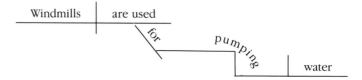

Subjective Complement: My favorite pastime is *reading* biographies.

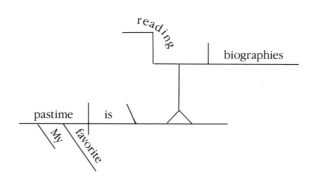

Index

505

Acknowledgments

Text

116 "Dreams" from *Selected Poems of Langston Hughes*. Copyright © 1932 by Alfred A. Knopf, Inc.; copyright renewed © 1960 by the author. Reprinted by permission of the publisher.

117 "All the World's a Stage" from *As You Like It* by William Shakespeare. Copyright © 1952 by Encyclopaedia Britannica, Inc. Reprinted by permission from *The Great Books of the Western World*.

118 "Southbound on the Freeway" by May Swenson. Copyright © 1963 by the author. First printed in the February 16, 1963, issue of *The New Yorker*. Reprinted by permission of the author.

120 "The Sea-Gull" from *Verses from 1929 On* by Ogden Nash. Copyright © 1940 by the author. Reprinted by permission of Little, Brown and Company.

121 "The Garden Hose" by Beatrice Janosco. Reprinted by permission.

121 "Steam Shovel" from *Upper Pasture* by Charles Malam. Copyright © 1930, 1958 by the author. Reprinted by permission of Henry Holt and Company, Inc.

121 "The Toaster" from *Laughing Time* by William Jay Smith. Copyright © 1953, 1955, 1956, 1959, 1968, 1974, 1977, 1980 by the author. Reprinted by permission of Delacorte Press/Seymour Lawrence.

124 "Hungry Mungry" from *Where the Sidewalk Ends: The Poems and Drawings of Shel Silverstein*. Copyright © 1974 by Snake Eye Music, Inc. Reprinted by permission of Harper and Row, Publishers, Inc.

127 "Foul Shot" by Edwin A. Hoey. Copyright © 1962 by Field Publications. Reprinted by permission of *Read Magazine*.

129 "Hark! Hark!" from *The Tempest* by William Shakespeare. Copyright © 1952 by Encyclopaedia Britannica, Inc. Reprinted by permission from *The Great Books of the Western World*.

130 "Cheers" from *It Doesn't Always Have to Rhyme* by Eve Merriam. Copyright © 1964 by the author. Originally published by Atheneum Publishers.

172 "When Dawn Comes to the City" from *Selected Poems of Claude McKay*. Copyright © 1981 by Twayne Publishers, a division of G. K. Hall & Co., Boston. Reprinted by permission of the publisher.

174 "Football" from *Walt Mason, His Book* by Walt Mason. Copyright © 1916 by Barse and Hopkins. Reprinted by permission of Grossett and Dunlap.

175 "Some People" from *Poems* by Rachel Field. Copyright © 1957 by Macmillan Publishing Company. Reprinted by permission of the publisher.

176 "Foghorns" from *I Thought I Heard the City* by Lilian Moore. Copyright © 1969 by the author. Originally published by Atheneum Publishers. All rights reserved. Reprinted by permission of Marian Reiner for the author.

176 "The Sidewalk Racer or, On the Skateboard" from *The Sidewalk Racer, and Other Poems of Sports and Motion* by Lillian Morrison. Copyright © 1977 by the author. Reprinted by permission of Lothrop, Lee and Shepard Books, a division of William Morrow & Co.

176 "War" by Dan Roth from *Literary Cavalcade*. Copyright © 1963 by Scholastic, Inc. Reprinted by permission of the publisher.

176 "Windshield Wiper" from *Out Loud* by Eve Merriam. Copyright © 1973 by the author. Originally published by Atheneum Publishers. All rights reserved. Reprinted by permission of Marian Reiner for the author.

177 "Ancient History" from *Lyric Laughter* by Arthur Guiterman. Copyright © 1939 by E. P. Dutton. Reprinted by permission of Louise H. Sclove.

177 "Whispers" from *Whispers and Other Poems* by Myra Cohn Livingston. Copyright © 1958 by the author. Originally published by Harcourt, Brace and World, Inc. Reprinted by permission of Marian Reiner for the author.

299 *Landscape, New Mexico* by Marsden Hartley. Oil on canvas (25³/₄ x 35³/₄ in.). The Cleveland Museum of Art, anonymous gift.

302 *Road to Lamy* by Andrew Michael Dasburg.

307 *Fire Down on the Labrador* by David Blackwood.

318 *Sedona,* 1986, from *Creatures* by Beth Van Hoesen. Copyright © 1986 by the artist. Reprinted by permission.

357 *Whaling off the Coast of California* by Coleman. Museum of Fine Arts, Boston; M. and M. Karolik Collection.

368 *Winter Moonlight* by Charles Burchfield. Henry Nelson, photographer. Wichita Art Museum, Roland P. Murdock Collection.

372 Samuel Morse, self-portrait. Addison Gallery of American Art.

414 *Portrait of Mademoiselle Violette Heymann,* 1910, by Odilon Redon. Pastel on cardboard (26 ³/₈ x 36 ³/₈ in.). The Cleveland Museum of Art, Hinman B. Hurlbut Collection.

423 *Self-portrait* by Leonardo da Vinci.

460 *Penn's Treaty with the Indians,* Bucks County, Pennsylvania, 1830–1835, by Edward Hicks. Abby Aldrich Rockefeller Folk Art Center, Williamsburg.

461 Antique navigational devices.

481 *Queen Elizabeth I,* c. 1575, by Nicholas Hilliard. The Tate Gallery, London.

483 Illustration from *A Christmas Carol* by Charles Dickens. The Bettmann Archive.

484 *Musical Forms* by Georges Braque. Philadelphia Museum of Art, Louise and Walter Arensberg Collection.

Photographs

Cover: Alan Shortall

i Jeff Lane. **ii** Comstock. **iii** Jim Brandenburg/Minden Pictures. **xvi–xvii** Frans Lanting/Minden Pictures. **xviii** Doug Lee/Tom Stack & Associates. **2** Brian Parker. **5** James L. Ballard. **20** Rod Planck/Tom Stack & Associates. **24** John Shaw/Tom Stack & Associates. **37** Elliott Erwitt/Magnum Photos, Inc. **37** Tom Stack/Tom Stack & Associates. **51** Wide World Photos, Inc. **56** Spencer Swager/Tom Stack & Associates. **77** Christopher Crowley/Tom Stack & Associates. **78** Tom Stack/Tom Stack & Associates. **96** Richard Nowitz/Black Star. **101** Microphotograph, courtesy Cargill Salt, Minneapolis, Minn. **112** William A. Seabright. **127** Rehabilitation Institute, Media Dept. **169** NASA. **171** The University of Illinois at Chicago, The University Library, Jane Addams Memorial Collection. **178** Tom Stack/Tom Stack & Associates. **182** Rick McIntyre/Tom Stack & Associates. **199** Eric Simmons/Stock Boston. **201** Rod Planck/Tom Stack & Associates. **211** Stewart Green/Tom Stack & Associates. **212, 214** James L. Ballard. **232** Margaret Bourke-White/Life Picture Service. **236–237** Pictor/Uniphoto. **243** Keith H. Murakami/Tom Stack & Associates. **244** Scott Blackman/Tom Stack & Associates. **285** Allen B. Smith/Tom Stack & Associates. **308** James L. Ballard. **353** Ron Watts/Black Star. **384** William A. Seabright. **400** The Bettmann Archive. **430** Gary Holheimer/Index Stock Photography. **433, 436** The Bettmann Archive. **438** NASA. **441** Stock Boston. **466** Erich Lessing/Magnum Photos, Inc. **475** Herman Kokojan/Black Star.

Illustrations

Frank Bozzo 175, 225(T). **Ted Carr,** 27(B), 48(B), 74(B), 156, 164(B), 168, 169, 250, 251, 255(B), 272, 273, 280, 284, 285, 288, 289, 336, 337(T), 394, 395, 404, 405(T), 425(B), 440, 441, 444, 454, 455. **Ralph Creasman** 1, 5(T), 6(B), 7(T), 8(B), 10(T), 11(T), 22, 23(T), 25, 26, 27(T), 34(M), 48(T), 49(T), 52, 53(T), 54(B), 60(B), 61, 67, 73, 79(T), 82, 83, 89, 90, 91, 100, 101, 104, 105, 108, 109, 113, 114(T), 115(T), 129, 135(T), 146, 147, 166, 167, 176(B), 200, 201, 210, 211, 214, 215, 216(T), 217, 222, 223(T), 226(T), 227(T), 228, 229, 242(T), 243, 290, 291(T), 292, 293, 344(T), 345, 358, 359, 370, 376, 377(T), 382, 383, 396, 397, 422,

423(T), 424, 425(T), 442, 461, 464, 465. **David A. Cunningham** xiii, xv(B), 98(B), 99(B), 170(B), 240, 241, 315(M), 474(B), 477(B). **Pat Dypold** 6(T), 49(B), 124, 125, 158, 159, 188, 189, 216(M,B), 224(M), 226(B), 227(B), 274, 275, 407(B), 456, 457. **Jean Cassels Helmer** 28, 29(M), 38(B), 42, 44, 47, 69(M), 86(T), 95(B), 103(B), 110(T), 116(B), 130(B), 180, 281, 303, 306, 310(B), 311(B), 312(B), 323, 324(B), 325(B), 338, 349(B), 371, 377(B), 379(M), 408(M), 412(B), 418, 419, 437. **Cynthia Hoffman** xiv(M,B), 3(M), 4, 14(T), 18, 19(T), 20, 21(T), 29(T), 38(T), 39, 40, 41, 50(T), 51, 54(T), 55, 58(T), 59, 62, 63(T), 68(T), 69(T), 77, 84, 85, 94, 95(T), 96, 97, 102, 103(T), 163, 312(T), 342, 370, 371. **Paul Hoffman** 172, 173, 337(B). **Mary Jones** 21(B), 32, 34(T,B), 35(T,M), 36, 45, 60(T), 72, 78(B), 106(T), 107(T,B), 135(B), 178, 179, 254, 298, 299, 300, 301, 302, 303, 321(M,B), 326(M), 350, 351, 384, 385, 386, 387, 410, 448, 449, 472(T), 473, 474(T). **Carl Kock** xi, xiv(T), xv(T), 2, 3(T), 8(T), 9(T), 12, 13(T), 15(T,B), 16, 17, 23(B), 30, 31, 33(T), 43, 56, 64, 65, 70, 71, 74(T), 75, 76, 80, 81, 87, 92, 93, 98(T), 99(T), 111, 115(B), 116(T), 117, 120, 121, 123(B), 126, 127, 130(T), 131, 132, 133, 136, 137, 138, 139, 140, 141, 142(T), 143(T), 144(T), 145, 148, 149, 154, 155, 160, 164(T), 165, 170(T), 171, 174, 176(T,M), 177, 182, 183, 184, 185(T), 186, 187, 194, 195, 204, 205(T), 218, 219, 220, 221, 225(B), 230, 231, 234, 235, 244, 248, 249, 252, 253, 255(T), 256, 257, 258, 259, 264, 265, 266, 267, 270, 271, 276, 277(B), 278(T), 279(T), 282, 283, 286, 287, 291(B), 304(T), 305(T), 309, 314, 315(T), 320, 321(T), 322, 323, 324(T), 325(T), 326(T), 327, 332, 333, 334, 335, 339, 343, 346, 347, 348, 349(T), 352, 353, 355, 356, 357, 360, 361, 374, 375, 380, 381, 390, 391, 392, 393, 398, 399, 402, 403, 406, 407(T), 411, 412(T,M), 413, 416, 417, 420, 421, 426, 427, 432, 433, 434, 435, 436, 437, 443, 445, 452(T), 453, 458, 459, 462, 463, 468, 469, 470, 471, 472(B), 475, 476, 477(T,M), 478, 479, 480, 482, 483, 486, 487, 488, 489, 490, 491, 492, 493, 494, 495, 496. **Laura Lydecker** 205(M), 206, 207, 208, 209, 304(B), 305(M), 438, 439. **Eileen Mueller Neill** xii(T), 86(B), 122(T), 123(T), 128, 150, 151, 152, 153, 196, 197, 198, 199, 202(T), 203, 232(T), 246, 247, 260, 261, 268, 269, 294, 295, 310(T), 311(T), 316, 317, 328, 329, 330, 340, 341, 344(B), 372, 373, 378, 379(T), 388, 389, 446, 447. **Barbara Nessim** 403(B). **Phil Renaud** xii(B), 5(B), 13(M), 19(B), 33(M), 53(B), 63(B), 142(B), 143(B), 144(B). **William A. Seabright** 14(M), 35(B), 48(M), 57, 106(M), 107(M), 110(B), 114(B), 122(B), 202(B), 223(B), 224(T), 241, 242(B), 267, 278(B), 279(B), 403(T), 408(T), 409, 452(M). **Slug Signorino** 58(B), 118, 119, 181, 185(M), 192, 193, 277(M), 405(B), 425(M), 428, 429, 450, 451. **Lynn Westphal** (handwritten letters) 137, 138, 141, 143, 144, 145, 148, 149, 151, 152, 153, 158, 159.

Editors for revision
Pam Bernstein, Stephanie Iverson, Suzanne Mazurek, Jane Samuelson, Richard F. Weisenseel.

Production Staff for revision
Nancy Gruenke, Mary O'Connor, Gloria Dallmeier.

The type for this book was set by Jandon Graphics, Inc.; the revised type was set on Macintosh computers; the film was made by H & S Graphics, Inc.; and the book was printed by R. R. Donnelley & Sons Company.

Loyola University Press has made every effort to locate the copyright holders for the text and images used in this book and to make full acknowledgment for their use.